The
STRATEGIC
MANAGEMENT
of COLLEGE
ENROLLMENTS

**Don Hossler
John P. Bean
and Associates**

The
STRATEGIC
MANAGEMENT
of COLLEGE
ENROLLMENTS

Jossey-Bass Publishers
San Francisco • Oxford • 1990

THE STRATEGIC MANAGEMENT OF COLLEGE ENROLLMENTS
by Don Hossler, John P. Bean, and Associates

Copyright © 1990 by: Jossey-Bass Inc., Publishers
350 Sansome Street
San Francisco, California 94104
&
Jossey-Bass Limited
Headington Hill Hall
Oxford OX3 0BW

Library of Congress Cataloging-in-Publication Data

Hossler, Don.
    The strategic management of college enrollments / Don Hossler,
John P. Bean, and associates.
      p.   cm. — (The Jossey-Bass higher education series)
    Includes bibliographical references and index.
    ISBN 1-55542-292-6
    1. College attendance — United States — Planning.   2. College
students — United States — Recruiting.   3. Universities and colleges —
United States — Admission.   4. Universities and colleges — United
States — Administration.   I. Bean, John P., date.   II. Title.
III. Series.
LC148.2.H68   1990
371.2'1973 — dc20   90-40146
                                         CIP

Manufactured in the United States of America

The paper in this book meets the guidelines for
permanence and durability of the Committee on
Production Guidelines for Book Longevity of
the Council on Library Resources.

JACKET DESIGN BY WILLI BAUM

FIRST EDITION

Code 9095

The
Jossey-Bass
Higher Education
Series

Contents

ix

For Don and Shirley, Bob and Barbara

For Barbara, David, and Jeffrey—
perhaps now we can go fishing.

Preface

The Emergence of Enrollment Management

The 1950s and 1960s were an era of unparalleled growth for American colleges and universities. World War II veterans and then the baby boomers created more demand for places in college and university classes than were available, and federal and state governments increased their level of funding to higher education. As a result, multiversities emerged and prospered, state teachers colleges became comprehensive universities, and the community college movement engendered the rapid growth of a new tier of institutions of higher education. On most campuses, faculty were granted tenure in short order, and the most important role for many admissions officers was to determine who would be admitted.

In the 1970s, however, the rapid growth that had characterized college enrollments in the previous two decades started to decrease. Cartter (1966) observed that the birthrate was no longer increasing, and by 1971, college and university administrators were beginning to discuss the impending decline in the number of traditional-age students.

By the late 1970s, federal and state funds for higher education also started to diminish. Competition for funds from the health sector, defense, and the federal deficit produced a decline in constant dollars of allocations to student financial aid. The recession of the early 1980s meant that many states also had to decrease their support for higher education.

Not surprisingly, college and university administrators started to show more interest in marketing and student retention. In the mid 1970s, the study of student retention became a focal point of research in higher education. Fueled by the theories developed by Spady and Tinto, the research of Bean, Noel, Pascarella, and Terenzini provided practical insights into institutional strategies to reduce student attrition.

About this same time, admissions officers began to employ marketing techniques borrowed from for-profit businesses. The works of Kotler, Kotler and Fox, and Ihlanfeldt became required reading for college admissions directors. On most campuses concerned about marketing and retention, however, the responsibilities for student retention and student recruitment were isolated from each other.

In the 1980s, a handful of practitioners and researchers realized the links between these two areas. Organizationally, it made sense to identify an administrative unit to coordinate recruitment and retention activities. These two functions came together under the umbrella term *enrollment management,* which refers to institutional efforts to influence the characteristics and the size of enrolled student bodies by directing the activities of the offices of admissions, financial aid, new-student orientation, career planning, retention, and a number of other student affairs areas. Through coordinated efforts, enrollment managers seek to enroll students who can succeed academically and who will find their educational experience to be satisfying and enriching.

Focus and Audience of the Book

The Strategic Management of College Enrollments provides an examination of research and practice related to enrollment management. Previous works on enrollment management have either focused exclusively on research in areas such as student college choice and student retention or tended toward organizational issues. This book discusses both enrollment management research and practice. It is the most comprehensive reference book currently available on enrollment management. It integrates current research on enrollment management topics and provides practical examples of every facet of enrollment management. It covers areas ranging from approaches to organizing an enrollment management division to nonprofit marketing and exemplary retention programs.

 This book is intended for college and university administrators and faculty who are interested in all aspects of enrollment management. Senior-level campus administrators are unlikely to be interested in every chapter; however, they will find the chapters in the first section, which provide a conceptual framework for enrollment management, very useful. They should also find Chapters Fifteen and Sixteen, which describe two functioning enrollment management systems and offer final recommendations for enrollment management, worthwhile reading. Faculty and student affairs administrators can learn about specific aspects of enrollment management, such as student retention programs or approaches to marketing and recruitment. Each chapter is written so that it can be used as a self-contained reference.

 The Strategic Management of College Enrollments will be most useful, however, for midcareer and experienced enrollment managers. Midcareer enrollment managers often come from the ranks of professional administrators in the areas of admissions, financial aid, institutional research, and other areas of student affairs. These managers may know a great deal about new student recruitment, financial aid, or new student orientation but lack an in-depth understanding of the many facets of enrollment management. For midcareer enrollment managers, this book can be invaluable as a comprehensive sourcebook. Experienced practitioners may not discover a great deal that is new to them, but the research and documented practices can help them to understand why some enrollment management practices that they do intuitively are so successful. They can learn to "make sense" out of what they do. Perhaps more important, experienced enrollment managers will find research that can provide outside support and validation for their requests for new institutional activities, additional staff members, or budgetary support. All senior-level administrators have found themselves at one time asking a staff member to quickly find some data or information that can be used to support a new initiative that is being proposed. Experienced enrollment managers will find this volume invaluable for such purposes.

Organization of the Book

Part One describes enrollment management, and then examines it in the context of strategic planning and presents four common organizational approaches to it. Chapter One looks at environmental and organizational factors that led to the development of enrollment management and discusses the organizational elements of an enrollment management system. Chapter Two presents an overview of strategic planning and discusses the ongoing role of enrollment management in an institution's strategic planning process. Chapter Three reviews the most common approaches to organizing enrollment management systems, pointing out that successful systems can have very different organizational structures. Administrators need to understand the organizational history and culture of their campus in order to implement enrollment management programs that use available personnel.

Part Two focuses on marketing and student recruitment. Chapter Four provides an overview of the college choice process. Institutions attempting to influence where students go to school should have a sophisticated understanding of the factors that shape college choice. Chapter Five introduces nonprofit marketing and explains its utility in higher education. The chapter's examination of the unique properties of marketing a college education is especially useful. Chapter Six discusses methods of conducting market research on student college choice. This chapter is intended to assist institutions in conducting their own market research. Chapter Seven provides an overview of current marketing practices. Part Two concludes with Chapter Eight, which presents case studies of how two institutions use marketing to influence their enrollments.

Part Three shifts the focus from attracting to retaining students. Chapter Nine reviews student attrition research. This chapter sets the stage for Chapter Ten, which describes a variety of approaches for conducting student retention studies. This

material can help institutions understand how to design retention studies. Chapter Eleven describes successful retention programs on a variety of campuses. This chapter is intended to
assist institutions that are designing retention programs to learn
from the successful efforts of other schools. The final chapter
in this part, Chapter Twelve, presents case studies from two
institutions that have successfully improved their retention rates.
The institutions are not similar and have taken different paths
to achieve their goals.

Part Four brings together the components of enrollment
management that have been presented in Parts Two and Three.
This section begins with an overview of student information systems and looks at the impact of such a system on a graduate
program at one institution. Discussing management information systems is an appropriate way to lead into this closing section because information is an important part of the "glue" that
enables a system to function. Management information systems
provide the baseline data that drive marketing and retention
activities. Data bases are the source of enrollment trends and
cohort studies of student attrition, and they can be used to help
evaluate the efficacy of marketing and retention activities.

Chapter Thirteen reviews the role of student information
systems in enrollment management and discusses key issues to
be considered when one develops a system. Chapter Fourteen
provides a look at the role management information systems
play in enrollment management. This chapter uses the setting
of a graduate business school to illustrate how student information systems can be used to improve both marketing and recruitment activities.

These chapters are followed by a case study of successful
enrollment management systems at two institutions. While the
case studies presented cannot be considered a blueprint for all
institutions, they provide insight into organizational structures
and strategies that can lead to successful enrollment management. Chapter Sixteen, the final chapter, summarizes what is
known about effective enrollment management systems and
challenges institutions to confront enrollment management in
terms of local issues. It also offers recommendations about staff-

ing and closes with a discussion of the future of enrollment management.

Acknowledgments

We would like to thank each of the chapter contributors for their efforts in bringing together this sourcebook. In addition, the insights and works of A. Steven Graff, Frank Kemerer, Robert Lay, Larry Litten, Ernest Pascarella, Patrick Terenzini, and Vincent Tinto have helped to shape this book.

We wish to acknowledge the helpful suggestions of Gale Erlandson and the editors of Jossey-Bass. In closing, we would like to thank Marilyn Ellis and Nick Vesper, who assisted with editing and manuscript preparation. We would also like to offer a special word of thanks to Joyce Regester, who assisted us at every step of this project and helped keep everything on track.

Bloomington, Indiana   Don Hossler
September 1990   John P. Bean

The Authors

Thomas D. Abrahamson is dean of admissions and records at DePaul University. A specialist in higher education marketing, Abrahamson is a frequent seminar leader at enrollment management conferences and has served as a consultant to the American College Testing programs and the College Board, for which he is presently a member of the National Advisory Committee on Research and Development.

Barry Abrams is vice-president for enrollment management at St. Mary's University of San Antonio, Texas. He has previously held the positions of admissions director and financial aid director, and he has published works and made presentations at workshops on enrollment planning issues.

Ernest W. Beals is currently dean of admissions at Georgia State University. He is a former high school teacher, guidance director, and director of guidance for the state of New Hampshire and for the University of Massachusetts, Amherst. He served fourteen years as a College Board staff member. He has been codirector of two summer institutes on enrollment management and has authored several admissions-related articles in professional journals.

John P. Bean is associate professor of educational leadership and policy studies at Indiana University. He has conducted over a dozen statistical analyses of student retention and student outcomes and published the results in such journals as the *American*

Educational Research Journal, Journal of Higher Education, Research in Higher Education, and the *Review of Higher Education.* He has served as a consulting editor to the latter three journals. His longtime interest in modeling student attrition culminated in the publication of an article (with B. Metzner) in the *Review of Educational Research* on nontraditional student attrition. He has consulted widely and conducted several workshops on implementing effective student retention strategies. He is currently studying the effects of diversity on student retention.

Trudy H. Bers is senior director of research, curriculum, and planning at Oakton Community College. In this capacity she is responsible for a variety of marketing activities, including conducting market research, producing numerous publications related to academic programs and services, and developing new programs and services. She has also served as acting director of enrollment management at the same time, which enabled her to direct admissions and financial aid functions as well.

John M. Braxton is assistant professor of higher education at Syracuse University. He has worked in offices of institutional research and admissions at Northeastern University in Illinois and Colgate University. One of his major research interests is the college student experience, including such topics as the college choice process, the student attrition process, and the effects of college on students. His recent publications in such journals as the *Journal of College Student Development, Research in Higher Education,* and the *Review of Higher Education* have focused on these topics. He also serves as a consulting editor for *Research in Higher Education.*

Catherine R. Clark is currently a doctoral candidate in higher education at Indiana University. She has held positions in student affairs at the University of Maryland and the University of Illinois. In addition, she has taught graduate-level courses and held administrative positions at Indiana University. She has served as the assistant editor of the *Enrollment Management Review.* Her interests include student development theory, student college choice, and enrollment management.

Don Hossler is associate professor of educational leadership and policy studies at Indiana University. He is the editor of *Enrollment Management Review* and the author of several books and articles on enrollment management and student college choice, including *Enrollment Management: An Integrated Approach, Creating Effective Enrollment Management Systems,* and "Understanding Student College Choice," which appeared in the fifth volume of *Higher Education: A Handbook of Theory and Research.* He has served as a consultant to more than twenty colleges and educational organizations and is currently engaged in a five-year longitudinal study of the factors that influence student college choice.

Marsha Krotseng is assistant director of planning and institutional research at the University of Hartford. She previously served as institutional research associate and as assistant professor of higher education at the University of Mississippi. She is active in the Association for Institutional Research and served on the board of directors of the Association for the Study of Higher Education. Her articles and reviews have been published in Jossey-Bass's *New Directions for Higher Education* series on faculty and in *Educational Studies* and the *Review of Education.*

L. Sandy MacLean is vice-chancellor for student affairs and adjunct associate professor of education at the University of Missouri, St. Louis. He has worked in student affairs for over thirty years, holding administrative positions at Eastern Michigan University; University of Missouri, Columbia; Indiana University; Northern Iowa University; and Michigan State University.

Mariea T. Noblitt is currently a marketing research analyst for higher education in the Academic Information Systems Division of the IBM Corporation. Prior to joining IBM, she was the director of admissions for the Johnson Graduate School of Management at Cornell University, where she designed and implemented their enrollment management software and developed their strategic marketing plans. She has over seventeen years of experience in college admissions and has developed and taught numerous workshops at the national level in the area of information management systems design for enrollment management. She continues to do consulting in higher education and specializes in helping institutions develop comprehensive enrollment management systems and marketing plans.

Faye D. Plascak-Craig is assistant professor of psychology at Marian College in Indianapolis, Indiana. She has been a full-time faculty member for five years, teaching research methods, statistics, gender issues, social psychology, and testing. Her work has focused on predictive and path analytical models of undergraduate attrition and of faculty job satisfaction. She does institutional research on student retention, student development, and faculty issues, often focusing on small college populations.

Frances K. Stage is assistant professor in the Department of Educational Leadership and Policy Studies at Indiana University. She has published articles and book chapters on college student satisfaction and retention, multicultural issues, research methods, and college choice. She has served as research consultant on many projects related to college attendance and retention and has experience working with community colleges and four-year commuter institutions as well as residential institutions in both the public and private sectors.

Robert O. Thomas is vice-president for student affairs at Westminster College in Pennsylvania, where his responsibilities include overseeing the admissions and enrollment management programs for the college. He has conducted research on enrollment management at liberal arts colleges.

Nick Vesper is a graduate student at Indiana University. Before pursuing his current interests in higher education and political science, he was an associate professor of mathematics and computer science and an administrator responsible for information systems, registration, and records at a private midwestern university.

The
STRATEGIC
MANAGEMENT
of COLLEGE
ENROLLMENTS

PART ONE

ENROLLMENT MANAGEMENT IN ACADEMIC SETTINGS

Part One is designed to introduce readers to enrollment management. Frequently college and university administrators want to know what enrollment management is and how they can create an enrollment management system. A recurring theme in this part is that there are no ideal approaches. Every successful enrollment management system reflects the unique characteristics of a campus and the particular strengths and weaknesses of the administrative staff who work at the institution.

Chapter One defines enrollment management both as an organizing concept and as a set of activities, and describes the administrative functions that should constitute an enrollment management division. One important perspective in this chapter is that of the enrollment management lens. Viewing the organization from different perspectives enables campus enrollment managers to better understand the matriculation and persistence patterns of students. More important, it enables them to better understand their own institutions.

Chapter Two examines the relationship between strategic planning and enrollment management. Strategic planning and enrollment management are not separate activities. They must be integrated in order for both to succeed. Enrollment management decisions should flow from a comprehensive strategic plan. Chapter Two provides an overview of strategic planning and then discusses how strategic planning should drive enrollment management activities.

Chapter Three reviews four basic organizational approaches to enrollment management that were first described by Kemerer, Baldridge, and Green in 1982. Each of these ap-

1

proaches has strengths and weaknesses. Furthermore, there are no examples of a "textbook" model of any of these four approaches. On campuses where one of these approaches has been successfully implemented, it has been intentionally and unintentionally adapted to fit local institutional needs.

Chapter 1

Principles and Objectives

Don Hossler
John P. Bean

A Perspective on Enrollment Management

Since 1973, the number of high school seniors graduating from high schools in our traditional marketing territories have dropped by 34%. In 1974 our
entering freshman class had 357 new students, in
1988 our class of entering freshmen had 273 students. In 1974 the average combined SAT scores of
our entering class was 967, in 1988 it was 759. . . .
In 1974 our admissions staff consisted of a director,
four professionals and one clerical position. In 1988,
our admissions staff includes a director, eight full-
time professionals, and two clerical positions [Sec-
tions from a report to the trustees at a liberal arts
college in the Midwest].

In 1971, after a hundred years of sustained growth, American colleges and universities began to project declines in student
enrollments. Demographic data indicated that the number of
new students entering college would diminish throughout the
remainder of the century. Initially these projections were ignored, but by the mid 1970s college and university administrators were searching for new ways to attract and retain students.
Marketing, a concept long viewed with disdain on campuses,
found its way into the admissions and recruitment practices of
many colleges and universities.

Faculty and administrators traditionally thought that their mission included "washing out" a certain number of students each year. With declining enrollments a real possibility, campus administrators quickly became interested in attracting and retaining students from a shrinking pool of applicants.

On most campuses, new marketing and recruitment activities took place in isolation from each other. Marketing was the responsibility of the admissions office alone and often meant little more than a larger printing and mailing budget. Retention activities were frequently assigned to a faculty committee or to an isolated student affairs official. The literature on marketing and student retention stressed the importance of information and research to help guide institutional activities, but such information was seldom used.

By 1980, several colleges and universities had discovered that attracting and retaining students requires the sustained and systematic use of institutional resources. Effective marketing requires institutions to know the characteristics of their applicants, how best to reach prospective students, and what prospective students value as they search for schools to attend. Similarly, campus administrators cannot develop effective retention interventions unless they know the characteristics of students who persist in school and those who withdraw. Retention efforts are complex and need to be tracked over several years.

Some colleges and universities discovered not only that information is necessary but also that the activities of financial aid, orientation, advising, and other academic and student affairs units influence student enrollments. Institutions of higher education, Boston College and Bradley University among the first, developed new administrative units — enrollment management divisions — to coordinate the activities of all administrative offices that affect student enrollments. By the mid 1980s, the term *enrollment management* became part of the lexicon of higher education. It was associated with a set of activities and an organizational framework that enabled colleges and universities to influence student enrollments.

Enrollment management has two goals. The first is to

exert more control over the characteristics of the student body, and the second is to control the size of the student body. Enrollment management has been defined in a number of ways, but in each case students are the focus of its activities. Kemerer, Baldridge, and Green (1982) note that enrollment management is not just an organizational concept; it is both a process and a series of activities that involve the entire campus. As a process, it includes tracking and interacting with students from the point of their initial contact with the institution until their graduation or departure from the institution. As an activity, enrollment management is designed to attract and retain students. Modifying Hossler's (1986) earlier definition, we believe enrollment management is an organizational concept and a systematic set of activities designed to enable educational institutions to exert more influence over their student enrollments. Organized by strategic planning and supported by institutional research, enrollment management activities concern student college choice, transition to college, student attrition and retention, and student outcomes. These processes are studied to guide institutional practices in the areas of new student recruitment and financial aid, student support services, curriculum development and other academic areas that affect enrollments, student persistence, and student outcomes from college.

This definition reveals the key attributes of enrollment management, which include:

1. The use of institutional research to:
   a. position the campus in the marketplace
   b. examine the correlates to student persistence
   c. develop appropriate marketing and pricing strategies
2. Developing appropriate marketing and pricing strategies through research
3. Monitoring student interests and academic program demand
4. Matching student demand with curricular offerings that are consistent with the institutional mission
5. Paying attention to academic, social, and institutional factors that can affect student retention

Enrollment management activities are broad in scope. Implementing enrollment management practices requires a campuswide effort and requires that senior-level policy makers be sensitive to the factors that influence student enrollments.

One of the most useful perspectives on enrollment management is that of George Rainsford, the president of a small liberal arts college in Virginia. Rainsford (1986) suggests that the emergence of enrollment management as a major administrative function in colleges and universities has been similar to the emergence of fund raising and development as a major campus function. Twenty years ago, senior-level policy makers realized the importance of fund-raising efforts in providing a margin of institutional excellence. Now that student enrollments can no longer be taken for granted, Rainsford asserts that college and university presidents need to realize that shaping the size and character of the student body also requires strategic decisions from senior-level administrators. Enrollment management has become an important part of the leadership's responsibilities in colleges and universities.

An increasing number of two- and four-year institutions have adopted some form of enrollment management (Novak and Weiss, 1985), but not all of these campuses describe their organizational structure as an "enrollment management system." In general, however, enrollment management practices have not been adopted by many colleges and universities. In a 1987 survey of enrollment management practices, conducted by Peat Marwick, 45 percent of the institutions surveyed reported that they did not have an enrollment management organization of any type in place (p. 13). On many campuses, enrollment management is not understood. Many faculty members and high-level administrators consider enrollment management to be the responsibility of the admissions office. Admissions programs are an important part of enrollment management, but enrollment management includes a wider range of activities.

Huddleston (1984) attempts to differentiate the role of an admissions manager from that of an enrollment manager. Admissions managers are only concerned with the enrollment of new students. Enrollment managers are concerned with attracting

new students as well as retaining students who are already enrolled. By emphasizing attracting and retaining students, enrollment managers are forced to ask two questions that move them
beyond recruiting. First, enrollment managers must determine
whether or not their recruiting activities attract students who
can succeed on the campus. Second, they must ask whether or
not the campus is making every effort to provide a positive
educational experience for students both within and outside of
the classroom—does the campus have a "staying environment"?

On many campuses, directors of admissions have been
given a title such as dean or vice-president of enrollment management, a salary raise, and perhaps a larger budget, but few
changes have been made in their responsibilities. These super-
ficial changes are an example of admissions management but are
not the fundamental changes necessary to create an enrollment
management system. As administrative units such as financial
aid, institutional research, orientation, and academic advising
become integrated with admissions, an enrollment management
system begins to emerge.

Functional Dimensions of Enrollment Management

Enrollment managers must be more than marketers and recruiters, the functions of primary importance to admissions
officers. Admissions, financial aid, orientation, academic advising, campus activities and residence life, career planning and
placement, learning assistance centers, institutional research,
and faculty development are all concerns of enrollment managers. In this section the functional areas of enrollment management are discussed in greater detail. This discussion is not a blueprint for all enrollment management systems. A recurring theme
in this book is that no single template serves for all enrollment
management systems; the most pressing campus concerns,
norms, politics, and informal networks and the skills of campus
personnel will dictate the activities and structure of enrollment
management systems on each campus. While the functions of
each system may be similar, the form (offices and personnel)
of enrollment management systems will differ widely at com-

munity colleges, liberal arts colleges, comprehensive colleges, and universities.

Admissions. The admissions office, through its marketing and recruiting activities, is the first point of contact between student and institution in an enrollment management system. Deans or directors of admissions must be able to find high school students or others who have the potential to become successful students at their institution. They must also be able to motivate these students to inquire about the school, apply to it, and matriculate.

To attract students to the institution, an admissions office needs an effective data storage, retrieval, and analysis system. It also requires staff members with skills in market research, financial aid, and counseling. DePaul University in Chicago, for example, has been developing a differentiated staffing pattern in which admissions staff members not only have different recruiting territories but also have special assignments in the areas of financial aid, marketing, alumni recruitment, graduate programs, and continuing education.

Financial Aid. With rising tuition and increasing competition among institutions, financial aid officers have become an important part of enrollment management systems. The director of financial aid and the financial aid staff must work closely with the admissions office. The activities of financial aid offices vary from school to school because many public institutions lack the resources to provide insitution-based financial aid. At most community colleges, the only aid available comes from federal and state programs. Some private institutions offer no-need aid while others do not. Regardless of the type of college or university, financial aid officers should work with admissions to ensure that students receive all aid for which they are eligible and that they receive their awards in a timely fashion. If merit and no-need aid is awarded, the admissions and financial aid offices must jointly identify the prospective students that they will target for special recruitment efforts.

The financial aid office must also analyze persistence trends among students to determine if aid policies affect student retention. At Carleton College in Northfield, Minnesota, the director of financial aid produces an annual report that assesses the college's financial aid programs. It includes information on the number of students awarded aid and the size of the awards, the financial aid awards of matriculants versus nonmatriculants, and even the debt burden of currently enrolled students. This report is used to help guide future policy decisions for admissions and financial aid.

Orientation and Academic Advising. Upon matriculation, new student orientation and academic advising often create a lasting impression of a school. The director of orientation must do more than introduce students to service providers on campus and help them learn the location of buildings and offices. Orientation directors should increase the anticipatory socialization of new students by introducing them to the norms and culture of the campus. Orientation should introduce new students to campus policies as well as important traditions. At the end of orientation, new students should have a sense of what it takes to succeed in their new environment.

The director of orientation should provide special orientation programs for returning adult students, international students, minority students, and transfer students. Each of these groups has unique needs that should be addressed to increase the likelihood that group members will successfully adjust to the campus and persist as students. Noel, Levitz, Saluri, and Associates (1985) indicate that freshmen, the most dropout prone students, often make their decisions to leave the institution during their first six weeks in school. Orientation programs can play an important role in helping students become a part of the institution they are attending.

Students' first contact with their academic advisers usually occurs during orientation. Most new students arrive on campus expecting to have meaningful interactions with faculty (Feldman and Newcomb, 1969) and to learn how the classes in which they will enroll are related to their career goals. For students, meaningful contact with faculty is characterized by faculty members who have a caring attitude toward students, a genuine interest in having the students succeed at the school, and the ability to answer students' questions about requirements for success on campus from the freshman year until graduation. It is incumbent upon colleges and universities to provide high-quality academic advising so that students feel connected to the institution and its faculty as early as possible after their arrival. Bean and Metzner (1985) suggest that academic advising plays an even more important role in retaining older students than traditional-age students.

Orienting students to an institution and bringing them into contact with faculty are especially difficult at community colleges. At many two-year institutions, few students attend orientation programs, and academic advising is provided by professional advisers rather than faculty members. Yet community college students also need orientation and can benefit from faculty contact. Orientation classes, required faculty advising sessions, and other incentives for both students and faculty to come together during the first weeks of classes can be helpful.

Bradley University was one of the first institutions to make orienation and advising an integral part of its enrollment management system. The associate vice-president at Bradley had a full-time staff member who worked exclusively with orientation and advising. This staff member was viewed as an integral part of institutional recruitment and retention activities.

Campus Activities and Residence Life. Residence-life and student activities programs provide important opportunities for students to develop friendships and to become involved in campus life. The positive relationship between student involvement and student persistence and development suggests that enrollment managers should make every attempt to provide high-quality activities and residence-life programs. Campus activity directors should attempt to involve every student in activities such as clubs and organizations, intramurals, and student government. Residence-life staff should also emphasize student programming in the residence halls.

At Drake University in Des Moines, Iowa, student activities and residence-life programs are directed by the same person — the chief student affairs and enrollment management officer. These programs provide the traditional services, but their importance in recruitment and retention is also acknowledged. This structure helps to integrate enrollment management into ongoing programs.

Career Planning and Placement. In an era of careerism, no college or university can afford to be without an effective career planning and placement office. During the 1970s, career planning and placement offices started to move away from placement and started to emphasize life planning. While life planning is an important developmental activity for students, these offices must also give attention to placement. Students want assurances that the school they are attending will help them succeed in the career of their choice. Only a small percentage of students actually get jobs as the result of on-campus interviews; nevertheless, career planning officers need to work hard at maintaining contacts with potential employers, helping students find jobs, and keeping track of both the rate of job placement and the rate of admission to graduate schools. These are student outcomes data that can be very useful in future marketing efforts.

Thomas (1988) found that liberal arts colleges that brought corporate recruiters to campus had higher rates of retention than those that did not. Placement programs can symbolize to students that the institution is of high quality ("IBM reps came *here!*") and that the institution cares about its students. High quality and a caring attitude are important factors in recruitment and retention.

Learning Assistance Centers. Some faculty and administrators decry the lack of preparation for higher education among today's high school students. While some students are excellently prepared, many who continue their education beyond high school are not prepared for the academic demands that will be placed upon them. Most colleges and universities, while selective, admit some marginal students. Underprepared students need tutoring and study skills development in order to succeed.

A comprehensive enrollment management system should include the learning assistance center. Administrators in learning assistance centers should track the success of underprepared students and provide data to the director of admissions. Such a tracking system can enable enrollment managers to determine if there are patterns among the types of students that succeed and those that consistently fail. When patterns of failure are evident, enrollment managers should ask if recruiting resources are being wisely spent. The consistent failure of an identifiable group of students suggests that the campus should provide more support for these students or that students with these characteristics should not be recruited and admitted.

The connection between learning assistance and enrollment management is very important at community colleges because community colleges are more likely to attract underprepared students. Miami-Dade Community College in Florida has received national attention for its computer-based academic assistance efforts. At Miami-Dade, students who earn poor grades receive a personalized letter that addresses their academic difficulties and offers suggestions for assistance. At the University of California, Los Angeles, the academic progress of students who are admitted in special programs for underprepared students is tracked carefully. Students who perform at acceptable or superior levels receive letters of congratulations and are encouraged to continue to work hard in their classes. This form of positive reinforcement for underprepared students who succeed is often missing. The approaches of both schools illustrate the ways in which learning skills centers should be linked with enrollment management.

Institutional Research. It is extremely difficult for enrollment managers to be successful without institutional research. *Institutional research* is a term that connotes a diverse set of analytical and planning activities. On large campuses, such as Tufts University in Medford, Massachusetts, or DePaul University, the enrollment management division may have its own institutional research office. At these campuses, institutional researchers devote their time to examining the factors that affect student enrollment and persistence. They also conduct evaluation studies of marketing and retention activities.

Small campuses may use a campuswide institutional research officer to conduct enrollment related studies. At Oberlin College in Oberlin, Ohio, one staff member devotes half of his time to enrollment-related research. Oakton College, a community college in suburban Chicago, has a centralized institutional research office with three staff members. One of the responsibilities of this office is to conduct marketing and attrition research.

On small campuses a full-time institutional research office is a luxury. On these campuses, enrollment managers may need to be more creative, seeking release time for a sociologist or psychologist to conduct research. Thiel College, in Greenville, Pennsylvania, has utilized a professor from the biological sciences who has a good research background to conduct some of its studies. Thiel has also contracted out some of its research to consultants. At Humboldt State University in Arcata, California, the former director of school relations conducted his own market research.

Who actually conducts the research is not as important as making sure that institutional data are collected and analyzed. Research is important for both strategic planning and policy analysis. Enrollment managers can no longer rely on intuition. They need to know where their students come from, what attracts students to the school, why students attend or fail to matriculate, and what factors affect students' persistence. Such information is only available through institutional research.

Faculty Development. While faculty play a critical role in attracting and retaining students, most faculty members are unlikely to respond to the directives of an enrollment manager. Faculty value their autonomy and freedom to help govern colleges and universities. They are accustomed to making decisions about curriculum and pedagogy and, at some colleges and universities, to setting the admissions policies.

Enrollment managers should attempt to educate and influence faculty by providing them with information, because faculty are socialized to make sensible decisions based upon information. Providing faculty with information about why students are choosing one campus over another, why students are withdrawing, or why they are dissatisfied with some of the outcomes of their education frequently provides the impetus for faculty to accept new policies that will positively affect student enrollments. Information can be used to convince faculty to adopt new policies that they might never be directed to make. The vice-president of enrollment management at St. Mary's University in San Antonio, Texas, credits much of his success in increasing both the number and the quality of students at St. Mary's to his work with the faculty. As the result of information provided to the faculty, curricular and pedagogical changes at St. Mary's were made voluntarily.

Enrollment Management and Institutional Effectiveness

The functional areas just discussed can play important parts in enrollment management systems. However, enrollment management must be viewed as more than an organizational restructuring or a set of activities designed to attract and retain students. Many campus administrators fail to recognize the strategic importance that student enrollments play in defining the image and the perceived effectiveness of an institution. For many reasons, the students who attend a college or university not only determine its financial health but also shape the image and future of the institution. Enrollment managers need to be able to influence student enrollments, but they also need to articulate the strategic role that student enrollments play in defining institutional character.

The most commonly accepted measure of organizational effectiveness is resource acquisition or financial viability (Price and Mueller, 1986). Given this definition, student enrollments are a major determinant of institutional effectiveness. The connection between student enrollments and tuition revenue is clear. At private colleges and universities, tuition revenues account for about 80 percent of all revenues. In the public sector, a variety of institutional funding approaches are used to determine the level of state appropriations or, in the case of some community colleges, the level of funding by the community college district. Some of these approaches are more tuition driven than others. At four-year public colleges and universities, tuition revenues typically account for 35 percent of all revenues (Jenkins, 1988). When state funding formulas based upon student enrollments are included, student enrollments represent more than half of the income at four-year public institutions. At public two-year colleges, tuition and enrollment-based funding formulas can account for nearly 70 percent of revenues (Martorana and Wattenbarger, 1986).

Another measure of an institution's effectiveness, the characteristics of enrolled students, is often overlooked. Trustees and administrators sometimes forget that colleges and universities are not-for-profit enterprises. Measures of this type of effectiveness are more elusive, but Bowen (1980) and others have observed that the achievement of excellence is one of the principal measures of prestige and success among institutions of higher education. For colleges and universities, quality is an important indicator of effectiveness. What campus administrators sometimes forget is the importance of enrolled students in determining perceptions of institutional quality. The characteristics and number of enrolled students greatly shape the image of a college or university. Perhaps the best way to illustrate the relationship between student enrollments and institutional image is to review the factors used by scholars to rate individual academic programs and entire institutions.

The characteristics of enrolled students are an integral factor in determining the quality and hence the image of both individual academic programs and entire institutions. Perhaps the criterion most widely used to rank schools is the quality of students at entrance. The most recent ranking of graduate programs (Jones, Lindzey, and Coggshall, 1982) used student scores on standardized graduate exams, such as the Graduate Record Exam, as one indicator of quality. Liberal arts colleges are ranked using student ACT or SAT scores, class rank, or high school grade point averages (Webster, 1986). *Peterson's Guide to Four-Year Colleges* uses the average SAT or ACT scores for entering freshmen to rank institutions along a continuum of competitiveness.

The academic quality of enrolled students is directly related to the quality of future applicants. Although college choice does not appear to be a completely rational decision, prospective students seldom apply to colleges or universities at which most students have significantly stronger or weaker academic abilities than their own (Hossler, Braxton, and Coopersmith, 1989). Images of quality based on the characteristics of students already enrolled thus influence the characteristics of future applicants.

The size of a student body influences an institution's visibility. Large institutions have more visibility and hence several advantages over smaller institutions in attracting prospective students. Large colleges and universities attract more attention and are mentioned more frequently in newspapers and on radio and television than smaller schools. Institutional visibility raises the level of awareness of a school among prospective students and their parents. Market research indicates that name recognition increases the likelihood that prospective students will respond to unsolicited mail from colleges and universities.

Besides student body size and quality, other student characteristics affect the image of colleges and universities. Church-related colleges frequently describe themselves on the basis of the proportion of enrolled students who are members of the sponsoring denomination. This information is then used to recruit prospective students. The percentage of commuter students, full-time and part-time students, and adult students and the extent and type of social life (Greek life, athletics, and vocational orientation) at an institution often define the culture of a college or university and thus its image.

Enrollment management focuses on student characteristics at entrance, student persistence, and student outcomes. Each factor is related to institutional image and the perceived value of attending a particular college or university. As the public started to hold institutions more accountable for students' success and failure, public policy makers and the general public started to look at student persistence in addition to student characteristics at matriculation. New Jersey provides incentive funding programs to state schools, from community colleges to research universities, that implement effective retention programs. The state funds a similar program to attract and retain minority students in these schools. Many high school counselors and published guides to colleges and universities now suggest that prospective students and their parents ask the admissions officers about retention rates.

Astin (1985) notes that the accomplishments of the graduates of individual colleges and universities have always been one way to measure institutional quality. Each time alumni win prestigious awards or receive public acclaim, their alma mater receives some credit.

Although faculty and administrators intuitively understand the impact that student enrollments have on a college or university, they seldom fully appreciate the strategic nature of the relationship between student enrollments and institutional image. Once perceptions of quality, selectivity, size, number of church members enrolled, student attrition rates, and so on are established in the public's mind, they are difficult to alter. A quick review of the quality rankings of graduate programs over the last fifty years reveals how little perceptions of institutions of higher education change over time. Without a carefully constructed strategic plan, the image of an institution, once established, usually determines the quantity and quality of future applicants.

The image students hold of a school becomes a self-fulfilling prophecy. For example, high-quality students will apply to a university that they perceive to be of high quality, and the institution will become one of high quality because it matriculates high-quality students. Enrollment managers, other administrators, and faculty members must be able to see the institution as the students see it. Enabling faculty and administrators to view the campus as the students see it is one of the most important outcomes of an effective enrollment management system.

The Enrollment Management Lens

Enrollment managers must be concerned with every facet of each student's experience, from the first point of contact with the institution through graduation and placement. They must adopt a wide-angle lens and view the entirety of the student experience.

Campus administrators and faculty often see students through too many narrow lenses that limit a comprehensive view. There is the admissions lens, the faculty lens, the student affairs lens, and occasionally the student outcomes lens. Seldom, however, is there one panoramic view of students.

Traditionally, admissions officers see students from the point of their first contact through matriculation. Admissions officers are concerned with how the institution makes its first impression. Students are seen as an annual cycle of prospects, applicants, matriculants, and "no shows." These administrators believe that a low persistence rate on campus is caused by the faculty or the student affairs staff not providing the classroom and out-of-classroom experiences that make attending the institution satisfying.

The faculty lens is equally narrow. Too many faculty are only concerned about what happens to students while they are in the classroom. Faculty often do not understand that how their department is perceived and the quality of their teaching, advising, and out-of-class contacts affect the attrition decisions of academically capable students. Frequently, faculty think that only students with poor grades drop out and that such students should leave anyway. All too often they believe that attrition results from poor admissions decisions, student incompetence, or poor student services. They do not see their own central role in attracting and retaining students.

Student affairs administrators often see students through student involvement in activities, student government, counseling needs, or residence life. On some campuses, the student affairs lens is so narrow that student affairs administrators may not be aware of the impact their programs have upon the external image of the campus. Some student affairs administrators would prefer to have little contact with offices like admissions or financial aid.

The student outcomes lens is altogether absent on many campuses. The impact that colleges and universities have upon their students should be an important element of an enrollment management system. Some college administrators might ask, "What do student outcomes have to do with enrollment management?" The response of enrollment managers should be, "Every-thing." Many prospective college students (both traditional and nontraditional) have come to view the college selection process as one more consumer decision. As a result they are concerned not only with initial costs, but with long-term benefits. Alverno College in Milwaukee, Wisconsin; Northeast Missouri State University in Kirksville, Missouri; and the University of Tennessee, Knoxville, can document how much their students learn. They have tracked the careers and incomes of their alumni and can explain how satisfied currently enrolled students are with their educational experience. These institutions are in a stronger position to market themselves than comparable institutions that have no information about these issues.

      This discussion of lenses has concentrated on viewing the student from the faculty perspective, the admissions perspective, and the student outcomes perspective. Enrollment managers should not only have a wide-angle lens that looks at students from all of these perspectives, but they and other administrators and faculty should also look at themselves and the institution as students do. Faculty may believe that they have the best math department in the region or the state. The student affairs staff may be confident that they have an excellent child-care program for adult students. The president may believe that students are very satisfied with their undergraduate experience. Through market research, retention research, and student outcomes research, however, faculty and administrators can test their perceptions against the perceptions of the students. In many respects, student perceptions are the only ones that matter. If students choose another college because they think the math department is better or if adult students drop out because of inadequate child-care provisions or if students tell their friends that they are not happy with their overall experience, then it does not matter what faculty and administrators think. Enrollments will decline because students perceive problems. By turning the enrollment management lens upon the institution, enrollment managers can provide data and insights that can create the impetus for changes that will positively affect enrollments.

      Enrollment management provides colleges and universities

with a new conceptual and structural framework for directing institutional activities to attract and retain students. It brings together a body of knowledge and research techniques that enable institutions to continually monitor their external image and internal environment for students. Enrollment management provides campus administrators and faculty members with an opportunity to develop a better understanding of how they influence students' perceptions of institutions and how students experience each campus after they enroll.

Chapter 2

Strategic Planning
and Enrollment Management

John P. Bean

Enrollment management must be planned. It must be planned not once but continually as an institution and its environment change. In this chapter several questions related to planning enrollment management systems are addressed: What is planning? Why is planning important for enrollment management? How do the scope of planning and the planning context affect plans for enrollment management? What is special about strategic planning? How can a college or university integrate strategic planning and enrollment management?

Defining Planning

Definitions of the term *planning* are abundant. They differ in emphasis, but typically refer to these elements:

1. Planning is planning for change. There is no need to plan to remain the same or to evolve slowly. People plan to attempt to influence some future activity.
2. Planning is future oriented. Planning is oriented toward the future, unlike decision making, which is oriented toward the present. Ackoff (1970) called this characteristic of planning anticipatory decision making.
3. Planning aims toward but often lacks rationality. Planners differ in the extent to which they believe they can act rationally. Rational action involves complete and accurate information, shared prioritization of alternatives, and complete

21

knowledge of the outcomes of any action taken. In the real world, none of these conditions can be met. Nevertheless, many planners act as if they could be rational.

4.   Planning can be seen as a process or a product. People can plan means (how to get there) or ends (where to go) or both. They can also look at the planning process (gathering information and talking) as most important or the planning product (the plan) as most important.

5.   Planning involves choosing between alternatives. Enrollment managers have limited resources and can engage in some but not all activities. Planning is a means to determine which alternative futures are preferred.

6.   Planning is the activity initiated formally by an organization and informally by organizational participants as a means to sense the future, understand the present, and rationalize the past (Clark, 1980).

7.   Planning is undertaken to achieve symbolic, advertisable, rationalistic, political, procedural, and futuristic ends (Clark, 1980).

The first five elements of this list form the core from which most definitions of planning are derived. They suggest that enrollment managers have to make decisions about (1) how much they will intervene in a campus or university as opposed to just allowing things to happen, (2) how far into the future they wish to extend their concern, (3) how rational they believe the planning process can be, (4) whether they are concerned with devising a plan as a final product or as a process for future action, and (5) how they will identify rules for choosing among alternatives and, especially, who will choose among alternatives.

Numbers 6 and 7 in the list suggest that enrollment managers also need to be aware that what they call planning may be similar to "retrospective sense making" (Weick, 1979). In some cases, planning becomes a rationale for what an organization has already been doing. For example, a university may begin planning by auditing its current situation with regard to students, faculty, resources, and so forth. The planners discover that the campus attracts large numbers of first-generation students. Then the school incorporates into its plan a program to attract first-generation students. In doing so it rationalizes its past action, advertises its intentions to continue attracting these students, and better understands (makes sense of) what it is currently doing. Planning in this case is really an attempt to reach a social consensus about what the organization or subunit does or should be doing.

Enrollment managers must also be aware that planning is a symbolic activity. Planning by an enrollment management office indicates the importance of attracting and retaining students externally, to potential students and competitors, and internally, to faculty, staff, and current students. Once in place, the strategies planned by enrollment managers, such as emphasizing quality or certain majors or cost, are also symbolic. The statement by a college, "Excellence first at Famous College," has nothing to do with the real quality of the institution, but it symbolizes a value. The symbols an institution uses become a vehicle for advertising the institution to the outside world as well as indicating to its members the school's priorities.

In considering the definition of planning, an enrollment manager is deciding what kinds of activities are legitimate. The manager identifies which activities can be taken seriously, which can have resources applied to them, and which are outside of the purview of the enrollment management office.

Scope of Planning and Planning Context

Two issues, the scope of the planning and the planning context, affect any type of planning. The scope of the planning sets the level of complexity in the planning process. The broader the scope, the more things considered in planning and the greater the complexity of the process. Common sense would indicate that planning something simple, like a workshop on enrollment management, is qualitatively different from planning a university. With a narrow scope, a manager can plan with more certainty, more control, and greater rationality; defining a narrow task over a brief time period means fewer things can go awry. In planning something of broad scope, little is stable, and any plan produced is based on dozens of assumptions that change in a dynamic and turbulent environment.

Johnson and Richard (1976) identify five elements that should be considered in defining scope: people, time, resources, programs, and ends and/or means. A plan of narrow scope involves few people, a short time frame, few resources, a single program or only part of a program, and either ends or means but not both. A plan of broad scope involves many people, perhaps thousands, a time frame of years as opposed to days or months, many resources, many programs, and both ends and means.

Certain aspects of enrollment management, student orientation, for example, may be fairly narrow in scope, but enrollment management as an institution-wide practice is broad in scope for just the reasons Johnson and Richard articulate. There are many players in enrollment management who attract and spend a lot of resources over a long time and operate several programs while deciding on new goals and new approaches to acheiving those goals. Its inclusive nature makes enrollment management planning complex and of limited rationality. Enrollment management planning demands an approach that can accommodate ambiguity, multiple beliefs about what is going on inside and outside the institution, and organized anarchy, while accomplishing some relatively simple and definable tasks. Strategic planning, described in a later section, offers such an approach.

Plans are developed at particular schools, at particular times, and in particular social, academic, political, and economic environments. Planners must be aware of their local context, a vital notion discussed further in Chapter Sixteen. External planning experts, that is, experts in the planning process, must be balanced against experts in the planning context.

What forms the context for planning in a college or university? Five areas are important: trends, values, power, stakeholders, and constraints. While trends constrain what is possible and identify opportunities to serve new students, the values of the most powerful stakeholders shape the ends and means actually pursued by a college or university and of which enrollment managers must be acutely aware.

An institution exists in a society in which general trends influence local action. Higher education has been affected by several trends, one of which is the movement over the past two decades away from a values-oriented social consciousness to a more materialistic and narcissistic orientation (Lasch, 1978). Trends like this one are reflected in changes in student responses to standardized questionnaires such as Astin's (1985) Cooperative Institutional Research Program (CIRP). Postsecondary education has become important for career preparation, and during the past century the matriculation rate has changed from 4 percent to over 50 percent. The curriculum of the 1960s, developed when there was a demand for relevant courses, has, ironically, little relevance in the culture of the 1990s. During the coming decade the relevant curriculum may again change. It is essential that enrollment management programs be planned taking national and regional trends into account.

Values are affected by trends but are usually more stable. They underlie everything people do but are notoriously difficult to define. An observer might recognize a person's values by noticing that the person always tries to behave in certain ways in order to achieve certain goals. Preferring certain modes of behavior (such as being logical or honest or loving or ambitious) indicates a person's *instrumental values,* while what that person seeks (such as wisdom, happiness, social recognition, or inner harmony) indicates the person's *terminal values* (a distinction made by Rokeach, 1968). Organizations can be thought of as having a similar set of characteristics: ends (terminal values) and means (instrumental values). When translating values into goals, enrollment managers must be cognizant of the stated goals of the institution, their own goals, and the real goals of other members of the institution. In a utopian world, all goals and value systems could coincide. In the real world, enrollment managers must deal with the values of the most powerful stakeholders in the organization — values that ultimately shape their work environments.

Power, therefore, also affects the planning of enrollment management systems. Put simply, power is the ability to affect outcomes. Powerful people can influence others to do what they want in order to get what they want from their organization. If President Smith wants to improve the quality of students at State College and Dean Jones wants a larger freshman class, and State College gets a larger but less-qualified freshman class, Dean Jones is more powerful than President Smith. Outcomes, not authority, indicate power. Power can be based on many things besides a person's rank in an organization: control of resources, possession of information, the ability to reward or punish, political power (control of votes), expertise, charisma, and so on. Enrollment managers with power have a lot of control over the characteristics and numbers of students enrolled at an institution and the processes used to attract and retain students. Enrollment managers with little power must do as they are told.

The next contextual element in planning an enrollment management system has to do with stakeholders. Any person with a vested interest in the performance of an institution or in a particular institutional process is a stakeholder. The stakeholders in a planning process are defined by who is included and excluded from the planning process and who is on the executive planning committee (the group actually doing planning) and who is merely consulted. The more people involved in decision making, the greater the commitment to implementing the decision. The fewer people involved, the less cumbersome the process and the more likely a plan will include something besides vague generalities. The trade-off between high levels of participation and high degrees of centralization is a difficult one to make — in fact, it is almost a catch-22. If a system is not centralized, it may not be able to act quickly enough to take advantage of an opportunity. But if it is centralized, the people who were excluded from the decision-making process may refuse to implement the activities required to take advantage of an opportunity. Since enrollment management ultimately concerns every member of an academic community, decisions about who to include in planning are critical.

The final contextual element, constraints, limits what an institution can do. Laws and executive orders, financial and personal obligations, and institutional traditions prescribe, permit, and prohibit certain courses of action. For example, at many institutions Title IX necessitated spending monies to rectify past discrimination against women's athletic programs. State and federal collective bargaining legislation permits collective bargaining at some institutions and not at others. Personal gifts to institutions sometimes require matching funds so that monies previously allocated to one program are reallocated in order to match the gift. The federal government can suddenly shift priorities from one area (such as physics) to another (such as cancer research). Resources previously available are no longer available. Plans must be made with constraints in mind and must be changeable when constraints change.

Trends, values, power, stakeholders, and constraints form the core elements of the planning context as indicated in Figure 2.1. Enrollment managers must understand these elements in order to have a sensible approach to planning. In addition to these contextual elements, several other aspects of planning should be discussed before addressing planning enrollment management.

Planning as Process or Product

Planning can be viewed primarily as a process or a product. As a process, planning involves gathering information and gathering people together to define the situation. During formal planning (informal planning is a constant activity), people come together and talk about what is important to them, exchange ideas, exchange pleasantries, exercise dominance and submission, and learn about what others think the college or university is or should be. Such activities define the meaning of organizational life and, ultimately, the organization. Through a continual planning process, ideas emerge around which different groups can coalesce, new rules are passed or new roles created, and a guided evolution of the institution takes place.

These activities do not necessarily produce a document called a plan. Enrollment managers need to quickly establish whether they are in an environment in which planning or the plan itself is most important. If the institution has a high tolerance

Figure 2.1. Factors Affecting the Planning Context.

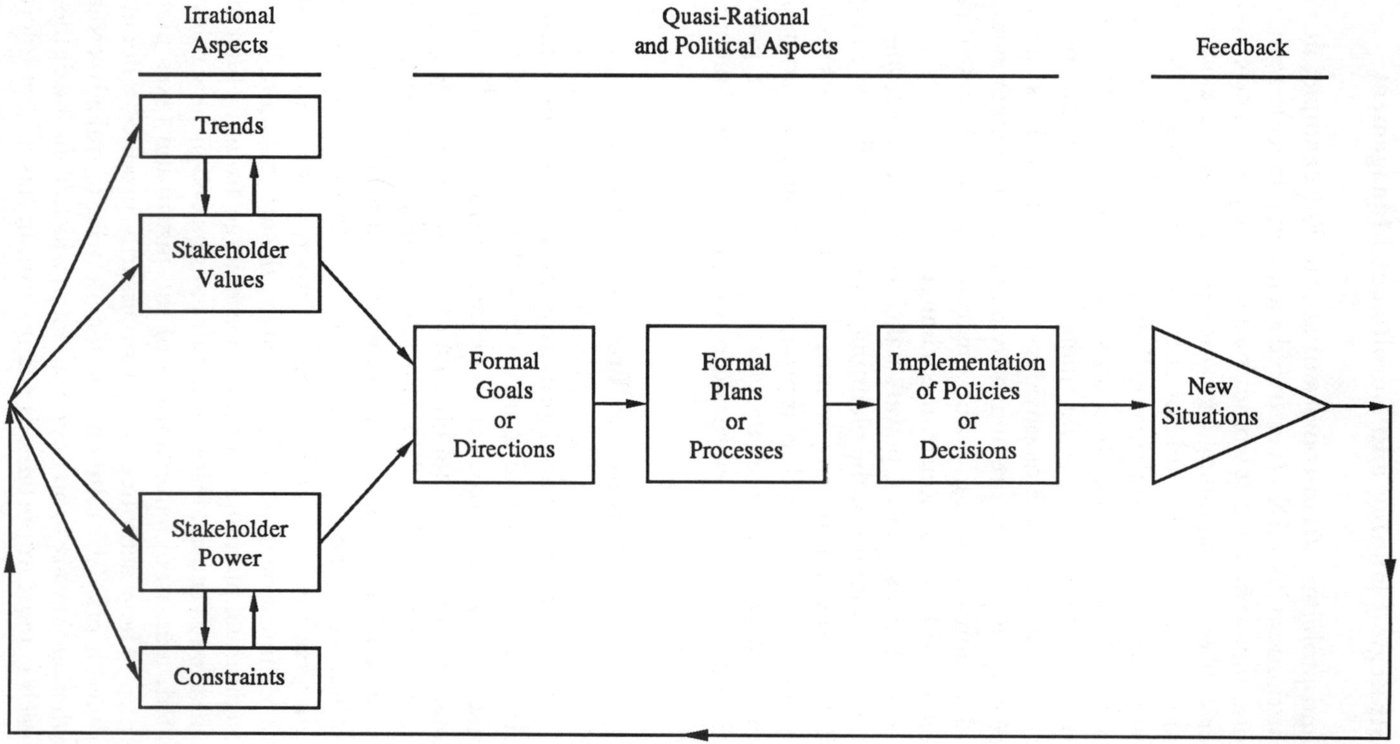

for ambiguity and risk taking, the planning process is likely to be most valuable. If there is little tolerance for ambiguity or failure, producing a plan may seem most important. Plans create the illusion of control: "Now that we have a plan, we know what to do and how to do it." Plans can also create part of the rigidity and centralization that Peters and Waterman (1982) were trying to avoid when they recognized the importance of "simultaneous loose-tight properties" as one element of excellent companies. A detailed plan emphasizes doing things right instead of doing the right things and sticking to process details as opposed to seizing opportunities as they occur, losing sight of core values in favor of attention to detail.

For example, an enrollment management plan might call for the identification of potential student markets. The plan might require detailed information about potential students at schools that send more than five students to the college. The enrollment management group might become so wrapped up in getting data about potential students that they lose sight of the fact that they are trying to enroll students. They gather extensive data on students that have already chosen to attend another college and fail to attract students outside of the target schools. The means (getting data) replaces the ends (enrolling students). Enrollment managers must be wary of focusing on detail as a way of controlling their turbulent work environments. President Franklin D. Roosevelt wanted memos to run no more than a single page. Perhaps plans should be so limited.

A plan (as a document) has to be implemented to affect organizational activities, while planning as a process affects organizational activities through changing people's beliefs about what they are doing, what is important, and who is powerful and by presenting new ideas. The Achilles' heel of a plan is its implementation since people are notorious for implementing only those parts of a plan that they like or agree with (that are consistent with their values). Whether a plan is detailed or general, enrollment managers must understand the costs involved in implementation (psychic and real) and the way in which implementation is likely to differ from the written plan. The greater the extent to which the plan indicates people should deviate from current practices, the less likely people are to implement the plan as written. Enrollment managers must be prepared.

Many definitions of planning imply that it is a purely rational process. It is not. Enrollment management planners cannot meet the criteria for rationality in a varied, politicized, and dynamic environment. Consider the following:

- The core contextual elements of planning — trends, values, power, stakeholders, and constraints — are not rational.
- Enrollment managers' knowledge of an institution and any given problem is imperfect.
- Planners cannot know everything that might affect a choice between alternatives.
- All alternatives cannot be fully developed because of the cost of generating full-blown alternatives and the limits of human imagination.
- A true and complete consensus about priorities at the operational level is technically possible but unlikely since endorsing one priority would cause some people to lose considerable resources (like their jobs) while others would gain control over the first group of people.
- Organizational members cannot predict all of the consequences of their actions.
- Organizational members cannot anticipate every important environmental change.

The implications for enrollment managers should be clear: They cannot expect miracles from planning. They must act consistently with a set of goals, but plan directions instead of details. They should hire people who value what the institution values. Since enrollment managers work in an open systems context, they should not plan a closed system (that is, one that acts as if there were no changes in the environment).

Enrollment managers must plan — their roles may not yet be clearly defined, but they will play a central role in shaping institutional quality and size. Strategic planning offers the most sensible approach to planning enrollment management, and it is strategic planning that will next be described.

Comparing Strategic Planning
and Traditional Planning

Although enrollment managers have a number of planning approaches to choose from, enrollment management should be planned strategically. It is important for enrollment managers to understand the differences between traditional approaches and newer strategic approaches to planning.

Strategic planning, derived from military planning and well known in business, began to enter into higher education after the long-range planning procedures of the 1960s and 1970s yielded fat plans but few tangible results. The general characteristics of strategic planning are, to paraphrase Cope (1981):

1. It is primarily (but not exclusively) a function of chief executive officers.
2. It involves planning across subunits — the unit of planning is the whole organization.
3. It emphasizes environmental conditions and the matching of institutional capabilities and environmental opportunities.
4. It is a continuous, iterative process.
5. It is more concerned with doing the right thing than doing things right — more concerned with achieving goals than following rules.
6. It seeks advantages from existing internal and external conditions, that is, synergistic effects.
7. It seeks to define an institution's mission, role, and scope and in doing so answers the questions "What business are we in? What business should we be in?"
8. It is concerned with the basic character of the organization, the core of special competence.
9. It emphasizes change through external and self-examination; hence it does not remain static.

Strategic planning differs from traditional approaches to long-range planning in several ways. Table 2.1 expands on the work of Cope (1981) and Bryson (1988) and summarizes some of these differences.

Table 2.1. A Comparison of Planning Procedures.

Conventional Long-Range Planning	Strategic Planning
Focus on goals	Focus on issues
Identify objectives to reach goals	Identify vision of success to shape work
Closed system	Open system
Internal orientation	Internal and external (environmental) orientation
Consensus-oriented (talk)	Action oriented (do)
Plan (blueprint)	Stream of decisions (process)

Source: Adapted from Cope, 1981, p. 7.

For the enrollment manager who comes from a quantitative orientation — one that measures success by numbers — the entry into the chaotic world of strategic planning may be dizzying. In strategic planning the illusion of control of the future is traded for the uncertainty of current opportunities.

The strategic planning of enrollment management is more appropriate than traditional planning approaches because of three central characteristics of planning enrollment management activities. First, enrollment management activities take place throughout an institution, not in isolation, and they are in dynamic and interdependent relationships with one another. Second, enrollment management activities depend on environmental scanning, in particular, identifying the ebb and flow of student markets. Third, enrollment management should be part of an institution's overall strategic planning. Students represent a major financial resource for a school, but, more important, they shape the character of the school. Thus, enrollment management plays a vital role in deciding "what business to be in," which is a major issue of strategic planners. The central purpose of enrollment management is to influence the size of the student body and to influence the types of students that enroll. These issues are strategic issues. In affecting the student body, enrollment management shapes the character, quality, and effectiveness of the institution.

Types of Strategic Planning

Chaffee (1989) makes a distinction between three types of strategic planning: linear, adaptive, and interpretive. Linear strategy is much like conventional long-range planning, in which people are expected to achieve a series of objectives in order to reach a goal. Adaptive strategy is much like the strategic planning described by Cope (1981). The primary characteristic of adaptive strategy is the attempt to match the capabilities of the organization and the opportunities in the environment. Since the environment and the organization are constantly changing, the organization must constantly adapt to this change.

The third type of strategic planning described by Chaffee is called interpretive strategy. This type is most closely associated with the "vision of success" aspect of adaptive strategy. The purpose of interpretive strategy is to plan how to affect the way stakeholders inside and outside of the organization interpret what the organization is and what it does. Interpretive strategy helps to make the college or university and what it does legitimate. Highly visible members of the academic community are the key players in interpreting strategy. They need to identify the purpose of the school and, ultimately, why it should continue to exist (or grow).

Chaffee and other organizational theorists have come to recognize that successful colleges and universities can build consensus among students, faculty, and administrators regarding the mission and goals of the institution. Campus leaders help develop a sense of institutional self-confidence and a strong institutional self-image. Later chapters on marketing and student retention strategies demonstrate that a strong institutional image can have a positive effect upon student recruitment as well as student persistence. Interpretive strategy involves the use of symbols, metaphors, rites, rituals, publications, press releases, public service announcements on radio and television, and other available means to develop a strong internal institutional culture and focus, and external legitimacy.

Interpretive strategy exists to make the institution legitimate in the face of change. When something unusual happens at an institution, what are stakeholders to think? Institutions should be prepared to explain new circumstances. For example, a 10 percent change in enrollments is usually a dramatic change. Consider the following hypothetical newspaper accounts of such a change:

> College A recently had a 10 percent increase in the size of its student body resulting in a crisis on campus. "We have no place to put all of these students," complained the director of housing. "The classes are already filled and we don't have qualified faculty to teach the extra sections of our introductory courses," the provost added.

> College B recently had a 10 percent increase in the size of its student body because of the creation of a new enrollment management program. As a result, increased tuition income will make possible the hiring of several new faculty members as well as the addition of new reference books to the library's already distinguished collection. Projections indicate that this enrollment increase will continue for some time into the future, and the board of trustees already has plans on the drawing board for two new dormitories.

Similar counter-intuitive arguments could be given for a decline in enrollments, which could be described in one instance as a harbinger of campus closure and in another as relief for overworked faculty and a chance for them to increase personal attention to students. While both versions report facts, the interpretation of those facts creates or fails to create legitimacy. In politics this is referred to as "spin control."

Two difficulties face interpretive strategies. First, it is difficult to know what emergencies will arise. Hence, a legitimizing philosophy must be in place so that strategic planners and decision makers can act consistently with this philosophy. Second, statements that might be very appealing to an external constituency might wreak havoc internally and vice versa. If a college reports to an external audience, as did College B in the example, that more students mean more faculty members and then class size is increased and few new faculty are hired, existing faculty may be justifiably outraged. Interpretive strategy may border on manipulation. On the positive side, being "value driven," driven by symbols of achievement and a core of excellence, is, according to Peters and Waterman (1982), very desirable.

Enrollment managers must be cognizant of the various forms of planning and the implications of using one type rather than another. The three types of strategy are not mutually exclusive. In fact, all three are probably required for different activities. Linear planning is required for routinized activities of limited scope, such as implementing a specific marketing or retention program. Adaptive planning can be used as a primary activity for developing a five-year marketing plan or retention plan, and interpretive planning can provide legitimacy for these other activities.

Implementing Strategic Enrollment Planning

In the context of strategic planning for an entire college or university, strategic enrollment planning directly affects an institution in two ways. The first is in terms of resources since enrollments are directly connected to revenues through tuition or head-count allocations. Second, the quantity, character, and quality of the student body shape academic life at a school and, hence, institutional mission. Faculty and curriculum depend on students (although the reverse is certainly true as well). Thus, two of the most important strategic issues for an institution are enrollment management issues.

In addition, enrollment management directly affects the offices, budgets, and activities of admissions and marketing, institutional research, financial aid, orientation, student services, and career planning and placement. When enrollment management offices coordinate retention activities, virtually every person and program on campus can be affected. Enrollment management is a central part of institutional strategy, and the strategic planning of enrollment management exists under the umbrella of institutional strategic planning.

Bryson (1988, p. 4) outlined an eight-step strategic planning process for public and nonprofit organizations. The steps are:

1. Initiating and agreeing on a strategic planning process
2. Identifying organizational mandates
3. Clarifying organizational mission and values
4. Assessing the external environment: opportunities and threats
5. Assessing the internal environment: strengths and weaknesses
6. Identifying the strategic issues facing an organization
7. Formulating strategies to manage the issues
8. Establishing an effective organizational vision for the future

Bryson and others have stressed that strategic planning is an iterative process, which may be a polite way of saying that it is chaotic. It might also be considered a hermeneutic process, in which each planning activity provides more information, which is then used to modify prior processes in an endless cycle. For example, enrollment planners could establish an organizational mission (step 3), assess the environment (step 4), and find part of the mission untenable due to environmental changes and go back and modify the mission (step 3 again). Although it can be described as an eight-step process, the procedure is not linear when actually used. Nonetheless, these eight steps provide a framework for raising planning issues that affect enrollment management.

Initiating and Agreeing on a Strategic Planning Process. Before initiating strategic planning, enrollment management planners have to answer the question: Is now the right time to proceed? The answer may be no for several reasons. If the institution has abundant resources and most stakeholders are delighted with the status quo, planning may be unnecessary. If a recent planning process was a disaster, a new planning process may be looked upon skeptically. If an administrative shake-up has occurred recently, no one may be able to take the risks necessary to make tough decisions about what is excluded from the institution's mission.

   If it is time to proceed, the next question to be answered is, Who should be involved and when should they be brought in? The answer depends on the history of enrollment management activities on the campus, local norms of decision making, management styles, and so on. An enrollment manager should be the chair of the planning committee if the manager has high status in the college or university. If not, a vice-president or provost should chair the committee while the enrollment manager does the lion's share of the work (setting the agenda, providing supporting information). The heads of all administrative subunits should be present, and representatives of constituent groups should have some mechanism for being included. The president and each vice-president should be represented. The directors of such programs as institutional research and financial aid and other deans or directors with a major role in student academic or social services should also be included, although the exact composition of the group will vary from campus to campus.

   After substantive membership is established, the committee needs a planning expert to help develop the strategic planning process. Experts within the institution may have a vested interest to protect. Outside experts need to be educated to the modus operandi and organizational sagas of the school or they may suggest planning systems that will not work in a particular case. Outside experts may have their own vested interests to protect in terms of promoting their products or services. A combination of inside and outside expertise is desirable to accomplish step 1.

Identifying Organizational Mandates. Most colleges and universities are obligated to certain mandates by federal regulations (such as affirmative action), state regulations (such as charters, laws), and benefactors' wishes (such as stipulations in large gifts). Institutions must thoroughly search the internal and external environment for the mandates that constrain their mission ("State University is not allowed to offer courses in veterinary medicine"), affect admission criteria ("You must admit all students wishing to attend who graduate in the top half of their high school class in this state"), and so on. A failure to adequately identify these mandates can cause embarrassment and even public ridicule.

Clarifying Organizational Mission and Values. Clarifying the organizational mission and values of an institution is the heart of interpretive strategy and answers the questions: What business are we to be in? What do we stand for? What is important to us? How shall we represent ourselves to the outside world? The mission and values represented in an enrollment manager's strategic plan must be compatible with those in the institution's overall strategic plan. If a school's overall plan values "quality" and an enrollment manager's plan values "big," conflicts will arise. There are internal and external consequences of choosing some values over others or emphasizing some missions above others. Poetic metaphors and symbols help impart institutional meaning to constituents. In one sense, the mission and values of the institution should have been decided at the highest (presidential or board) level. On the other hand, the values of the enrollment management players should be considered. In steps 2 and 3, enrollment managers are deciding what they would like to do in their work and in shaping their school. Successful enrollment managers must meet the expectations that key stakeholders have for enrollment management. When enrollment management is no longer viewed as legitimate by these stakeholders, it will vanish.

Assessing the External Environment: Opportunities and Threats. The external environment is the definitive element in adaptive strategic planning. The Harvard Policy Model, developed to match firms to their environment, organizes its central activities around "SWOT" analysis — systematically assessing internal strengths and weaknesses and external opportunities and threats (Bryson, 1988). Enrollment managers need to identify opportunities and threats in the external environment. Environmental factors are usually considered an opportunity or a threat depending on the extent to which they exist. For example, another college in the institution's area might represent the opportunity for joint programs, increasing enrollments at both schools, while five colleges in the area might represent stiff competition for entering freshmen.

Members of organizations create their own environments (Weick, 1979) by deciding what is and what is not important in the infinite complexity of events that go on around them. Only things that they recognize can provide opportunities. Threats have a way of making themselves known whether they are recognized or not. This implies that the richer an institution's understanding of its environment, the greater the number of opportunities for success the institution will have. Although the prescription to look carefully sounds simple enough, people consistently fail to recognize new things — they see only what they have seen before. For example, orientation programs and course schedules are often designed for residential students, even though the majority of students may now be commuters. Recognizing diversity in the student body might lead to orientation programs for commuter students who are mothers, commuter students with full-time employment, full-time traditional-age residential students, full-time traditional-age residential students from foreign countries, upper-class black students, black students from inner cities, and so on. Each group might have unique orientation needs. Stereotypes result in lost opportunities.

Among the factors that need to be considered by enrollment managers in assessing the external environment are: demographic trends (age, educational level, numbers, race, ethnicity, and gender of students or potential students); economic trends (employment rate changes, size of tax base, probability of foundation gifts, pricing strategies); student markets (sources of current students, potential new sources); salient characteristics of market segments (students' interests, students' abilities to pay); educational and noneducational options for potential students; competitors; and nontuition sources of income. Interpreting a factor after it has been recognized is equally important to enrollment managers. Recognition and interpretation create people's environments — they constrain what people take seriously.

Assessing the Internal Environment: Strengths and Weaknesses.
Internal assessments are usually more difficult than external assessments. Often staff and faculty think that they know much more than they actually do about themselves and their institution. They are often surprised to find out what others in the institution are doing — faculty are often ignorant about what student services personnel do and vice versa. Some individuals are reluctant to admit or are unaware of their skills and limitations, yet these people can have a direct impact on the success of enrollment management efforts. Frequently, the most meaningful assessment is for each person concerned with enrollment management to describe his or her work, purpose, the purpose of his or her subunit, and the purpose of the institution. This step is often taken for granted, but when a new office of enrollment management is developed, everyone needs to be educated as to what the office can and cannot do.

Other parts of internal assessment are more mundane but very practical. They involve routine gathering of data and creation of information about the activities of the organization. IPEDS (Integrated Postsecondary Educational Systems) and NCHEMS (National Center for Higher Education Management Systems) data are of this sort. Information of primary interest to enrollment managers is baseline data (how many people are taking what courses, living in what dorms, attending what events, and so on) and trend data (in what programs or majors are enrollments increasing or declining and by how much). Studies can also be used to find out the types of students (age, race, gender, major) enrolled in each class or program or major or living arrangement. Other studies can look at how students with different characteristics or from different high schools fare in different majors and how many persist until graduation. The information generated from such assessments can be used to assess the demand for and cost of programs in light of the programs' centrality to the mission of the school and its quality.

Identifying the Strategic Issues Facing an Organization. The previous five steps should identify the major strategic issues that an institution must confront. These issues include major policy questions related to the collegiate mission, the purpose of enrollment management, stakeholder values, power relationships among stakeholders, constraints, mandates, resource availability, market segments for existing and new students, curricula, retention programs, financing, and management activities. These issues should be succinctly described and analyzed in terms of SWOT—organizational strengths, weaknesses, opportunities, and threats. The way in which particular issues affect enrollment managers as opposed to other members of the college or university needs to be clarified.

Formulating Strategies to Manage the Issues. Strategies define institutional action, both means and ends, for the long and short term. The way to develop strategies is idiosyncratic to institutions and to people. If there were an algorithm for generating effective strategies, managers would have little to do. Good strategies solve problems, create opportunities, resolve conflicts, find resources, and translate the mission of the school into action. Good strategies can be accomplished by the staff at hand, are efficient, and make sense in terms of the environment. They must be politically possible and serve the overall mission of the institution.

This book is filled with marketing and retention strategies that make sense in a given context and with the proper personnel and circumstances. The local context is the one that counts, a point made again in the concluding chapter.

Establishing an Effective Organizational Vision for the Future. The planners' vision of what the successful institution would look like is the part of interpretive strategy that provides meaning for present activities. Current activities can be evaluated in terms of their consistency with this vision. The tight coupling between current activities and this vision of the institution is the "tight" part of Peters and Waterman's (1982) simultaneous loose-tight properties. Frequently, however, routine tasks should be tightly monitored, but an overemphasis on correctness may be counter-productive if it limits flexible responses. The vision indicates the right thing to do without being prescriptive about how to accomplish the task. Just as in other aspects of interpretive strategy, this vision has both an internal and external impact.

Enrollment management must fit within the vision of the future of the entire school, but it should also have a vision of itself. An internal vision should include: structures (Where should the director of enrollment management be placed in the organiza-tion? What offices should report to the director?), actors (Who should constitute the enrollment management staff? How should others, such as faculty members, be engaged in enrollment man-agement?), and targets (What should be the mean SAT or ACT scores of incoming classes for the next five years? What should be the size of the student body and what should be its composi-tion in terms of age, race, gender, full-time/part-time status, and so forth?). Employees who share the vision of a particular school's enrollment management process need little supervision. These employees also feel more freely invested in their work since they understand how their small acts help create a desir-able future for the college or university.

Enrollment management has a particular concern for the size and character of the student body, and, therefore, part of the vision for enrollment management needs to include students as benchmarks of strategic success. Changes in numbers, rates, and percentages are more important indicators of programmatic success than cross-sectional one-time data. Answers to the fol-lowing eight groups of questions can indicate levels of strategic success for most enrollment management programs. Answers to the first five should be provided for the student body as a whole and for each meaningful group of students that attends a particular school — groups such as those based on age, gender, race, religion, full-time/part-time status, high school (or college or university in the case of transfer students) of origin. The ques-tions are: (1) Size: How many students are in each group? How many credit hours are generated by each group? (2) Quality: What is the scholastic quality of each group? (3) Trends: How have the numbers of students in each group changed over time? Do their reasons for attending differ? Are there changes in enrollment patterns in target groups because of new enrollment management practices? (4) Retention: Have retention rates changed for each group of students? (5) Graduation rates: Have program completion and graduation rates changed for each group of students? (6) How successful has this school been against its competitors? (7) How well has the school been able to segment its market? (8) How well has the school been able to match faculty and curricular resources with students' or potential students' needs and interests?

Answering these questions, especially examining changes in the answers over time, brings visionaries to earth. It grounds strategic planners of enrollment management in the fundamental indicators of institutional success.

Chapter 3

Organizational Approaches

Don Hossler

In the first two chapters, enrollment management was defined and the strategic planning process was examined. These two chapters provide a conceptual overview, but enrollment management also requires an organizational structure. Functional areas such as admissions, orientation, and institutional research need to work within an organizational structure that will facilitate communication and efforts to achieve enrollment goals. This chapter examines the approaches for organizing enrollment management systems. It also discusses the necessity for enrollment managers to be flexible in organizing enrollment management efforts and looks at important staffing and support issues.

In Search of a Template

Many campus-based administrators who become interested in establishing an enrollment management system at their institutions look for an organizational template that will quickly create an effective system. The kinds of questions they explicitly or implicitly ask include: What kind of organizational structure should be put into place? Who should coordinate or direct enrollment management activities? Should the chief enrollment manager come from admissions, student affairs, institutional advancement, or the faculty? How can we develop a successful system during the next year?

    An examination of successful enrollment management systems over the past ten years indicates that there is no one right answer to these questions. Like planning, enrollment management must be adapted to the needs, organizational climate, and administrative skills available on each campus. Enrollment management activities, like any organizational task, need to be compatible with local campus issues, management styles, and traditions and culture.

Some colleges and universities that have been successful in influencing their student enrollments do not even use the term *enrollment management*. DePauw University in Greencastle, Indiana, has an informal working relationship, developed over time, among the assistant to the president, the dean of students, and the registrar that helps DePauw to attract and retain an increasingly more qualified student body. The system that has emerged at DePauw is coordinated by the assistant to the president and director of admissions, who came to the school with several years of experience in admissions. DePauw did not set out to create the system that is in place; it evolved over many years.

Similarly, at Wichita State University in Kansas, there is no enrollment management division in the formal organizational chart. The associate vice-president for academic affairs directs the enrollment related activities. Admissions and financial aid report directly to the vice-president, as do the offices of orientation and student retention. The senior enrollment management officer was previously the associate vice-president for student affairs at the school. Wichita State intentionally set out to establish an enrollment management system and the vice-president was moved into his current role. However, he would be the first to acknowledge that Wichita State is still in the process of developing the kind of enrollment management system it wants. Building a successful system usually takes time.

Drake University in Des Moines, Iowa, has developed an enrollment management system that is housed within the student affairs division and run by the vice-president of enrollment management and student services. The current vice-president had previously been the vice-president for student affairs for many years before expanding his responsibilities. Drake created an effective organization in just two years. For several reasons, however, Drake is an anomaly in this regard. The vice-president has been at Drake for many years. He was well established and respected. Also, both the number and the quality of enrolled students at Drake had been declining in recent years, and the faculty and administrators had become concerned. When a new president was appointed, he identified enrollment issues as a major campus concern, giving them legitimacy and gaining them resources. The resulting campus climate allowed for change much more quickly than usually is possible at most colleges and universities. The new enrollment management system was able to bring about immediate results.

Each of these institutions employed different strategies to exert influence over student enrollments. Enrollment managers need to keep in mind that there are a variety of successful models and that even successful models grow and evolve. For institutions that are beginning to build an enrollment management system, however, it can be useful to consider some basic frameworks for developing an organizational model. Kemerer, Baldridge, and Green (1982), in their book *Strategies for Effective Enrollment Management*, describe four archetypal models: the enrollment management committee, the enrollment management coordinator, the enrollment management matrix, and the enrollment management division. These models should not be considered as blueprints for individual institutions but rather as points of departure for a model that will fit the conditions on different campuses.

The Enrollment Management Committee. When a problem or issue arises at most colleges and universities, the first step taken is to establish a committee. On many campuses, the first step in the creation of an enrollment management system is the creation of an enrollment management committee. The committee is usually charged with looking at the institution's current marketing and student retention efforts. Sometimes two separate committees are established, one for marketing and one for student retention. As in most campus committees, the membership of an enrollment management committee includes faculty, administrators, and students. Usually, the director of admissions, a student affairs administrator, or a faculty member is asked to chair the committee.

Kemerer, Baldridge, and Green (1982) accurately identify the advantages and disadvantages of the committee model. An enrollment management committee can be an effective vehicle for educating large numbers of faculty and administrators about marketing and retention, which can be a good way to build campus support for enrollment management activities. In addition, a committee is less likely to raise issues of administrative jurisdiction because no administrative restructuring is required. It also does not require as much administrative support from senior-level administrators to implement. Nor does it require a large investment of institutional money. A committee is a good model for exploring enrollment related concerns if the problems are not so severe that they require quick actions.

There are, however, a number of disadvantages to the committee model. At most colleges and universities, committees have little influence over institutional policy making. Committees have to report through several layers of faculty or administrative bureaucracy, so any feedback mechanism they have to senior-level administrators is slow. It is also hard for committees to engage in sustained efforts. The membership of most committees completely rotates every two to three years. The enrollment management committee may spend more time educating new members than it does developing enrollment management strategies. Since this approach does not require high levels of administrative support to implement, it may also lack sufficient support to bring about any needed changes. Although there are several advantages to establishing an enrollment management committee, this approach is seldom a long-term organizational solution. It can be a good place to start, but over time enrollment management systems usually need to evolve into more centralized organizations.

The Enrollment Management Coordinator. Another common response to enrollment concerns on many campuses is to designate an enrollment management coordinator. The Peat Marwick (1987) survey of enrollment management practices indicated that 13 percent of all responding institutions had only a committee in place, while 42 percent had some combination of a committee and a director or dean of enrollment management (p.15). The enrollment management coordinator is charged with organizing recruitment and retention activities. The coordinator is often a midlevel administrator, such as the director or dean of admissions. Sometimes the coordinator will also have responsibility for financial aid.

Like the committee model, the coordinator model requires little organizational restructuring and less administrative support than more centralized models. As a result, administrative units such as orientation or student activities may be less threatened and more likely to cooperate with the coordinator on a voluntary basis. The coordinator should also work with an oversight committee so that the benefits of educating large numbers of administrators and faculty are retained. This model is less costly than the next two models that will be discussed.

An important disadvantage to this model is that it provides no formal mechanism for linking enrollment concerns and the decision-making agenda of senior-level administrators. Again, the lack of administrative support required to implement this approach may exacerbate the problem; enrollment concerns remain problems only for midlevel administrators. In addition, the success of this model is highly dependent upon the coordinator who is appointed to the position. If the person has a good deal of internal credibility and can work effectively as a facilitator, this model can work. However, a coordinator who lacks respect and interpersonal skills may not be able to implement the necessary enrollment management initiatives.

The Enrollment Management Matrix. The enrollment management matrix requires more centralization than either the committee or the coordinator model. In the matrix model, an existing senior-level administrator such as the vice-president for student affairs, academic affairs, or institutional advancement directs the activities of the enrollment management matrix. In this model, administrative units are not formally reassigned to a new vice-president. Instead, the administrative heads of these units continue their existing reporting relationships, but they also become part of the enrollment management matrix. In essence, these administrative units work with two senior administrators.

One of the important advantages of the matrix model is that enrollment management becomes the direct concern of a senior administrator. This also means that to implement the model will require higher levels of administrative support than needed to implement the previous two models. If implemented, the model ensures that enrollment related issues will have a hearing at the top levels of the campus administration. In addition, in this model the senior administrator relies less on personal persuasion to achieve goals. The administrator is more likely to have the resources and the authority to make decisions in a timely fashion. Although a more centralized model than the first two, this approach also does not require administrative restructuring, which can be costly and antagonize administrators and faculty who do not wish to see major changes take place.

The primary disadvantage of the matrix model is that the vice-president who is assigned to direct the activities of the matrix may not have the time to devote to enrollment management concerns. In addition, the vice-president may not be knowledgeable about this area. Either of these factors could reduce the effectiveness of the matrix model. Jurisdiction issues can also be a problem. If midlevel administrators who are part of the matrix report to another vice-president who is not in agreement with the enrollment management goals, problems will arise.

The Enrollment Management Division. The most centralized of the models is the enrollment management division. In the division model, a vice-president or associate vice-president is assigned the responsibilities for all enrollment management activities (see Chapter One for a full description of an enrollment management division). The vice-president houses most or all of the administrative areas that influence student enrollments within one large functional unit. This model requires high levels of administrative support; usually the president or a senior vice-president of the institution has to become a strong advocate of this model.

There are several advantages to this model. It brings all

of the administrative units that can influence student enrollments into one division. Enrollment management strategies are easier to identify and implement. A senior-level administrator is given full responsibility to direct administrative activities that affect the recruitment and retention of students. Cooperation among key offices, such as admissions and financial aid, is more likely to occur. An enrollment management vice-president can carry enrollment related concerns directly to the president and the board of trustees.

This centralized approach, however, is not without its drawbacks. Unless a campus is in the midst of an enrollment crisis, it is difficult to create a new administrative division. Existing vice-presidents do not like to have administrative units removed from their divisions. For example, taking financial aid from a vice-president for finance, and career planning from a student affairs division could alienate both the units being moved and the vice-presidents to whom they had previously reported. As a result, an enrollment management division that looks good on paper may not function smoothly. On many campuses that put an enrollment management division into place quickly, staff turnover has been high and the staff members who remained suffered extended periods of low morale.

Most existing successful enrollment management divisions either were put into place during a crisis (such as the division at DePaul University) or developed slowly over several years (such as the one at the University of Wisconsin, Oshkosh). Seldom are comprehensive enrollment management divisions implemented effectively and quickly.

Creating enrollment management divisions can also be costly. In most instances vice-presidents for enrollment management are hired from outside the institution. There is a strong demand for senior administrators with the skills needed for enrollment management, and they can command large salaries. In addition, a new vice-president will often determine that new directors of admissions or financial aid are needed. Directors of research may also be added to enrollment management divisions. Enrollment management divisions may be more effective than other models, but they are also more costly. Institutions that are exploring this model are well advised to be certain that they are willing to pay the political and economic costs associated with it.

Emphasizing Substance over Form

Successful enrollment management systems can be found that employ variations of each of the four organizational models. It is important to note that there are few textbook examples of any of these models. At the University of Wisconsin, Oshkosh, and DePaul University, the vice-presidents of enrollment management do not oversee most of the student affairs divisions that might influence student retention. Therefore, the enrollment management divisions operate more like a matrix or coordinator model when working with student affairs units. Almost all institutions continue to have marketing, retention, or enrollment management committees even after a more formalized system is put into place.

In addition, institutional size and complexity can determine which model will be the most appropriate. Large research universities may have several systems in place. At the undergraduate level, a centralized enrollment management system may work. At the graduate level, however, individual departments and schools have much greater control over marketing activities and retention is usually not a major problem. Therefore, at the graduate level, an associate dean for marketing or recruitment who may work with several departments in a consultative and coordinating role may be more appropriate. It is probably easier for small campuses to have variations of the coordinator, matrix, or division models because smaller size permits enrollment managers to know all of the people involved in enrollment management activities. The institutional mission and subsequent priorities are clearer at small schools. Community colleges may find it easier to develop a centralized enrollment management division because they traditionally have had stronger administrative leadership than four-year institutions.

More important than formal organizational structure are the relationships between key administrative units and the skills of the staff members in those units. Many new enrollment managers seem more concerned about finding the right structure rather than making sure that an institution has administrative staff with the requisite skills in key positions. If the right people are in key positions, the structure of the enrollment management system may not matter.

Some of the staffing questions that need to be asked include:

- Do we have someone with expertise in mail and telemarketing?
- Do we have someone with expertise in market research?
- Does the financial aid office segment student markets and make targeted financial aid awards?
- Do we have someone who can function as an effective retention officer?
- Do we have the staff capabilities to conduct retention research?
- Do we have staff that can manage data bases and retrieve student information in a timely manner?

These skills are essential to effective enrollment management.

In addition to skilled personnel, enrollment management cannot succeed without computerized information systems. Storing, sorting, and analyzing information are the backbone of enrollment management. Smaller campuses can probably use microcomputers and appropriate software to support their efforts. Larger campuses will require access to minicomputers or large mainframes in order to maintain an adequate student data base.

The Enrollment Manager

The remaining question to be addressed in this chapter is, Who should serve as the senior enrollment manager? Once again, there is no one answer to this question. Successful enrollment managers have come from admissions, institutional research, financial aid, student affairs generalist positions, and the faculty.

St. Mary's University in San Antonio has developed a successful enrollment management system that is described in more detail in Chapter Fifteen. At St. Mary's the vice-president for enrollment management has a doctoral degree in higher education with an emphasis in curriculum studies. He also served as the director of financial aid at a liberal arts college. John Maguire, formerly at Boston College, who developed the first documented enrollment management system, was originally a faculty member in the Physics Department at Boston College. The current vice-president for enrollment management at Boston College has a background in institutional research. The vice-president for enrollment management at DePaul University worked in admissions for several years before joining DePaul. It is difficult to find a pattern in the backgrounds of successful enrollment managers. In each case they are good managers, and they all use student information in an analytical framework to make decisions.

To date there is a shortage of people who have the requisite skills and background to fill senior-level enrollment management positions. A viable strategy for many campuses is to train their own enrollment manager. If student enrollment concerns are not at the crisis stage, institutions can identify an internal candidate who has proven to be an effective administrator, who is comfortable with market and retention research, and who is respected across the campus. By attending conferences, reading, and visiting campuses with successful enrollment management programs, administrators or faculty members can be trained to assume enrollment management positions.

Spending time on campuses that already have successful systems may be the most important part of the training process. Institutions that are implementing an enrollment management organization should consider sending administrators who are being trained for senior-level positions to visit a successful system for a week or more. They should spend time with a successful practitioner, serve as consultants on their own campuses, and study in detail how a successful system works. In this way, new enrollment managers have the opportunity to see successful practices in action. New enrollment managers can learn more this way than by bringing a consultant to their campus for one or two days.

Successful enrollment management systems require an organizational structure. The structure, however, should follow from the degree of perceived need for change, the skills of administrators in key units, such as admissions, financial aid, and student retention, and the resources available to develop a system. Forcing centralized systems on institutions that are not in crisis or that have strong resistance to changes may be counterproductive. Successful implementation requires not only that those developing the system know something about enrollment management, but also that they be good organizational diagnosticians as well. In most instances, successful enrollment management requires time to mature.

PART TWO

THE MARKETING DIMENSION
OF ENROLLMENT MANAGEMENT

Part Two describes relevant research and strategies related to the marketing and recruitment function of enrollment management. It provides the knowledge base enrollment managers need to devise effective marketing strategies. This section also provides a practical look at marketing strategies.

Chapter Four is a comprehensive review of research on student college choice. During the past fifteen years, a great deal of knowledge about the factors that influence the enrollment decisions of students has been accumulated. This chapter shows the possibilities of influencing students' choice of college as well as the limits of an institution in affecting that choice.

Chapter Five reviews the literature on nonprofit marketing. It also examines the unique characteristics of marketing an intangible product, like a college education. Choosing a college is a risky decision for many students and families. This chapter provides a conceptual overview that can help guide the marketing practices of enrollment managers.

In Chapter Six, market research techniques are discussed. Successful enrollment management efforts are based on the ability of colleges and universities to segment markets. This chapter describes the most effective approaches for conducting market research. The chapter is accurate and informative yet written in a nontechnical style so that practicing administrators can grasp the concepts behind each technique.

Chapter Seven is a hands-on examination of marketing techniques that are currently in use. It covers topics ranging from videotapes to direct mail campaigns. It can be used as a reference for enrollment managers who wish to determine if they are using all available marketing strategies.

Chapter Eight presents two marketing case studies. Marketing must ultimately be organized and well planned and include a generous portion of attention to detail and follow-through. These two case studies demonstrate the process of marketing as well as providing a look at what a comprehensive enrollment management plan should entail.

Chapter 4

How Students
Choose Colleges

John M. Braxton

Enrollment management is a proactive approach to ensuring the continuous supply of qualified students needed to maintain the vitality of individual colleges and universities (Kemerer, Baldridge, and Green, 1982). Thus, effective enrollment management entails a full range of activities designed not only to attract prospective students but also to retain those students who matriculate (Hossler, 1984). Marketing, recruitment, admissions, and the awarding of financial aid are enrollment management activities conducted to influence the size and characteristics of the student body (Hossler, 1984). In other words, such activities are performed to influence the college choice behavior of prospective students.

For enrollment managers to perform such activities effectively and professionally, they must understand the college choice process. The purpose of this chapter is to review research findings on the student college choice process and to suggest possible ways that colleges and universities might apply these findings. Specifically, the limits and possibilities of enrollment management activities for influencing students' choice of a particular college or university will be identified.

Stages in the College Choice Process

Student college choice has been defined as a "complex, multistage process during which an individual develops aspirations to continue formal education beyond high school, followed later by a decision to attend a specific college, university or institution of advanced vocational training" (Hossler, Braxton, and Coopersmith, 1989, p. 7) This chapter is guided by this definition. A three-stage model of the college choice process posited by Hossler and Gallagher (1987) provides an organizing framework for the research findings summarized in the chapter. The three stages are predisposition, search, and choice.

During the predisposition stage, students decide whether or not they would like to continue their formal education beyond high school. This stage entails the development of aspirations for college attendance (Hossler, Braxton, and Coopersmith, 1989). The search stage is characterized by students' development of knowledge of the attributes and values of colleges and universities and also their identification of the right attributes and values to consider. In the choice stage, students develop a set of colleges to which applications will be made and decide which institution to attend.

As the fostering of aspirations for college is not within the scope of influence and concern of enrollment management, no attention will be devoted here to the predisposition stage. The search and choice stages will be the focus of the following summary of research findings.

Search. In an extensive review of literature on the student college choice process, Hossler, Braxton, and Coopersmith (1989) found few studies that focus on how students identify a desirable set of institutional characteristics. However, this review of literature identified some research that has directed attention to the process through which prospective students engage themselves in the search stage. This research has addressed the timing of, the information sources used in, and the limits placed on the search process.

The junior year in high school appears to be the time during which prospective college students begin the search process (Gilmour and others, 1978; Stewart and others, 1987). The taking of the PSAT is a significant event in this process, because students develop a potential list of institutions when they take the test (Gilmour and others, 1978). However, many students continue the search process into their senior year of high school (Lewis and Morrison, 1975).

A variety of information sources are used by students during the search stage. These sources include college guidebooks, friends, campus visits, and college publications (Gilmour and others, 1978; Cibik, 1982). In rank order, the most frequently used sources of information are catalogues, campus visits, guidance counselors, current college students, and admissions officers (Lewis and Morrison, 1975). The information desired from such sources includes indications of academic quality, cost, career availability, criteria for awarding financial aid, and the helpfulness of instructors (Cibik, 1982). Students from low socioeconomic backgrounds tend to use fewer sources of information than do students from high socioeconomic backgrounds (Tierney, 1980).

Prospective students also develop parameters for the search process. Most students establish limits on geographical location and costs (Gilmour and others, 1978; Tierney, 1983; Astin and others, 1980). Once such limits are established, prospective students seek out institutions that offer programs they desire (Gilmour and others, 1978).

Choice. Various characteristics of prospective students have been found to be associated with the type of college or university selected for enrollment. Family socioeconomic status is related to the quality of the institutions students apply to and attend (Tierney, 1980, 1983; Hearn, 1984; Spies, 1978; Maguire and Lay, 1981; Zemsky and Oedel, 1983). Students from high socioeconomic backgrounds are more likely to apply to and attend selective colleges and universities than are students from low and middle socioeconomic backgrounds. However, the cost of the colleges and universities students select does not appear to be related to family socioeconomic status (Hossler, Braxton, and Coopersmith, 1989).

Student academic ability is another student characteristic associated with the choice of colleges and universities. High-ability students are not only more likely to attend selective institutions (Dahl, 1982; Hearn, 1984; Jackson, 1978; Zemsky and Oedel, 1983) but also are more likely to select out-of-state colleges and universities (Dahl, 1982; Zemsky and Oedel, 1983). Conversely, low-ability students are more likely to attend less selective in-state institutions.

The educational level of students' parents and the parents' encouragement of college attendance are also associated with the type of college or university students apply to and select. As parental educational level increases, students are more likely to apply to and attend more selective institutions (Hearn, 1984). Moreover, students whose parents have a high level of education tend to select private colleges and universities (Litten and others, 1983). Students who receive a great deal of encouragement to attend college from their parents are also more likely to attend selective private colleges and universities (Conklin and Dailey, 1981; Keller and McKewon, 1984). However, encouragement from peers has little relationship to the type of institution selected (Jackson, 1978; Gilmour and others, 1978).

Few studies have addressed the influence of ethnicity on the choice stage (Hossler, Braxton, and Coopersmith, 1989). However, Hearn (1984) found that black students are less likely to apply to more selective institutions, even when their academic ability and socioeconomic status are high.

Various institutional characteristics have also been found to be important in the choice stage. When students have been asked to rate the characteristics of institutions important in their decision to apply to or attend a particular college or university, the characteristics cited most often by them are (in rank order): special academic programs, tuition costs, availability of financial aid, general academic reputation or quality, location or distance from home, size of student body, and social atmosphere (Douglas and others, 1982; Dahl, 1982; Keller and McKewon, 1984; Konnert and Giese, 1987; Maguire and Lay, 1981; Litten, 1982; Litten and others, 1983; Stewart and others, 1987; Chapman and Jackson, 1987).

However, the weighting of these factors varies for different types of students (Hossler, Braxton, and Coopersmith, 1989). For academically able students, perceived quality is the most influential institutional characteristic in the choice stage (Chapman and Jackson, 1987; Litten and others, 1983; Keller and McKewon, 1984). However, costs are more important than quality for academically talented students who are considering attending an in-state institution (Keller and McKewon, 1984).

Students' decisions to attend particular types of colleges and universities are also influenced by state policies and the types of institutions that predominate in a given geographical region. In states having state scholarship programs that provide a generous level of aid, students are more likely to attend private colleges and universities (Astin and others, 1980). Students are also more likely to attend private institutions if they reside in states in which a large number of private colleges and universities are located (Zemsky and Oedel, 1983). Moreover, prospective students living in a state with many and diverse colleges and universities are more likely to attend an in-state institution (Zemsky and Oedel, 1983).

The institutional characteristics that have been discussed thus far — academic quality, costs, and geographical location — are "fixed" institutional characteristics (Chapman, 1981). Such characteristics are difficult for institutions to alter. However, financial aid is a "fluid" institutional characteristic and is subject to change by individual colleges and universities (Chapman, 1981).

Although students suggest that financial aid influences their choice of a college or university, research indicates that this influence is modest. In general, receiving financial aid increases the chances that an accepted applicant will enroll by 8.5 percent (Jackson, 1978, p. 568). The effects of aid, however, are greater in certain situations for particular types of prospective students. Although perceived quality of an institution has a greater effect on choice than does financial aid for academically talented high school students (Chapman and Jackson, 1987), the amount of financial aid awarded plays a significant role in the decisions of such students when their second- and third-choice institutions offer more aid than does their first choice. Specifically, it takes $4,000 more in financial aid for students to select their second-choice college or university and $6,000 more in aid for them to select their third-choice institution. If an academically talented student is undecided between two institutions, however, $1,000 more in financial aid from one of the institutions can influence a student's decision in favor of that institution (Chapman and Jackson, 1987, p. 38). Most of this research has been conducted using samples of academically talented students. Thus, the effects of aid on less-able students are unknown.

Implications of Research for Enrollment Management

Marketing, recruitment, and the awarding of financial aid are enrollment management activities conducted to influence the enrollment decisions of prospective students. The research reviewed in this chapter suggests both limitations to and possibilities for the probable success of these activities.

Limitations. Such proponents of enrollment management as Hossler (1984) and Kemerer, Baldridge, and Green (1982) are generally optimistic about the success of enrollment management activities in influencing student enrollments and institutional vitality. Kemerer, Baldridge, and Green, in particular, contend that if institutions take an active and assertive stance they can influence their own futures. Nevertheless, these proponents do have some concerns about the success of enrollment management. Kemerer, Baldridge, and Green urge institutions to make realistic assessments of possible barriers to success. Hossler cautions that enrollment management is not an elixir for some institutions, given their situations.

With the exception of research on financial aid policies, researchers have focused on student characteristics and such fixed institutional characteristics as location, public or private support, and admissions selectivity. From this research, it is possible to identify some barriers or limitations to enrollment management activities for different types of colleges and universities.

Less-selective institutions are limited in the academic qualifications and geographical location of prospective students. Less-selective institutions are not as likely as more selective institutions to enroll highly qualified high school students. Thus, the probability of meeting faculty demands for better-qualified students in such institutions is not high. Less-selective institutions are also not likely to experience a high degree of success in attracting students able to pay all or part of their college expenses because students from high socioeconomic backgrounds are more likely to enroll at more-selective colleges and universities. Neither are less-selective institutions seeking to maintain their enrollments by recruiting out-of-state students likely to experience a high degree of success.

Limitations for enrollment management activities for more-selective colleges and universities are also suggested by the research. Such colleges and universities that seek a more socioeconomically diverse student body or desire an increase in black student enrollment are not likely to experience a great deal of success in these goals.

The state in which a college or university is located serves as an additional limiting force for enrollment management activities. The enrollment prospects of private institutions located in states with poorly funded state scholarship programs are dimmer than those of private colleges located in states with well-funded programs. For private institutions located in states dominated by state-supported higher education, the probabilities of success for enrollment management activities are less than for private institutions located in states with a diverse system of higher education.

Possibilities. The research also suggests possibilities for influencing student enrollments. For example, as previously indicated, research has found the junior year in high school to be the time during which prospective students become familiar with the characteristics of different colleges and universities. Moreover, taking the PSAT also appears to be an important event in the search process. These findings suggest that admissions officers should seek out juniors possibly interested in their institution during fall as well as spring high school visits. In particular, PSAT takers who have expressed an interest in an institution could be contacted prior to the high school visit by an admissions officer. Institutions that use direct mail programs such as the American College Testing Services' Educational Opportunity Service and the Student Search Service offered by the College Board should seek student mailing information for junior test takers as well as senior test takers.

Moreover, colleges and universities that currently host campus days for accepted students (Murphy and McGarrity, 1978) should consider inviting high school juniors to such events or holding a separate campus day for juniors only. The basic idea undergirding these suggestions is that enrollment management activities should be directed toward high school juniors currently in the search or preapplication stage not only in the spring and summer months after the current freshman class has been recruited but throughout the year.

Although college quality is a fixed institutional characteristic that has been found to be influential in the choice stage of the student college choice process, student perceptions of college quality can be influenced in part by such enrollment management activities as high school visits, campus interviews, and various admissions publications (Chapman, 1981; Hossler, 1984; Kealy and Rockel, 1980). Thus, enrollment managers are urged to inform students about the quality of their institutions through such enrollment management activities.

Perceptions of college quality are related to perceptions of academic quality, social life atmosphere, and campus location (Kealy and Rockel, 1987). Information about these dimensions should be communicated to prospective students, parents of prospective students, and high school guidance counselors. Kuh and Wallman (1986) suggest that enrollment managers inform students about the effects or outcomes of attending a specific college or university. They place outcomes information into four categories: knowledge and intellectual development, social development, personal development, and career and vocational development. Kuh and Wallman suggest indices of student development in each of these categories that could be communicated. Information demonstrating gains by students in critical thinking could be presented as an index of knowledge and intellectual development. Aspects of social development, such as students' increased political and social sophistication and increased confidence in working with others, could also be communicated. Students' increased self-assurance and self-sufficiency and greater awareness of their values, interests, emotions, and aspirations are dimensions of personal development that could be included. Information on the proportion of students placed in fields related to their college major and postcollege salaries of graduates are possible indicators of career and vocational development that could be presented through various recruitment activities.

Indices of institutional quality such as high admissions rates of graduates who apply to top graduate or professional schools, the presence of students who were academic achievers in high school, a large variety of courses and programs, many small classes, and advanced laboratory equipment and library resources should be communicated to high-ability students. These indices were identified by Litten and Hall (1989) through research they conducted on how high-ability students view quality in colleges and universities.

Information on institutional quality could be communicated in college catalogues, viewbooks, and fact sheets; conferences with guidance counselors held by admissions officers; interviews with prospective students; presentations at college fairs; and high school visits made by admissions officers. Such information should become more readily available to specific institutions as increasing attention is given to the assessment of college student outcomes (Jacobi, Astin, and Ayala, 1987).

The awarding of financial aid is another activity over which enrollment managers can exert some control. As previously indicated, financial aid can influence the choices made by high-ability prospective students who have ranked a given institution as their second or third choice for attendance (Chapman and Jackson, 1987). To apply these findings, enrollment managers could obtain information on the characteristics of the students who typically rate an institution as their second or third choice. Additional information on the financial aid packages such students received from the institution they decided to attend could also be gathered. Both forms of information could be collected over time using surveys of accepted students so that historical averages could be developed. With such information, enrollment managers could award financial aid packages to currently accepted high-ability students who fit the profile of characteristics of past students who have rated the institution as their second choice. The financial aid awarded should exceed by at least $4,000 the average award made in the past by the first-choice school to such students. For students fitting the profile of those who rate the institution as their third choice, the aid awarded should exceed by at least $6,000 the average award made by first-choice colleges and universities. Over time, such practices might increase the selectivity of an institution by increasing its proportion of high-ability students. For less-selective institutions, these practices could serve to overcome to some degree the improbability of attracting out-of-state and high-ability students.

Despite the appeal of luring high-ability students through generous financial aid awards, this practice can be quite costly. Chapman and Jackson (1987) caution that such aid needs to be awarded to all students fitting the type of profiles suggested because the intentions of recently accepted individuals are unknown. Many institutions do not have the financial resources necessary to make these awards. For such institutions, the efficacy of the suggested financial aid practices may be limited. Instead of using financial aid to attract students, such colleges and universities should seek to understand the types of students their institution is most likely to enroll and graduate. Marketing practices that can be effective in attracting such prospective students will be discussed in Chapter Seven.

Although financial aid has its limitations, other fluid institutional characteristics can be effective in attracting prospective students. For example, research by Buffington, Hossler, and Bean (1987) suggests that altering course schedules and student relationships with faculty and administrators exerts an influence on enrollment maintenance for private, less-selective liberal arts colleges. Specifically, choices in the number of days and times courses are offered appear to be effective. Also, a campus atmosphere marked by faculty and administrator concern for the individual student positively affects the maintenance of enrollments.

Both course scheduling and faculty and administrative relationships with students are institutional characteristics that can be altered to some degree. However, many enrollment managers may not be able to directly control or influence these forms of fluid institutional characteristics. Enrollment managers should first develop a knowledge of the days and times courses are desired by prospective students, as well as a knowledge and understanding of the nature of student relationships with faculty and administrators. Enrollment managers could work with institutional research officers or other research units charged with enrollment management research to develop studies designed to gather such information. The results of such research could, in turn, be used by enrollment managers to influence administrators and faculty not only to develop favorable course schedules but to foster a caring campus atmosphere.

Some of the research findings summarized in this chapter may not be a surprise to experienced and perceptive observers of the college choice process. Some of the findings, however, may be unexpected or may seem novel. Nevertheless, the research summarized does provide knowledge needed to reduce the trial-and-error nature of enrollment management. More certainty can be obtained in the practice of enrollment management by recognizing the possibilities and probabilities of influencing student enrollments through such enrollment management activities as marketing, recruitment, and financial aid. Success can be increased by the application of the findings summarized and the suggestions made herein. Thus, costly errors can be kept to a minimum.

Although enrollment management is not a panacea, it can influence student enrollments, especially if enrollment managers apply the knowledge and understanding of the college choice process provided by the research summarized in this chapter. Sound market research used to collect data about student college choice (at the institutional level) in conjunction with sound nonprofit marketing practices allows enrollment managers to develop marketing strategies to exert more influence over student enrollments.

Chapter 5

Marketing in Nonprofit Organizations

Catherine R. Clark
Don Hossler

Colleges and universities have been slow to accept the need for marketing. For many years, academics resisted marketing because they believed that it was not consistent with the goals or image of institutions of higher education. Although the term has become widely used in academic circles, it remains widely misunderstood by many campus administrators. Marketing has an almost mystical aura surrounding it. Too many administrators believe that they need only hire someone who understands this mysterious science and the numbers of qualified applicants will increase. Marketing, however, requires goal-oriented planning, research, and consistent follow-through. Effective marketing requires resources and hard work.

This chapter introduces marketing concepts from a broad perspective and discusses these concepts in relation to higher education. Although the marketing problems faced by nonprofit organizations have some similarities with those faced by for-profit organizations, nonprofits also have some unique problems.

Definition of Marketing

Kotler (1982, p. 6) defines marketing as "the analysis, planning, implementation and control of carefully formulated programs designed to bring about voluntary exchanges of values with target markets for the purpose of achieving organizational objectives. It relies heavily on designing the organization's offerings in terms of the target markets' needs and desires, and on using effective pricing, communication, and distribution to inform, motivate, and service the markets." A key concept in this definition is that marketing is aimed at target populations and not the broad public. Furthermore, a primary purpose of marketing is to ensure the survival of the organization by more effectively responding to the public's needs.

Marketers have employed the following concepts to think about marketing strategies: production, product, selling, marketing, and societal marketing (Kotler, 1986). This section will discuss these five concepts and a marketing framework developed by McCarthy and Perreault (1984) that combines these concepts.

The concept of production has a basis in the belief that "consumers will favor those products that are available and highly affordable, and therefore management should concentrate on improving production and distribution efficiency" (Kotler, 1986, p. 14). Kotler notes that this philosophy proves useful when the demand is high and the supply is low or when the cost of production is high. Henry Ford's use of the assembly line production method illustrates the concept of lowering production costs and increasing efficiency, thus making the product more available and more affordable. The development of community colleges is an example of this in higher education.

The concept of product is based on the belief that "consumers will favor those products that offer the most quality, performance, and features, and therefore the organization should devote its energy to making continuous product improvements" (Kotler, 1986, p. 14). This belief may push organizations to improve products, but it does not necessarily push organizations to change to better products.

Selling is a concept grounded in the belief that "consumers will not buy enough of the organization's products unless the organization undertakes a substantial selling and promotion effort" (Kotler, 1986, p. 15). The selling concept appears to be more prevalent in businesses in which the product is seldom bought or purchased only once. For many faculty members and college administrators, the selling concept may best define how they view marketing. This concept leads colleges and universities to expend large amounts of money and resources on promotion.

The concept of marketing has a basis in the belief that "the key to achieving organizational goals rests in determining the needs and wants of target markets and delivering the desired satisfactions more effectively and efficiently than competitors" (Kotler, 1986, p. 15). In contrast to selling, which focuses on the sellers and what they have to offer, marketing focuses on the needs of the buyer and challenges organizations to service these needs. The marketing concept also involves strategies of assessment to determine the needs and wants of consumers and then to develop more effective and efficient ways to meet those needs and wants.

The most recent addition to these marketing concepts is that of societal marketing. Societal marketing is the concept most closely associated with higher education. It is grounded in the belief that "the organization's task is to determine the needs, wants, and interests of target markets and to deliver the desired satisfactions more effectively and efficiently than competitors in a way that preserves or enhances the consumer's and the society's well being" (Kotler, 1986, p. 17). Three considerations underlie the societal marketing concept. The first consideration, which is not descriptive of most institutions of higher education, is that organizations are concerned with profits. The second is that organizations are concerned with consumer needs and wants. The third is that organizations are beginning to recognize and consider society's interest in their strategies.

McCarthy and Perreault (1984) describe a perspective on marketing that combines more traditional approaches to marketing with societal marketing and environmental concerns. In order to understand their perspective on marketing, the traditional approach to marketing must first be explained.

The traditional approach, the four P's, was first described in 1960 as an innovative marketing approach. The influence of the four P's marketing concept is still prevalent in many organizations. The four P's are product, place, promotion, and price (Kotler, 1986; McCarthy and Perreault, 1984).

The term *product* describes the development of the right product for the target market. *Place* describes the distribution of the right product to the target market. *Promotion* describes the development of strategies to tell the target market about the right product. Finally, *price* describes setting an appropriate price for the right product. Inherent in the four P's approach are the strategies of defining the target market and assessing the needs, wants, and desires of the target market. This approach combines the earlier marketing concepts of production, product, selling, and marketing, which constitute the emergence of modern marketing theories.

McCarthy and Perreault (1984) extended the four P's to include environmental and organizational factors that affect an organization's ability to utilize marketing strategy. These include the goals and objectives of the organization, competitors, economic and technological environment, political and legal environment, and cultural and social environment. These factors interact to influence marketing strategy. For instance, when the constant dollar value of federal financial aid decreased during the Reagan administration, both public and private colleges embarked upon ambitious campaigns to raise money for student scholarships. These scholarships helped to make higher education affordable to students who were adversely affected by the economic and political factors that influenced federal financial aid.

The historical basis for the current marketing strategies shows the evolution of marketing from production and product based, to consumer based, to the current structures that combine production, product, and consumers with environmental influences. Marketing activities in higher education reflect this same evolutionary pattern. Current marketing strategies utilized by colleges and universities are integrated processes that involve strategic planning, assessment, research, and evaluation.

Basic Principles of Marketing

Several authors have discussed the basic principles of marketing. In general these principles can be organized around the following five areas: (1) strategic planning and research; (2)

analyzing markets; (3) selecting target markets; (4) developing a market mix; and (5) planning, implementing, and managing the marketing effort (McCarthy and Perreault, 1984; Kotler, 1982, 1986).

These integrated activities are the foundation of marketing in higher education. Although these activities are not restricted solely to marketing in colleges and universities, the discussion in the next section will be limited to practices in higher education.

Strategic Planning and Research. Strategic planning has already been discussed in detail in Chapter Two. In the planning process, strategic planning, enrollment planning, and marketing overlap. Many institutions of higher education now incorporate marketing plans and enrollment plans into their overall strategic planning process. Marketing can help to guide strategic planning by providing a framework, identifying the market, assessing the institutional potential for the market, and guiding the development of objectives.

The "organizational portfolio," as developed by Kotler (1986), is a tool for assessing the strengths and weaknesses of colleges and universities and a vehicle for providing the big picture of institutions. The organizational portfolio involves analyzing such areas as market size and growth rate, market share, price, competitors, product quality, knowledge of consumer and market, and sales effectiveness (Kotler, 1986). Techniques for analyzing student markets will be discussed in greater depth in Chapter Six.

McCarthy and Perreault (1984) define marketing as a way for the organization to understand its target populations and the related marketing mix. A strategic marketing plan developed through research can guide colleges and universities in the implementation and management of their marketing efforts. McCarthy and Perreault suggest the four P's as a useful tool to delineate the major aspects of marketing. They provide a framework for evaluating current practices and attempting to plan for future marketing efforts.

As part of the strategic marketing plan, the institutional administrators should first make decisions about the school's current product and if the product is meeting the needs of the target populations. College administrators should list all products, ranging from the curriculum to ancillary products, such as entertainment and community services. Market research may be needed for administrators to identify target populations. On many campuses this has not previously been done.

Next, the institution needs to determine if the product distribution is effective, is efficient, and meets the needs of the consumers. This involves determining if the "place" of the product is appropriate (McCarthy and Perreault, 1984). Administrators then need to look at current promotional activities and determine if these activities are matching the target populations. For both of these steps market research and program evaluation may be required.

Research into promotional activities may also help enrollment managers determine the best way to attract a new population. Finally, marketing research can aid campuses in determining if adjustments in the price of the product are necessary. For example, many institutions are concerned that they may be pricing themselves out of the market. On the other hand, research has suggested that students may associate a high price with high academic quality (Hossler, 1984). Institutions of higher education need to understand their target populations and provide education at a price that not only meets the needs of the institution but is affordable to students and is consistent with the academic image the institution wishes to project.

Analyzing Markets. Each college and university exists in a marketing environment that is separate from the management function of marketing activities. The marketing environment involves both the microenvironment and macroenvironment of the institution (Kotler, 1986). These environments are determined by potential consumers and other outside individuals and groups who can influence the ability of an institution to present itself in ways that will satisfy consumer needs.

The microenvironment includes organizational functions, such as manufacturing, finance, or personnel. For colleges and universities these other activities include: teaching, research, student services, service to the community, and finance. From a microenvironmental perspective, enrollment managers need to consider the mission and needs of these activities when planning marketing activities.

Also within the microenvironment are the consumer markets. Kotler (1986) defines five consumer markets. However, some of them are not relevant to institutions of higher education. Some categories have been deleted here and others added. The consumer markets relevant to higher education are:

1. Individuals who purchase the product for individual use, that is, college students.
2. Industries that buy products in order to utilize those products to achieve profits or other organizational objectives. For colleges and universities this consumer market group is represented by public and private firms that contract with colleges, universities, and other educational vendors for degree and nondegree educational programs and services.
3. Surrogates, represented by parents, spouses, and others who may help their daughter, son, or spouse pay for postsecondary education and may influence educational choices.
4. Individuals who purchase the other products of higher education, such as research, service, and entertainment.

To successfully stimulate consumers in the microenvironment, marketers must identify their competition, including direct competitors who market very similar products, indirect competitors who market a more generic product, and peripheral competitors who market within a product framework. For example, the state board of realtors could compete for continuing education students by offering noncredit courses. For-profit research labs might compete with a university's research labs. Other universities compete for graduate students, although the extent of the competition will vary according to the reputation of individual graduate programs. Community colleges often compete with full-time work opportunities rather than other colleges or universities.

The macroenvironment is similar to the external environment that is frequently discussed in the strategic planning literature. An organization's macroenvironment is defined by McCarthy and Perreault (1984) as those environments outside the organization that affect marketing but over which the organization does not have control. These environments are defined as cultural and social, economic, technological, and political and legal (McCarthy and Perreault, 1984; Schoell and Ivy, 1982).

The cultural and social environment includes such variables as demographics, structure of the American family, buying patterns, geographical distribution of population, education, and income. For colleges and universities, these variables include student preferences for private or public institutions, public policy affecting financial aid, inflation, technological trends that can affect the cost of instruction, and employment trends. Additionally, public interest groups and consumer advocacy can contribute to the changing political and legal environment for higher education.

Selecting Target Markets. For institutions of higher education, identifying target markets is an important step. Target markets are identified by analyzing and forecasting demand and identifying market segmentation and positioning (Kotler, 1986). In order to analyze demand, organizations must first define their current market (Guiltinan and Paul, 1988), including who currently buys the product, where they buy it, and how they use it (Kotler, 1986). This analysis provides the organization with a picture of the current market. Kotler (1986) has further refined current markets into five subgroups. Four of these are relevant for colleges and universities: potential market, qualified available market, served market, and penetrated market. The potential market includes those individuals who have expressed an interest in the services that particular colleges and universities provide. For individual institutions, the qualified available market includes only those interested individuals who could be admitted and could afford (with financial aid) to enroll. For commuter campuses, geographical accessibility would also be a factor. The served market then becomes the part of the qualified market that the organization decides to target with the marketing strategy. The penetrated market consists of those consumers who have already purchased the product, that is, students who have enrolled. The penetrated market should be carefully analyzed as the characteristics of these students can be used to identify served markets for future years. Unless there is a shift in the image of the institution or student interests, the characteristics of enrolled students and recent graduates provide the best indicators of the types of prospective students who will be the most receptive to future marketing initiatives.

By identifying these four market areas, an organization can change the direction of its marketing strategy to focus on one of these groups. For example, a university may attempt to utilize initiatives that emphasize improved quality to move customers from the potential market into the qualified available market. For example, a state vocational institute may highlight its low cost to increase the size of its available market. Higher education institutions frequently define their qualified available market as high school graduates who meet certain admissions criteria. Some institutions, however, have effectively increased their qualified available market through such programs as open admissions, remedial learning centers, evening and weekend classes, and varied course offerings.

Information on student market characteristics can be gathered using techniques such as mail surveys, observation, focus-group interviewing, telephone surveys, and in-depth personal interviews. Once the data are collected, they must be analyzed to search for patterns that might identify relevant market segments and their characteristics. Although this sounds straightforward, campus administrators should understand that no research is exact and that various factors may influence a consumer's response. After the data are collected and analyzed, institutions can develop strategies to best meet their situation. Market research, however, is not a panacea that can resolve problems such as poor instruction or little student demand for academic programs offered.

The second part of selecting a target market involves market segmentation and positioning. Market segmentation is "dividing a market into distinct groups of buyers who might require separate product or marketing mixes" (Kotler, 1986, p. 263). Guiltinan and Paul (1988) note that market segmentation is important because different segments of buyers are likely to respond differently to price and promotion. Segmentation not only defines who buys the product (Buell, 1986) but also differentiates the consumers to allow for target marketing. Popular ways of segmenting markets include geographical segmentation, demographic segmentation, and behavioral segmentation, discussed in Chapter Six.

Segmentation provides enrollment managers with ways of identifying groups of students who are most likely to respond positively to the mission and image of their school. Furthermore, knowledge of market segments can help enrollment managers to determine how to best present their institution to qualified available markets. Market segmentation has allowed institutions to target their marketing to audiences more effectively and to establish a market position among potential students.

Ries and Trout (1980) assert that marketing is really a process in which organizations battle for position in the consumer's mind. While the image of a battle may not sit well with many academics, this is an apt description of the marketing process. Choosing a college or university has become a consumptive decision for many students and parents, and they can consider a wide array of educational options. From a marketing perspective, the goal of enrollment managers is to establish a position of dominance in the minds of their target market segments. Basically, colleges and universities attempt to position themselves among competing institutions so that consumers will view them as different and more desirable (Buell, 1986). A term that is useful in conceptualizing market position is *image potency*. Institutions with a strong market position vis-à-vis their competitors have a potent image in their target markets. To develop a potent image, marketers must identify salient institutional characteristics and identify those characteristics that consistently have meaning for target markets. If an institution lacks these characteristics, its administrators must try to develop them. A consistent image is an important attribute of image potency. Many campuses have publications, designed by individual departments or programs, that lack visual and thematic consistency. Consistency, a key point in marketing, is one of the points in which creativity gives way to methodical, well-organized marketing activities.

A school can position itself along several lines. A college may position itself as an elite college, equating admission with acceptance into an exclusive club. Only a few students have "the right stuff." A university might position itself as the low-cost pathway to upward mobility for first-generation college students. Other institutions might emphasize their vocational programs or a special mission (such as that of a church-related school). Perhaps the most important attribute institutions should and do emphasize is quality since perception of quality is the most important reason for selecting a school (see Chapter Four).

Postsecondary educational institutions need to develop strong market positions with respect to quality; however, enrollment managers should recognize that quality is an elusive attribute. Does quality mean the same thing to a high-income student with a 4.0 GPA as it does to a first-generation college student with a 2.75 GPA? Does quality mean the same thing to a nontraditional adult student pursuing a vocational certificate at a community college as it does to a traditional-age student attending a small church-related college? Probably not. Here again market research should play an important role. The task of enrollment managers is to discover the characteristics of a quality institution for their target markets. Little published research addresses this question. Ingersoll (1988) reports some results from a study that suggests that traditional-age students of high ability equate quality with acceptance to graduate programs, while less-able students may equate quality with an education that leads directly to a good job. Litten and Hall (1989) examine the institutional characteristics that students applying to elite private colleges believe to be important. They conclude that characteristics such as high acceptance rates to graduate schools, large variety of courses and programs, and advanced laboratory and library resources are some of the best indicators of institutional quality.

The authors of this chapter conducted some market research for one school in which the faculty decided that they wanted to attract a larger and more-able student body. The faculty was convinced that if they changed their recruitment literature to look more like an elite ivy league school's literature they would be able to attract more high-quality students. The student market segments this small school attracted were not similar to those attracted by ivy league institutions. The recruitment material did not help to attract more students from the school's traditional markets nor did it attract students who attend more prestigious institutions. The material was changed against the wishes of the admissions office, and new freshman enrollment dropped that year. It is unlikely that the changes made in the recruitment literature alone accounted for the enrollment drop; nevertheless, market research suggested that this was not a wise tactic.

An overall measure of quality, however, is not the only institutional attribute prospective students consider. Most colleges and universities position themselves along several attribute lines because the college selection process is multidimensional. Institutional quality, price, special academic programs, and student life each influence students' decisions. Again, the importance of market research cannot be overemphasized. Faculty and administrators may like to think of their campuses as elite schools or research universities or as having excellent placement records, but if their target markets do not have these perceptions, marketing materials that overemphasize these attributes will fail. Colleges and universities need to find that fine line that represents them as they aspire to be seen while staying reasonably close to their image in the student marketplace.

The Unique Characteristics of Marketing in Higher Education

Although enrollment managers have learned a great deal about marketing from the business sector, colleges and universities have unique characteristics that must be considered in any marketing efforts. Lovelock (1984) identifies the important differences between marketing products and services. Products are tangible; they can be examined and tested and often come with a manufacturer's guarantee. Services, however, are intangible.

Frequently, the consumers do not know exactly what they are purchasing until after the service has been provided, and services are less likely to come with a guarantee.

Marketing higher education is a form of service marketing. Higher education is not a product in the way people traditionally think of products. What are the products of higher education? Are students the raw material or are they the products? Are faculty members part of the capital that transforms the raw material or are they products (faculty research and service are often referred to as a product of higher education)? For traditional-age students, going to a college or university is the first noncompulsory educational decision they have made. It is a purchase they have not made before, they do not totally understand what they are purchasing, and the benefits of that decision will not accrue to them immediately but instead over a lifetime. Furthermore, there are many surrogates who shape the purchasing decision. Parents, employers, siblings, teachers, counselors, and peers can influence, sometimes even determine, the outcome of the college choice process. These factors present a number of unique marketing problems. How do institutions market something that the consumer does not understand? How can they make something that is intangible tangible? Who are the target audiences for marketing activities? Students? Parents? Counselors?

The purchase of a college education is a risky decision when compared to the purchase of many products (Litten, 1986). Since a college or university education is not well understood and buying one is not a purchasing decision that students, parents, and others routinely make, selecting a college involves more risk (Lovelock and Weinberg, 1984). The task of enrollment managers is to reduce the risk. When purchasing services, consumers often look for proxies or indirect indicators of the quality of the service. For example, Litten and Brodigan (1982) found that prospective students and parents consider currently enrolled students and alumni to be good sources of information about schools they are considering. Alumni and enrolled students can provide testimonials that make the benefits of higher education more concrete and tangible, thus reducing the element of risk in the decision.

Campus appearance can also be an indirect indicator of quality, especially when prospective students and others are not quite sure what a college or university should look like (Huddleston and Karr, 1982). Similarly, Zeithaml (1988) found that consumers are more likely to equate cost with quality when they are purchasing an intangible product. This may help to explain why families have been willing to pay for a college education even though college costs have been rising faster than the rate of inflation for most of this decade.

Another way for enrollment managers to make a college education more tangible is to track the outcomes of attending a college. Each time admissions officers can discuss in detail the job placement rate, the acceptance rate to graduate schools, or the average earnings of alumni who graduated ten years ago, they are helping to reduce the risk of school choice. Each time recruitment brochures document how much students learn, report low attrition rates, or describe the level of student satisfaction, they make a higher education more tangible. This kind of information can be an important part of marketing efforts.

Developing a Market Mix. After completing market planning, research, and segmentation, enrollment managers must develop a marketing mix that links service marketing concepts with the four P's and effectively presents the institution to prospective students. Marketing mix involves combining all the elements of marketing to determine the process of marketing (Borden, 1964). The elements discussed earlier in this chapter — research, planning, and determining markets and target markets — become essential elements in the marketing mix. McCarthy and Perreault (1984) combine product, place, promotion, and price with the consumer to determine the marketing mix.

The product quotient of the marketing mix involves defining the product, packaging, product management, and development of new products (Kotler, 1986; Lovelock and Weinberg, 1984; McCarthy and Perreault, 1984). In higher education, faculty members, administrators, students, and others deal with an intangible product, education. Levitt (1981) notes that in defining the product it is important for the consumer to understand the product. Since a higher education is an intangible product, the definition and development of the product become more cumbersome. In addition, the product of most vocational schools, colleges, and universities is not very flexible. Hossler (1984) suggests that postsecondary institutions have many fixed characteristics that cannot readily be altered. The product of institutions of higher education is the curriculum, and the curriculum is not easily altered in significant ways. A liberal arts college is unlikely to ever become known as an excellent engineering school. Few institutions that have a strong technological orientation are also known as places where the humanities thrive. Schools may add new majors to alter product, but these ventures are often unsuccessful unless they add programs in areas related to traditional strengths. Even when schools do develop strong programs in new areas, it usually takes several years for those programs to develop reputations that attract students. Curricular focus tends to be a fixed characteristic of most institutions.

Place in the marketing mix for higher education involves where instruction will be offered and, sometimes, how it will be offered. Such instructional innovations as computer-based instruction, interactive videodiscs, radio, and television can affect the place where instruction is offered. For a variety of reasons that are beyond the scope of this chapter, these innovations have not been heavily utilized by colleges and universities. Therefore, in higher education, place involves the campus and any branch campus or services that are offered in locations other than the campus. Again, as with product, place is difficult for institutions of higher education to change. Instructional locations are also fixed characteristics for most schools. Schools may offer courses in a nearby city, but they are unlikely to offer courses in other states. Place factors also include availability of services and the physical attractiveness of the environment. Enrollment managers can exert more influence over these factors and they should make every effort to ensure that services are available at convenient times and that the campus locations are attractive.

Promotion in the marketing mix includes communication, selling, advertising, recruitment, and sales management (Kotler, 1986; McCarthy and Perreault, 1984). Institutions of higher education have begun to utilize market segmentation and targeted marketing to reach different populations. Additionally, admissions offices have become more creative in their marketing efforts to students. Admissions officers are developing promotional approaches that will stimulate student interest and that set their marketing activities apart from those of other campuses. One example is the Knox Box distributed by Knox College in Galesburg, Illinois. The Knox Box is a videotape about the college that arrives in a sleek black box that high school students have found attractive. Knox College reports that this approach has been very successful in stimulating student interest. After introducing the Knox Box, the conversion rate from student inquiries to applications increased significantly. More examples of creative marketing approaches are discussed in Chapter Seven.

Price in the marketing mix involves pricing strategies and pricing objectives (McCarthy and Perreault, 1984). Except for privately operated for-profit technical and vocational institutes, institutions of higher education are not concerned with profits, but they are concerned with meeting the operating expenses and long-term needs of the campus. Price involves many different considerations. A problem for institutions is that students considering higher education tend to overestimate the cost of schooling or have incomplete information about the net price. Federal and state financial aid plays a major role in determining the cost feasibility for many students. Many students exclude institutions from serious consideration on the basis of cost long before they know how much financial aid they may receive. Price, too, tends to be a fixed characteristic. Institutions of higher education may affect the price in some areas, by discounting evening courses, offering special scholarships to a wide market segment, or "freezing tuition," but most institutions cannot significantly alter their costs. Nevertheless, these costs have an impact upon student enrollment decisions.

McCarthy and Perreault (1984) include the consumer as the fifth factor in the marketing mix by including all the information about consumers and consumer behaviors with the target marketing information. Clearly, in a marketing mix, the consumer becomes the focal point around which the four areas of product, place, promotion, and price revolve.

Planning, Implementing, and Managing the Marketing Effort.
This final step in the marketing process involves how the organization combines all aspects of the marketing process into
a strategy that is effective. If enrollment managers are not careful
they can become so enamored with the marketing concepts and
research that they fail to do the hard work and follow-up required to implement an effective marketing plan. The final step
involves utilizing the information obtained through research and
market analysis to plan and implement and evaluate the marketing effort.

Marketing should be an ongoing process that is the result
of strategic planning and research, defining the markets, developing a target market, and developing a marketing mix. The
marketing strategy is not as linear as it might appear in this
chapter; it is an iterative process. Institutions are continually
researching, reassessing, and redefining markets and changing
and updating promotions, price, place, and the product. The
current status of market research and planning determines how
an institution's marketing strategy will look for any given period
of time.

Colleges and universities may opt to create a marketing
niche for themselves that clearly distinguishes them from their
competitors. Institutions of higher education have utilized this
technique by designing academic programs that are unique.
Another strategy may be to compete openly with the competitor or to imitate a competitor's strategy that has been successful.

At this stage in the marketing process, schools need to
make a commitment to support the marketing functions. Publications should present a consistent image that is attractive and
describes the institution accurately in ways that will motivate
target markets. Mailing campaigns should communicate with
prospective students often, in a timely manner, and at times
when they are making important decisions as they move through
the admissions process. All contacts, mail, personal, and via
phone, should be personalized so that the prospective students
feel like they are being courted by the institution (Lewis, 1987).
Braxton, in Chapter Four, points out that these personalized
approaches may be just as effective as more costly forms of finan-

cial aid for many students. Campus tours, communication with parents and other surrogate consumers, and contacts from faculty may not be as exotic as market segmentation studies, but they are the activities that must be supported. Prospective students of all ages respond positively to marketing activities that are personalized and that answer the particular questions raised by each prospective student. Timely responses, with a delay of not more than a few days, are also important to successful marketing. Adequate professional and support staff are crucial as are computerized data information and retrieval systems.

The interrelationships between marketing and the other functions of the institution are also important. Without desirable academic programs, quality teaching, and an involving student-life program, enrollment managers have nothing to market. Marketing and enrollment management cannot be the responsibility of one office or functional area. Nevertheless, on many campuses, marketing has not become an integral part of the administrative decision-making process. For some people in higher education, the notion of marketing higher education runs counter to the academic ethos. For many administrators in higher education, marketing is associated with business and is an area with which they are not familiar. However, higher education has changed significantly over the past twenty years, and the idea of marketing has evolved over that time to mean more than simply selling products. A strong marketing effort can provide institutions with valuable information about their target markets, identifying their needs, wants, and interests. A concerted marketing effort is an essential element of an enrollment management system.

Chapter 6

Doing
Effective Market Research

John M. Braxton

In previous chapters, research on college choice has been reviewed and nonprofit marketing concepts have been discussed. These topics provide a context for a closer examination of how enrollment managers can use market research to better understand their market niche. Effective marketing strategies, which are discussed in Chapter Seven, are dependent on sound market research.

Student marketing and recruitment are among the major areas of responsibility for the enrollment manager (Hossler, 1984). For enrollment managers to effectively exercise their responsibility, they should develop a marketing and recruitment plan. Such a plan outlines specific recruitment goals and specific strategies for the implementation of these goals (Kemerer, Baldridge, and Green, 1982).

Such marketing techniques as institutional positioning and the identification of segments of the student market are fundamental to the development of a marketing and recruitment plan. Effective utilization of these techniques requires systematic studies of the institutional market. Thus, the purpose of this chapter is to discuss an array of approaches individual colleges and universities might use to conduct institutional market studies.

Although market studies require the use of various research procedures, a nontechnical discussion of these methods will be offered. The discussion of each approach will focus on the type of information that can be derived from it and how

86

the approach can be used to develop institutional marketing plans. Thus, a strong background in statistics and research methods is not required for readers of this chapter to understand the utility of the approaches. Administrators or enrollment managers who read this chapter should acquire a knowledge and understanding of these approaches sufficient to seek the technical assistance of their institutional research offices or other offices responsible for conducting marketing research. A discussion of the terms of institutional positioning and segmentation will be presented before the chapter looks at research useful for positioning and segmentation.

Positioning and Segmentation Defined

Positioning refers to the identification of the characteristics of a given institution and the comparison of these characteristics with the characteristics of competing colleges and universities (Kemerer, Baldridge, and Green, 1982). Through such comparisons, it is possible to differentiate or position an institution with respect to its competition.

Moreover, positioning can help provide answers to the following questions: How do prospective students perceive the institution? What position does the institution want to have and to be associated with? Which competing institutions hold a similar position? Does the institution have the ability to attain and hold a desired position? Answers to these questions are requisite to development of effective recruitment activities.

Markets consist of prospective students who are likely to differ on one or more factors (Kotler, 1982). Segmentation entails the identification of distinguishing factors among prospective students and the targeting of recruitment strategies to each identified segment (Grabowski, 1981). Segmentation can be geographical, demographic, psychographic, and behavioral (Kotler, 1982). In geographical segmentation, the market is divided into different geographical locations, such as states, regions, counties, or cities. The underlying assumption of geographical segmentation is that the college choice process varies across different geographical locations. Demographic segmentation is the division of the market into groups based on age, gender, ethnic group membership, and parental income. As in the case of geographical segmentation, the undergirding presumption of demographic segmentation is that the college choice process varies across students of different demographic characteristics.

Kotler (1982) distinguishes psychographic from demographic segmentation by pointing out that demographic characteristics reveal little about the attitudes and life-styles of individuals, as individuals within the same demographic group can differ on psychographic variables. Of the psychographic factors suggested by Kotler, social class is the most potent as a segmenting variable for markets of prospective students (Hossler, Braxton, and Coopersmith, 1989). Thus, the assumption underlying psychographic segmentation is that the college choice process will vary for students from different social classes.

Behavioral segmentation entails the division of markets into groups based on their knowledge, attitude, or use of a particular product (Kotler, 1982). Parental education level and high school quality have been found by researchers to be associated with college enrollment (Hossler, Braxton, and Coopersmith, 1989), and behavioral market segmentation along the lines of the quality of the high school attended by prospective students and the level of education attained by the parents of prospective students is a possibility.

Research for Institutional Positioning

Before institutional positioning can be accomplished, competing colleges and universities need to be identified. Although most college and university officials have an intuitive sense of who their competitors for students are, they may have little understanding of how their own institution compares to competing institutions. Two major approaches have been used by researchers to develop an understanding of the structure of competition. One approach estimates the "drawing power" of an institution in comparison to its competitors (Lay and Maguire, 1980; Lolli and Scannell, 1983). The other approach compares the focal institution with other colleges and universities on a series of attributes (Lay and Maguire, 1980, 1981).

Draw Rates. The computation of drawing power will be illustrated using accepted students as an example, because drawing power among competing institutions for accepted students has been the principal interest of proponents of this method. Lay and Maguire (1980) report the use of a survey instrument that is administered to accepted students. An item on this instrument asks students to list all of the colleges and universities for which they completed applications. For each of the institutions listed, the students are asked to indicate whether they were accepted or rejected for admission. Moreover, each respondent is asked to indicate the name of the college or university he or she selected to attend.

The "draw rate," a measure of drawing power, is obtained through this information (Lay and Maguire, 1980; Lolli and Scannell, 1983). It is the ratio between the number of students accepted at two institutions who chose the focal institution and the number of students accepted at both institutions who chose the competitor. A ratio of 1.00 indicates an even draw, whereas a ratio considerably above 1.00 means that the competitor is being outdrawn (Lolli and Scannell, 1983). In contrast, a ratio greatly below 1.00 signifies that the competitor is outdrawing the focal institution. Draw rates may be computed for each of an institution's top competitors for accepted students. Top competitors can be identified by the number of common applications shared.

Draw rates can also be computed for other groups of prospective students. For example, draw rates could be derived for students who make inquiries. In this case, the draw rate would be a ratio between the number of students making inquiries to both institutions who decide to apply only to the focal institution and the number of students making inquiries to both institutions who decide to apply only to the competitor. A survey instrument could collect the data necessary to compute this draw rate. On the instrument, students would be asked to list the colleges and universities from which they had requested information. For each institution listed, respondents would be asked to indicate the institutions to which they had submitted applications for admission. The volume of inquiry overlap among competing institutions could also be estimated from such a survey instrument.

The calculation of these draw rates could raise the intriguing issue of differences in competition at the inquiry stage and at the stage when applicants have been accepted. More specifically, an institution might learn that it competes with a wider range of institutions at the inquiry stage than at the accepted-applicant stage. This range might be characterized by institutional size, admissions selectivity, and control (public or private).

Draw rates can provide a realistic assessment of how an institution fares against its major competitors, thus demonstrating a need for institutional positioning. Moreover, unfavorable draw rates might stimulate such questions as: Why do colleges X, Y, and Z greatly outdraw our institution? What can we do to improve our draw rate with respect to colleges X, Y, and Z? How do we compare with colleges X, Y, and Z on such institutional traits as academic quality or reputation, campus social life, academic facilities, and campus appearance? Not only do such questions provide the beginning steps in institutional positioning, but they also can be used to sharpen the focus of research studies that are designed to compare an institution with its competitors on selected attributes.

A determination of the important characteristics or attributes underlying an institution's current position is also a requisite step in institutional positioning (Leister, 1975). Such a concern characterizes the second approach to the identification of an institution's structure of competition (Lay and Maguire, 1980).

Comparison of Attributes. Several techniques have been used by researchers to identify the important factors that differentiate an institution from its competitors. These techniques are best suited for studies on students who are making inquiries or applications to schools rather than those making enrollment decisions. These techniques are perceptual analysis (Leister, 1975), the ideal point preference model (Coombs, 1964; Kuntz, 1987), the expectancy value model of preference (Cook and Zallocco, 1983; Muffo and Whipple, 1982), and focus groups (Bers, 1987).

Perceptual analysis produces a "map" that graphically portrays an institution's position with respect to competing colleges and universities (Leister, 1975). Institutions are represented as points on this map, and their similarity or dissimilarity to competitors is indicated. These maps are produced using student ratings of all pairs of institutions on a numerical scale (such as a nine-point scale) representing the degree to which the pair is perceived to be similar or dissimilar. These dissimilarity ratings are then processed by the statistical procedure called nonmetric multidimensional scaling (Leister, 1975) to produce a visual model of an institution's position relative to its competitors.

Enrollment managers wishing to use perceptual analysis to assist in the process of institutional positioning could develop a survey instrument to be administered to either students who make inquiries or applicants for admission. Respondents to this instrument would be asked to rate pairs of colleges and universities on their degree of similarity or dissimilarity using a nine-point scale. Each competing institution would be paired with every other competing institution, as well as the focal college or university. These ratings could then serve as input to statistical routines using nonmetric multidimensional scaling. Researchers or statisticians at the institution could conduct the analyses needed to produce the perceptual maps of interinstitutional positioning.

Enrollment managers wanting a more fine-grained sense of how their institution compares to its competitors may wish to have survey respondents assess pairs of institutions on traits other than global similarity or dissimilarity. Researchers of the college choice process have identified the following characteristics as important in student decisions to apply to or attend a particular college or university: special academic programs, tuition costs, availability of financial aid, general academic reputation or quality, location or distance from home, institutional size, and social atmosphere (Douglas and others, 1982; Dahl, 1982; Keller and McKewon, 1984; Konnert and Giese, 1987; Lay and Maguire, 1981; Litten, 1979; Litten and others, 1983; Stewart and others, 1987; Chapman and Jackson, 1987). One or more of these characteristics could be selected for ratings of similarity and dissimilarity. Specific academic programs might be selected for perceptual analysis as institutional positioning can involve the differentiation of an institution from its competitors on the basis of academic programs (Grabowski, 1981). For example, a college or university wishing to stress its computer science program may wish to conduct similarity ratings on other institutions' computer science programs.

With the development of subsequent marketing plans, enrollment managers may want to single out specific concerns for perceptual analysis. Such concerns may be identified through the general program of marketing and recruitment research conducted by an institution. For example, campus appearance may be a concern, and similarity ratings among competing institutions on this dimension may be in order. A college or university with poor athletic facilities for intramural and recreational use might also wish to use similarity ratings to assess this perceived problem.

The expectancy value model is another technique used to make comparisons between a college or university and its major competitors (Cook and Zallocco, 1983). This model is most useful in ascertaining global attitudes of students toward a particular institution. However, it is different from a general perceptual analysis approach because the general attitude or preference for a given institution is based on several different institutional traits. The overall preference for a given college or university is predicated on two dimensions: the importance an individual places on particular traits and the individual's belief that a given institution possesses those traits.

Cook and Zallocco (1983) posit that importance and belief are components of preference that cannot be ignored. Thus, an individual's preference for an institution is established by multiplying importance ratings by belief ratings for each trait of interest. These cross products are added across all traits to derive the overall preference an individual has for a given college or university. Preference scores for each institution can then be used to make comparisons between the focal college or university and its major competitors.

The data source for such preference scores would be a survey instrument administered to prospective students who are making inquiries or those applying to the school. The instrument would contain two basic categories of items. One category would ask respondents to rate each trait as to how important it is to them in the selection of a college or university. Cook and Zallocco (1983) provided a rating scale that ranged from 1 (not important) to 7 (very important). The second category of items would serve to measure belief. Respondents would be asked to rate each selected competing institution and the focal college or university on the extent to which they agree that each institution possesses each selected trait.

Among the traits used by Cook and Zallocco (1983), which enrollment managers might use in such an instrument, are excellent academic reputation, existence of a specialized program of study exactly suiting a student's needs, closeness to home, low cost of attendance, close faculty-student association, excellent physical facilities, and an active social life. Other traits could be gleaned from the literature on student college choice.

Enrollment managers could use the institutional preference scores to gain an understanding of the attitudes prospective students hold toward the target institution in comparison with competing institutions. This approach differs from perceptual analysis in two ways. First, preference scores are based on several traits rather than a global, unspecified sense of similarity or dissimilarity. Second, an enrollment manager can rank institutions according to how much each institution is preferred by prospective students. Perceptual analysis can locate the proximity of one institution to another, but it cannot indicate which institutions are preferred over others.

Unlike perceptual analysis or expectancy value modeling, the ideal point preference model (Coombs, 1964; Kuntz, 1987) is best suited for use with prospective students making inquiries to schools. The logic of this model, when applied to student college choice behavior, is that preference for a college is a function of its perceived attributes weighed in comparison to an ideal conception of the attributes a college or university should possess. Thus, the more closely a college or university resembles the ideal, the more it is preferred by a prospective student (Coombs, 1964).

Like perceptual analysis, the ideal point preference model also uses nonmetric multidimensional scaling to visually depict the proximity of competing colleges and universities to the "ideal college." A survey instrument could be administered to students who had made inquiries to the focal college or university. The survey instrument would instruct respondents to rate pairs of competing institutions, the focal institution, and the ideal college on their degree of similarity or dissimilarity to each other.

Enrollment managers interested in a greater degree of specificity of the components of an ideal college may wish to include various institutional attributes on such a survey instrument. Respondents would be requested to assess each competing college, the focal institution, and the ideal college on the degree to which they possess each selected institutional trait. These ratings could, in turn, be statistically related to the dimensions that graphically locate the position of selected colleges and universities in relationship to the ideal college produced by the multidimensional scaling procedure. Enrollment managers could consult with institutional researchers or other applied statisticians at their college or university for statistical assistance.

Application of the ideal point preference model would assist enrollment managers in institutional positioning by visually displaying how their college or university and its competitors are perceived in relationship to an ideal college. Institutional positioning might take the form of differentiating the focal institution from its competitors, and would seek to demonstrate how various of the institution's traits resemble those of the ideal college.

Perceptual analysis, the ideal point preference model, and the expectancy value model of preference are quantitative tools useful in institutional positioning. However, the perceptions of respondents that underlie their responses to survey items are sometimes not detectable through such quantitative methods. Focus-group interviews provide another method to assist enrollment managers in the task of institutional positioning. They generate new insights and develop a deeper understanding of the perceptions that prospective students hold of competing institutions. Thus, focus-group interviews can be used either to further understand the findings of quantitative techniques or to identify new variables to be used with such techniques (Bers, 1987). Bers also asserts that focus-group interviews can yield an in-depth picture of the deeply held perceptions of prospective students or other persons influential in the college choice process. Moreover, this approach seems suitable for use with students at all stages of the process.

Bers (1987) urges careful attention to the selection of individuals to participate in such focus groups. The group members must be members of the population of interest. For example, high school counselors selected should be those individuals who routinely counsel college-bound students on the college choice process. At a minimum, two groups pursuing the same topics should be formed to reduce the chances of an aberrant group biasing the information gained from focus-group interviews.

Focus groups are moderated by an individual who probes and explores the topics or issues germane to the session with the members of the group. A guide is prepared that lists the topics to be covered by the moderator (Bers, 1987). And the moderator can seek group elaborations on relevant topics not anticipated in advance.

The information gained from focus-group interviews should be analyzed to identify broad themes and elaborations on them. Bers (1987) believes that the broad themes and ideas identified can prevent an institution from making costly errors in marketing. The information gleaned from focus-group interviews can also help enrollment managers to better understand their institution's position within its group of competitors.

However, an institution's market position is not always static. Another variant of market position is what Straumanis (1987) describes as repositioning. Repositioning refers to the efforts of campus administrators to alter an institution's image in relation to its competitors. Efforts might include attempts to be perceived as more selective or more student oriented. Information gained from the approaches discussed thus far, especially the quantitative approaches, is not as helpful in the development of repositioning strategies.

The goal of repositioning is to change the perceptions of an institution that are held by prospective students, parents, high school guidance counselors, and others influential in the college choice process. Straumanis suggests the use of trade-off analysis (TOA).

Trade-off analysis allows respondents to indicate those attributes of an institution that they are willing to relinquish in exchange for improvement in other attributes. TOA differs from other methods in that attributes are considered as a group rather than one at a time (Straumanis, 1987). To gather data through TOA, important attributes affecting institutional positioning can be used in the development of profiles of the institution. Each profile uses different values of the attributes, and respondents are asked to indicate their degree of preference for one profile over another. Profiles are presented in pairs. For example, one profile might depict a college as having a moderately attractive campus and being high in academic quality. The alternative profile might characterize a college as having a very attractive campus and being moderate in academic quality. Further combinations of different values of these two attributes would be very attractive campus and high academic quality compared with very attractive campus and low academic quality. Ultimately, all combinations of the discrete values of each attribute would be profiled. Using cue cards containing each profile is the standard method for conducting TOA (Straumanis, 1987). Straumanis notes, however, that there are currently microcomputer software packages available for TOA.

Thus, the idea of TOA is to identify the specific levels of each important attribute that respondents prefer the most and are willing to exchange for different levels of the other important attributes reflected in each of the paired profiles. Values called "utility scores" are computed for each level of a given attribute. These utility scores represent the preference or weight a level of a given attribute has in comparison to the various profiles a respondent has assessed. The utility scores generated through TOA can be added across levels of each of the variables to find the combination of attributes and their levels that most students prefer.

From this information, enrollment managers can develop strategies for institutional repositioning along the lines of these preferences. For example, a preference that might emerge could be for high academic quality and a moderately attractive campus. In other words, prospective students might be willing to exchange campus attractiveness for high academic quality. Therefore, an institution that previously had emphasized the attractiveness of its campus might reposition itself by giving more emphasis to its academic quality. Straumanis (1987) also points out that utility scores can be calculated for various market segments. Thus, TOA can be useful for the development of repositioning strategies designed for particular market segments.

Research for Market Segmentation

The underlying assumption of market segmentation is that prospective college students in different segments — geographical, demographic, psychographic, and behavioral — vary across aspects of the college choice process for different colleges and universities. Through a knowledge of such variations, enrollment managers can develop recruiting activities targeted specifically for a given segment. Thus, the identification of the ways in which prospective students vary across different segments is the principal objective of research conducted to assist in market segmentation.

Litten (1982) suggests four demographic market segments for the college choice process: race, gender, student ability level, and parents' educational level. Geographical location is the other market segment he identifies. He also suggests six different dimensions of the college choice process on which market segments might differ. These dimensions are: (1) timing of the process, (2) the number of colleges considered and the number of colleges to which applications were made, (3) types of information desired, (4) college attributes considered, (5) information media used or preferred, and (6) persons influential in the choice process.

Segmentation research could be used to identify similarities or differences between different market segments on the dimensions of the college selection process. Survey instruments could be developed that would measure the various dimensions of choice. They could be administered to prospective students when they are inquiring to schools, when they are applying to schools, or when they are enrolling in a school.

Perceptual analysis, the ideal point preference model, the expectancy value model, and focus-group interviews could also be used in segmentation research. Perceptual analysis could be employed to determine if students of various levels of academic ability differ in their perceptions of similarity and dissimilarity between the focal college or university and its competitors. More simply put, maps could be generated for groups of students of different academic ability. The ideal point preference model could be used to learn if students from different ethnic groups differ in their perceptions of the degree of similarity between the ideal college and the focal institution and its competitors. The expectancy value model could be utilized to ascertain whether male and female students differ in their preferences for the focal college or university and for competing institutions. Focus-group interviews could be used to see if different themes emerge from different focus groups that represent varying student character-istics. Different student market segments could be viewed from the perspective of each of these techniques, and information use-ful to the development of recruitment strategies for each mar-ket segment could be obtained.

An additional technique is the Chi-Square Automatic In-teraction Detector (CHAID). This technique is specifically de-signed to identify market segments (Wakstein, 1987). CHAID is a statistical procedure that uses the chi square statistic to as-sess the association of variables and the interactions between specific categories of such variables. Categorical or nominal data are used when applying CHAID. This technique can identify, if present, categories or subgroups of two or more independent variables that have a stronger association with the dependent variable of interest than do other categories of independent vari-ables. For example, the association between social class and high school class rank and the choice of a particular college or univer-sity could be assessed using this technique. As a categorical vari-able, social class can be divided into low, middle, and upper class and high school class rank can be divided into top quarter, second quarter, third quarter, and fourth quarter. A possible interaction that CHAID might detect is that prospective stu-dents who are from upper-class backgrounds and who are in the third quarter of their graduating high school classes are more likely to choose a particular college than are students from other social-class categories and high school class rank intervals.

The output of CHAID is depicted in the form of tree diagrams that express the percentage of responses falling into each category represented by the "branches" of the tree displayed. From the branches of this tree diagram, market segments can be identified.

An array of approaches useful to institutional positioning and market segmentation have been presented. Different approaches can yield distinctive patterns of knowledge and understanding that may provide enrollment managers with a deep and subtle understanding of their institution's place within the structure of its competition. Without such an understanding, effective marketing plans cannot be developed.

Chapter 7

Applying Marketing Strategies in Student Recruitment

Thomas D. Abrahamson
Don Hossler

Successful marketing not only requires an understanding of the unique problems of marketing in higher education and market research but also ultimately rests on the ability of enrollment managers to develop a set of integrated, systematic marketing activities. Enrollment managers employ a variety of marketing strategies. The goals of these strategies are more complex than they seem to faculty and administrators unfamiliar with marketing. Marketing strategies can be designed to enhance name recognition, to provide exposure for a college or university among target markets. They can also be designed to motivate prospective students to request information about an institution or to apply. Yet other marketing strategies can be designed to motivate students to matriculate. It is misleading to suggest that every marketing activity can readily be classified as an inquiry strategy or a name-recognition strategy. Nevertheless, enrollment managers must be certain of the objectives they hope to achieve with each marketing strategy.

This chapter will review key marketing strategies commonly used by marketing-oriented colleges and universities. It has been organized into eight broad categories of marketing strategies: publications, network marketing, direct mail, electronic media, telemarketing, marketing in the field, on-campus programming and activities, and pricing and aid strategies. In addition, staff development and training will be discussed, because without an effective staff training program it is impossible to implement effective marketing strategies. A further examination of the need for classifying the purposes of marketing strategies and evaluating marketing strategies will also be presented.

Publications

Hundreds of different publications are available to assist in the college marketing process. Although a great deal of research has been conducted on the types of institutional characteristics students consider when choosing a college (see, for example, Litten and Hall, 1989), little research has been done on the efficacy of the various types of publications. The most common goals of publications include increasing a school's exposure or name recognition, motivating students to inquire, or motivating them to apply. Three types of publications will be discussed in this section: guidebooks and reference books, advertising publications, and college-generated publications.

Guidebooks and Reference Books. At least twenty-five guidebooks list numerous colleges. Perhaps the most widely recognized are the *Peterson's Guide* series and *The College Blue Book.* Most guidebooks utilize extensive annual surveys that generate descriptive statistical pictures of each college and university. Institutions are listed at no cost if they provide the requested information. Some guidebooks also have paid advertising sections, in which institutions can exert more control over the information presented. Guidebooks and reference books are frequently used by prospective students as sources of information during the search and choice stages of the college choice process (see Chapter Four for a discussion of these stages). Enrollment managers should take advantage of opportunities to be listed. The usefulness of paying for advertising space in these guidebooks is unclear. Enrollment managers may wish to pay for larger descriptions of their institutions in one or two widely used reference books. The success of these advertisements, however, is not established, and caution should be exercised before committing large amounts of institutional funds to them.

Accurate, consistent, on-time responses to reference-book surveys will ensure that prospective students are reading the same description of the institution in each guidebook. It is in the best interest of enrollment managers to keep track of when questionnaires are received and, if necessary, contact the publisher in the event that the survey was not received or was misplaced. Guidebook publishers usually welcome feedback, listen to suggestions, and correct inaccuracies when they occur.

Advertising Publications. There are many advertising opportunities available in magazines, newspapers, and education supplements in newspapers. There are several issues to consider when selecting advertising publications.

1. What target market are you trying to reach? Local newspapers may be very good for reaching nontraditional adult students, but ineffective for reaching high-ability traditional-age residential students.
2. What is the distribution method of the publication? Is it effective in reaching students? Is it well targeted? To answer these questions, it is necessary to have a clear demographic picture of the target markets you are trying to reach and to gather information about the distribution efforts of the publication.
3. What experiences have colleagues at similar institutions had with this publication?
4. How effective is the publication in accomplishing its intended purpose? Is it a lead, or inquiry-generating device, or a general purpose image-promoting piece? How does the publisher of the magazine or newspaper measure success with the product?
5. What kind of response mechanism is built into the publication? If it is a response card, does it provide enough information for a segmented marketing approach?

In recent years a variety of publications have been developed to reach traditional students in general or to reach students considering private colleges and universities. The utility of these publications should be evaluated by considering the previous questions. Church-related schools may find that denominational magazines are useful marketing devices. Here again questions of target markets are important. For traditional-age students, the target for some advertising might be parents rather than students because parents exert a strong influence over students during the early stages of the college choice process (Hossler, Braxton, and Coopersmith, 1989). Several years ago, a consortium of public and private two-year and four-year colleges in the Philadelphia area developed a cooperative marketing campaign. It was designed to increase exposure and inquiries for all institutions in the geographical region (Lamden, 1982). Advertising publications were an important part of this effort.

College Generated Publications. The quality and quantity of marketing publications utilized by institutions have increased dramatically in recent years. Viewbooks, catalogues, departmental brochures, residence-life brochures, newsletters, scholarship materials, and so on have become essential tools for enrollment managers. They can serve purposes ranging from promoting the institution's image to motivating prospective students to move from inquiry to application. In each case, these materials must be written for the specific purpose and target audience the institution is trying to reach.

In a previous chapter, the importance of visual and thematic consistency of publications was emphasized. Consistency is essential for all forms of institutional publications. One of the goals of each publication is to reinforce a desired image of the college or university.

As market segmentation has become more sophisticated, institutions have discovered that they can be more successful if they have publications developed for specific target markets (Litten and others, 1983). Butler University in Indianapolis, Indiana, has developed viewbooks targeted at black students. In the early 1980s, Carleton College discovered that it needed to develop different publications for students on the East Coast and in the Midwest. Carleton was perceived to be too costly in markets in the Midwest but too inexpensive on the East

Coast. New developments in desktop publishing make it possible to develop a basic publication piece that can be modified to meet the needs of different market segments. Of course, the danger in this is that institutions may try to be all things to all students and attract large numbers of students who are unlikely to persist.

The value of having publications developed by specialists versus developing them in-house cannot easily be determined. Outside specialists bring expertise in graphics, copyediting, and so on that can be invaluable to institutions. Outside specialists, however, are more expensive. On the other hand, if enrollment managers have access to internal expertise in these areas and they field-test their publications with appropriate target audiences, it is possible for them to develop high-quality publications internally. On many campuses, however, the necessary expertise is lacking, or materials are not field-tested. Additionally, on many campuses, departments develop their own material without attention to visual and thematic consistency.

Network Marketing

Network marketing and publications serve similar purposes. Network marketing uses high school counselors and teachers, alumni, parents, and others to help create an institutional image and to convert prospective students to applicants and matriculants. Research suggests that high school counselors, teachers, and others (except for parents) do not exert a strong influence upon where most students go to school (Hossler, Braxton, and Coopersmith, 1989); nevertheless, they may be important sources of information about schools. In a longitudinal study of college choice, Hossler and Schmit (1990) report that these "networks" can be where students first learn about a college or university. Thus, they can be an important source of information during the search stage of college choice.

High School Counselors. High school counselors are responsible for assisting their students in the college choice process. It is very important to inform counselors about the institution—

particularly any changes in programs, admissions criteria, cost, financial aid, and scholarship opportunities. Mailings to counselors, on- and off-campus briefings, and informal contacts are used to keep counselors well informed.

High School Faculty and Private Teachers. High school faculty and private teachers exert a weak to modest influence upon the college enrollment decision (Hossler, Braxton, and Coopersmith, 1989; Litten, 1989). Students often ask teachers to suggest institutions that they should consider. Teachers are also asked to write letters of recommendation. Two- and four-year institutions that draw heavily from local student markets can develop relationships with high school faculty and private teachers that can work to an institution's advantage. Schools that attract students from a wide geographical area should develop follow-up mechanisms such as thank-you notes or some form of recognition to teachers who make referrals.

Alumni. Alumni are utilized in the marketing process in a variety of ways. Some institutions have well-established alumni networks in which hundreds of volunteers serve as information or referral sources for prospective students or conduct admissions interviews. The key to effective alumni programs is good training for volunteers. They need to know about the campus as it exists today, about admissions and financial aid programs, and about the students they are working with (that is, they need information about prior student contact, follow-up information about application status, and so on). Alumni can communicate personal and local perspective to students and can tangibly demonstrate the value and benefits of the education they have received. They are considered by prospective students to be good sources of information (Litten, 1989).

Parents. Parents are very influential in the college choice process. The information they need must be provided in a variety of ways. All on- and off-campus marketing programs should include a focus on parents. Issues of importance to parents are different from those of importance to students and include cost, job placement, quality of teaching, campus safety, and distance from home (Hossler and Schmit, 1990; Litten, 1989). Marketing programs should be designed specifically to reach parents. In group settings, the parents of currently enrolled students can also be very good representatives of a college or university. Many institutions have active parent networks, similar to alumni networks. Parent volunteers can provide a form of reassurance to other parents that cannot be provided by any other group.

Current Students. Targeted peer recruitment can be one of the most effective means of marketing (Hossler, 1984). Its success can be attributed to the fact that current students are current consumers, are close in age to the prospective students, and usually "tell it like it is" when discussing the college. Litten (1989) notes that prospective students regard currently enrolled students as one of the best sources of information about a school. Many admissions offices run well-organized student-ambassador programs. These programs provide a range of services including letter writing, telephoning, conducting tours, hosting students overnight, assisting with campus events, visiting high schools, and assisting with college-night programs. The potential drawbacks are that the students' experiences at the institution may be too narrow, and the program may not be well organized. Therefore, student volunteers should receive ongoing training and some form of special recognition. Student volunteers should also be encouraged to provide feedback to the admissions office because they can see the campus from a student's perspective. In addition, the questions prospective students and parents ask often reflect "the word on the street" about an institution.

Campus Faculty and Staff. Campus faculty and staff are often overlooked as an important source of prospective students. Because of their familiarity with the institution, they can be a rich source of student referrals. Strategies can be devised to encourage the referrals of the children of friends, relatives, neighbors, and so on. Good service to a referred student is always important, especially for those referred by faculty and staff members. Keeping them posted on the application process is not only good for internal relations but can also avoid embarrassing situations (for example, the referred student is denied admission and the faculty member first hears of it from the neighbor). The admissions office may wish to allow the staff member to convey the acceptance decision. This can be satisfying and will likely result in more referrals.

Direct Mail

Direct mail strategies focus on three goals: stimulating inquiries, converting inquiries to applications, and converting applicants to enrolled students. It is not unusual for a direct mail program to encompass hundreds of thousands of personalized letters during a year. These letters are usually produced in-house or sometimes by outside mailing houses.

Direct mail, along with telemarketing and on-campus visits, is one of the most commonly used approaches to personalizing marketing activities. Although some marketing experts would disagree, the authors believe that all letters, from the first contact to the last, should be personalized. As much as possible, letters should address the individual concerns students raise. Often, when students request more information about a college they ask for information about specific academic programs. Although research has shown that students respond more positively when their requests for specific information are answered (Geller, 1982), many institutions continue to respond with form letters. The letters may be addressed to the student, but the content remains a standard form-letter response.

Enrollment managers are fortunate to have access to powerful and accurate lists of potential students. Lists can be purchased from such services as the College Board, the American College Testing Program, and Educational Testing Services. In addition, specialized lists can also be purchased that contain, for example, names of students who go away to college and have permanent addresses in the institution's town (for summer school marketing efforts) or students who subscribe to particular magazines or journals.

Mass Mailings. Mass mailings are those in which all or most members of the mailing list are sent the identical information.

They often include catalogues and admissions materials sent to high schools and colleges and universities; mass distribution admissions materials, such as financial aid newsletters; student newspapers; activities calendars; invitations to on- and off-campus programs; and new-student-profile mailings.

Individual Correspondence. A tailored response to a student's inquiry can be accomplished by creating a library of letters that allow for individual tailoring. It is not uncommon for a direct mail marketing program to include hundreds of form letters that can be personalized. As stated earlier, individually crafted letters are the most effective; however, the number of inquiries often prohibits such letters because of the large amounts of professional and clerical staff time involved. A well-informed clerical letter coordinator with access to a comprehensive letter library can satisfy most of the requests for information.

Electronic Media

Electronic media include videotapes, radio, and television. Each of these media has distinctive uses for different target markets.

Videotapes. Videotapes are usually designed to help establish a market image and to induce students to request more information. Many colleges have created videotapes about their institutions. The videotape format lends itself to higher education marketing for many reasons. First, most students (of all types) are visually oriented; they spend more time watching television than reading. Most homes have videocassette recorders, as do high school guidance libraries. Students probably prefer watching videotapes to reading brochures. Videotapes can more effectively portray action and provide visual images than other media. Second, videotape has been described as a linear medium, one that communicates in a straight line from start to finish. Catalogues and viewbooks, on the other hand, can be scanned and sections or pages read out of sequence. Enrollment managers therefore have more control over the way their institutions are presented in videotapes.

In theory, a videotape presentation is more controlled and has more impact than a print presentation. In practice, however, college videotapes have several limitations. Students are accustomed to watching television in ten-to-fifteen-minute intervals. An entire university is a difficult product to condense into a twelve-minute presentation. Also, the videotape must be professionally produced. If a videotape appears to be amateurish or cheaply made it may do more harm than good. Videotapes are expensive to produce and distribute, but they have a shelf life of at least two years and they can be reused. This helps to reduce the long-term costs of producing a videotape.

Videotapes should be part of a comprehensive set of marketing strategies. They may be especially effective in high school guidance libraries. For most institutions, however, videotapes are not primary marketing tools, and money should not be diverted from key direct mail, telemarketing, or on-campus visitation programs to fund videotapes.

Radio and Television. Radio and television marketing has grown during the past decade. Marketing through these media is most effective in increasing institutional visibility and image when a college or university has a local and well-defined geographical market. Vocational schools, as well as two- and four-year institutions, in metropolitan areas can effectively use radio and television to make their programs known to prospective students. Radio advertising usually consists of spots of fifteen, thirty, or sixty seconds and requires frequent repetition to have an impact. For this reason it can be expensive. It is most often used to market undergraduate and graduate programs for adult students. Television advertising is usually employed in ways similar to radio advertising. Some institutions have used television marketing to reach more geographically distant markets. Drake University has purchased time on MTV in the Chicago metropolitan area, which is one of its primary markets. Although it is difficult to evaluate this approach because Drake has introduced several new marketing strategies in Chicago, enrollments from Chicago have increased (Adams, 1987).

Care should be taken not to use radio and television marketing indiscriminately. Some students react negatively to this form of marketing, while others report that it simply has no impact upon them (Hossler and Schmit, 1990). For example, high-ability students may find such forms of advertising inconsistent with their image of the mission and purpose of an institution.

Telemarketing

Telemarketing has become a powerful tool to motivate students to move from making inquiries to applying and enrolling (Lewis, 1987). Colleges and universities are employing an increasing array of telemarketing strategies in their marketing programs. Institutions are developing an "open telephone line" philosophy in student recruitment, which includes using WATTS lines and encouraging students in brochures, letters, and contacts in the field to call any time a question arises.

In addition to using the telephone to respond to student-initiated contacts, a number of institutions have developed proactive telemarketing strategies. Since prospective students respond positively to individualized attention, it is not surprising that the telephone has become a useful tool in efforts to personalize the recruitment process and to respond to inquiries in a more timely fashion. Some of the telemarketing strategies that are being employed include:

1. Follow-up calls to written inquiries
2. Calling campaigns to applicants
3. Reminder calls to students confirming on-campus appointments
4. Notification calls to students confirming appointments at their high school
5. Congratulatory calls to admitted students
6. Status-checking calls to students who have not responded to application materials, letters of admission, invitations to on-campus programs, or requests for additional credentials

7.   Faculty calls to students interested in particular academic
     programs

Marketing in the Field

Marketing in the field includes a diverse set of activities that
can be used to increase visibility, attract student inquiries, move
inquiring students to apply, and motivate applicants to enroll.
These activities include individual visits, college days and fairs,
and hotel programs and interviews.

Individual Visits. Individual visits by admissions representatives to high schools, community colleges, and companies can
be useful methods of recruiting students, provided the locations
are carefully selected. Appointments are usually scheduled several months in advance, permitting ample time to notify prospective students of the admissions representative's visit. Reminders
of visits should be made by mail or telephone within one to three
days of upcoming visits. When the desired students are seen
in a setting conducive to individual discussion, the visits are well
worth the effort. Unfortunately, there are many variables that
are out of the control of the admissions office, and when visits
are bad they can affect the image of the institution. Sites at which
visits are consistently bad should be avoided.
     There is considerable debate among enrollment managers
about the efficacy and cost effectiveness of these visits. Some
institutions, such as Carnegie Mellon University and Brown
University, have moved away from high school visits because
their marketing research suggests visits are not effective. Other
institutions continue to see visits as an effective marketing tool.
The task for enrollment managers is to carefully evaluate the
role of visits in securing leads and applications.

College Days and Fairs. A major component of field work is organized, convention-style college days and nights at high schools,
community colleges, four-year colleges, companies, and con-
vention centers. These are usually staffed by an admissions staff

member and alumni or other volunteers. These events range in size from a dozen local schools to hundreds of colleges and universities. The National Association of College Admissions Counselors sponsors several programs held in major cities throughout the United States.

These types of programs can be an efficient method for generating leads. Like high school visits, however, the quality of the event is dependent upon the organizing group and logistical issues, such as the location of the booth each institution is assigned. The effectiveness of these events has also been questioned. Some colleges and universities no longer participate in college fairs. Here again, evaluation is the key. One recent institutional study conducted by one of the authors found that approximately half of the entering freshmen at a liberal arts college first heard of the institution at a college fair.

Hotel Programs and Interviews. Many colleges host an annual series of off-campus informational programs in hotels or other locations. Sometimes called seminars or receptions (or internally referred to as "road shows"), these events are attended by prospective students and their parents, admissions representatives, invited alumni, selected faculty, and sometimes the institution's president. Often slides, a film, or a videotape is shown, and the perspectives of alumni and parents of currently enrolled students are shared. The advantage of this approach is more control over the environment. Only highly motivated students will take the time to attend these events, similar to campus visits. Therefore, the events should be of high quality.

On-Campus Programming and Activities

One of the tasks of marketing in higher education is to make an intangible product tangible. Levitt (1983, p. 27) notes, "Tangible products can usually be directly experienced — seen, touched, smelled, tasted, and tested. . . . You can test drive a car, smell the perfume . . . . Intangible products . . . can seldom be experienced or tested in advance." The managed campus visit is the closest schools can come to actual prepurchase testing of their product. Research has shown that the campus visit is the most influential factor in a student's decision to enroll in a college or university (Hossler, Braxton, and Coopersmith, 1989).

On-campus programming is usually intended to motivate students to apply or to enroll. The primary goal of the campus visit is to enable students to intensely explore all aspects of the institution and to gain a thorough understanding of the academic, cultural, and social dimensions of the campus. A positive experience is critical. In one consulting project in which one of the authors was involved, there appeared to be a cause-and-effect relationship between a negative campus visit and the decision to enroll at another institution.

A variety of strategies can be used to simulate the college experience during a campus visit, including

1. All-university open houses
2. Focused open-house programs for specific colleges, departments, or programs within the institution
3. Large-scale overnight programs for students and parents who live out of the area
4. Group visits by high school students, community agencies, and so on
5. Scholarship interviews and award ceremonies
6. "Sidebar" programs associated with campus events such as concerts, lectures, and athletic events

In addition to these activities, admissions counseling, campus tours, classroom visits, and early registration are important.

Admissions Counseling. The admissions counseling session is part sales situation, part selection interview, and part counseling session. A well-trained counselor can sell the school on an individualized basis during this session to the prospective student's family. The counselor can also screen the applicant in regard to likely fit and success at the institution. Counseling occurs when the staff member either starts to prepare the student for what life might be like after enrollment or counsels the student to seek out other institutions because the student does not have a strong chance of being admitted.

Campus Tours. If small and led by a knowledgeable guide, the campus tour can be one of the most influential student-to-student marketing activities. The most effective tours are those that give the student perspective on the campus, are informative, and allow for individual questions and requests. Campus tours should be well organized, with attention to detail. The tour is the best opportunity a college or university will have to convince students that the campus is a good place to be. Programs run entirely by student volunteers, or that are one of several responsibilities of a junior member of the admissions staff, may not show the campus in the best light.

Classroom Visits. It is important for visitors to see the faculty in action and to learn more about academic areas in which they have an interest. To an extent, classes should be preselected to ensure that the subject matter is at an appropriate level. Faculty members must be contacted in advance so they know about their prospective student guests and to be certain the date and time are appropriate (for example, no quizzes or tests are scheduled that day). Faculty should also be encouraged to spend a few minutes before or after class with guests.

Early Registration. At one time, most colleges and universities could assume that a student would enroll once an application had been accepted and a deposit was paid. This is no longer true. Institutions must continue to recruit students right up to the time students arrive for classes in the fall. One way of doing this is to plan late spring and early summer registration sessions in which students can come to campus (this also can be done at off-campus locations or over the telephone), receive academic advising, and register for courses. At the end of registration, students should leave with a completed class registration that lists the courses, instructors, and class times and locations. Early registration can help to seal the commitment to enroll and provides a good opportunity for a preorientation program for students and parents or spouses.

Campus visitation programs should be viewed as the culmination of marketing strategy. Most campuses appreciate the importance of campus visits, yet at many institutions they are assigned to a student coordinator who may not receive adequate training or compensation. The more important marketing activities are left to the professional staff. While on-campus visits do not necessarily have to be assigned to professional staff, their importance should not be taken for granted.

Pricing and Aid Strategies

The net cost of attending an institution is one of the most important determinants of where students go to school. Among traditional-age students, next to quality, cost is the most important determinant of where students enroll (Hossler, Braxton, and Coopersmith, 1989). Among adult student populations, cost is second to convenience and location (Grahm, 1985). Tuition costs have been described earlier as one of the fixed characteristics of an institution (Hossler, 1984). One of the intriguing aspects of tuition costs is that they affect prospective student markets in different ways. For example, low cost is one of the principal advantages that community colleges offer students. For some students, however, low cost is equated with low quality. Enrollment managers need to understand their target markets and the institutions with which they compete in order to determine how their tuition costs influence the enrollment decisions of students. This section will discuss some of the most common pricing and merit-aid strategies employed in colleges and universities. It will not examine new loan programs or packaging policies that go beyond the scope of this chapter.

Pricing and Payment Strategies. Many colleges and universities have developed sound marketing strategies within the limits of their fixed pricing structures. Many schools that attract large numbers of adult students now permit students to pay by credit card. Most institutions offer extended payment plans to students and parents. The effects of these strategies should not be overlooked. Students and parents look at the effects that college costs have on their monthly cash flow, not just at the overall costs.

Consumers have become so accustomed to thinking about monthly payments that college costs have become another monthly expense (Litten, 1986). Monthly payments reduce the "sticker shock" associated with going to college.

Some private institutions have also adopted price-freeze, or guaranteed-tuition strategies: if entering students pay a premium above the costs of their first year's tuition, they are guaranteed that their tuition will not increase during the two or four years in which they are enrolled. In an era in which costs at private institutions have been rising faster than the consumer price index, guaranteed-tuition plans can have a positive influence on the enrollment decisions of students.

Merit and "Vanity" Aid. Although research has not established that merit aid is effective, its use has grown dramatically (see Chapter Four). Merit aid is used to induce students to enroll in an institution that they might not have otherwise attended because of cost differentials or perceived differences in quality. Merit aid programs are used to reward academic achievement, musical talent, athletic talent, leadership skills, and other special abilities valued by institutions. Merit aid awards can range from full scholarships to small financial aid awards.

Enrollment managers should be cautious about investing large sums of money in merit aid to individual students. Many administrators who insist that merit aid works simply count the number of merit aid students who enroll. If all forty merit aid scholarships are eventually accepted and the students enroll, then the program is presumed to work! In fact, the number and size of merit aid awards have been increasing during the past five years. Careful research designs often show, however, that students may have been considering the campus already (Chapman and Jackson, 1987; Freeman, 1984), or as Freeman (1984) and Jackson (1978) point out, that the special "courtship" activities that accompany merit aid awards are as influential, or more so, than the actual amount of the aid award. For these reasons, more modest individual merit aid programs, used in conjunction with special recruitment programs, appear to be a more prudent investment of institutional resources.

Many private colleges and universities also have discretionary aid funds that the financial aid office or the admissions office can award to students. These funds are described as gift aid, vanity aid, or discretionary awards or by a number of other phrases. These funds are awarded when members of the admissions or financial aid staff believe that a prospective student is wavering and that just a few more dollars may convince the student to enroll. There are no documented investigations of the effects of these types of awards. In most instances, enrollment managers can never determine with certainty that a vanity award was the deciding factor. Students frequently say that it was the deciding factor, but without knowledge of the other colleges or universities that the students were considering and how the institutions were ranked in order of preference, the effectiveness of such programs cannot be determined.

The uncertain effects of merit and vanity aid are weighed against some of the ethical issues that are discussed in the last chapter of this book. In total, the evidence suggests that merit and vanity aid should be used judiciously and awarded in small amounts. Research suggests that schools might spend large amounts of aid dollars and yet have a limited impact upon the enrollment decisions of students.

Staff Training and Development

Effective marketing is dependent upon a strong admissions staff. Admissions staffs on many campuses are made up of a large number of relatively new professionals and student help. Except in large universities, where salaries are better, many admissions staff members leave the field after just one to three years of experience. Yet, the admissions office must employ increasingly sophisticated technology and strategies to enroll the desired mix of students. Given this high staff turnover and the heavy reliance on student assistance, it is essential that staff members are trained in counseling techniques and are well versed in the institution's academic programs and student support services. It is important that staff members are aware of broader institutional issues and that they have a good understanding of the institution's mission. Some of the areas in which staff members require ongoing training include public speaking and effective writing, new recruitment software packages, new tracking or marketing strategies, financial aid policies and trends, the needs of different student populations (such as handicapped students, minority students, returning adult students, and so on), and topics such as effective management, program evaluation, and educational research related to admissions.

A Word About Evaluation

The focus of this chapter is on marketing strategies. Earlier in the chapter, the goals of marketing strategies were identified: strengthening market image or position, attracting student inquiries, moving inquiring students to apply, and motivating students who have applied to enroll. For every marketing activity, the goals must be identified so that the activity can later be evaluated. The goals determine the measures that are used to evaluate marketing strategies. Mass mailings designed to identify leads should be evaluated on the basis of how many inquiries are received. Newspaper advertisements that are intended to stimulate more applications for an evening program that enrolls adult students should be evaluated on that basis. If activities are not evaluated, decisions regarding which activities to repeat next year cannot be made on a sound basis.

Although all activities should be evaluated, enrollment managers should realize that, ultimately, their ability to conduct evaluations is imprecise. Letters intended to motivate students to convert from an applied student to a matriculated student may end up attracting the student's spouse or younger sibling. A radio advertisement designed to stimulate inquiries from adult students may be the deciding factor in motivating a traditional-age student to matriculate. Nevertheless, enrollment managers should attempt to classify each of the marketing strategies they employ. Failure to do this may result in ineffective strategies. The real work in marketing takes place in marketing strategies. Organization, follow-through, personalization, and evaluation are the cornerstones of effective marketing strategies.

Chapter 8

Case Studies
of Successful Marketing
in Two Institutions

Trudy H. Bers
Ernest W. Beals
Don Hossler

Previous chapters have examined the factors that influence college choice, nonprofit marketing, market research, and marketing activities. They provide enrollment managers with the tools to implement a marketing plan. This chapter looks at the marketing plans of two institutions: Georgia State University and Oakton Community College. Like each of the case studies in this book, these institutions have been selected because they illustrate different aspects of enrollment management plans.

Most of the literature on marketing suggests that successful marketing requires a strategic planning process in which marketing is fully integrated into the campus plan. This makes intuitive sense, yet many college administrators have worked on campuses at which strategic plans or formal marketing plans are never produced. Recent research on organizational culture, however, asserts that successful organizations are those in which patterns of doing things, organizational norms, have been fully integrated into the thoughts and actions of all members of the organization (Kuh, Whitt, and Shedd, 1987; Schein, 1985). These norms, values, and accepted ways of doing things become part of the invisible culture of an organization. From this perspective, successful marketing might not require a centralized planning process.

The two case studies presented in this chapter illustrate aspects of noncentralized approaches to marketing. The marketing plan at Georgia State, developed by Ernest Beals, emphasizes what a comprehensive marketing plan should include. Trudy Bers, the senior director of research, curriculum, and planning at Oakton Community College, explains the marketing perspective that has resulted in a decentralized approach to marketing. Together, these case studies provide a realistic picture of both the processes and outcomes of marketing plans.

This chapter will begin with an examination of marketing activities at Georgia State University, which is followed by a discussion of marketing at Oakton Community College. Issues that readers should keep in mind include:

1. What was the impetus for marketing at each institution?
2. How can enrollment managers know if their marketing efforts have been successful?
3. At which organizational units within an institution must marketing be accepted and used?
4. How can information be used to assist marketing efforts?
5. What problems can be anticipated?
6. How formalized are the marketing plans?

Georgia State University

Georgia State University (GSU) was formed in 1913 as an offshoot of Georgia Tech. It was called Georgia Tech Evening School of Commerce, and 27 students were enrolled. For a period in its history it was also affiliated with the University of Georgia. From its first small class of students, Georgia State has grown to its current size of 23,000 students. Located in Atlanta, the university has grown in parallel with the city.

Like many urban institutions, Georgia State serves a large number of adult students. Currently, 30 percent of each entering group of newly enrolled students can be classified as adult learners. In addition, 56 percent of each group of newly enrolled students are transfers. Georgia State is moderately selective; the average SAT score for entering nonadult freshmen was 990 in

1989. Since Georgia State is an urban institution, 62 percent of its students come from a ten-county area that includes Atlanta and surrounding communities. The campus does not own any residence halls.

Georgia State offers both undergraduate and graduate degrees, including doctoral programs. It has a fine reputation in many areas and has built some excellent graduate programs. The programs in business and education are very highly regarded. Nevertheless, many state residents continue to see the university as of lower quality than the University of Georgia, located in Athens, Georgia.

The campus is relatively new and some of the buildings are modern, attractive-looking buildings while others are temporary buildings that the administration has never quite been able to retire because of the rapid growth of the university. Three years ago a new dean of undergraduate admissions was appointed. One year ago a new president was appointed. Therefore, the entire market planning process at Georgia State is changing. The market planning activities described in this case study are still in the process of evolving. Currently, enrollment management is not centralized at Georgia State, but a Presidential Task Force on Enrollment Management has recently been commissioned. Graduate admissions efforts are decentralized. Each graduate program handles its recruitment programs separately. The Office of Undergraduate Admissions is responsible for all undergraduate programs. The dean of undergraduate admissions reports to the vice-president for student affairs.

The Marketing Plan at Georgia State

The marketing plan at Georgia State University can best be described as a process, not a plan that has been settled. At Georgia State, the marketing plan is a document that outlines a set of goals and activities for the university for a five-year period. The plan was developed by the dean of undergraduate admissions, who has the primary responsibility for reviewing and updating the plan. The plan becomes a formal document each year when it is approved by the newly appointed Steering Committee of the Presidential Task Force on Enrollment Management.

The plan, based upon a marketing planning model developed by Kotler and Fox (1985), consists of the following sections: (1) executive summary, (2) situational analysis, (3) goals and objectives, and (4) marketing strategies, activities, and budget. Except for the executive summary, which is self-explanatory, each of the sections will be reviewed to provide an overview of the elements of a comprehensive marketing plan.

Situational Analysis. This section of the Georgia State marketing plan addresses the internal and external environments that are described in Chapter Two. The current status of student enrollments is described. Also, future demographic projections for the geographical regions that make up the school's traditional and nontraditional student markets are presented. These projections have been integrated with enrollment trends at the university and provide a context for a discussion of strengths and weaknesses and opportunities and threats for Georgia State.

The Office of Undergraduate Admissions at Georgia State University relies heavily upon the Enrollment Planning Service (EPS), available through the College Board, to analyze each student market. The counties described by EPS have been used to identify the university's core markets. Future enrollments and draw rates from each market have been predicted. The admissions office has identified each high school in its primary, secondary, and noncore markets.

EPS is also used in the marketing plan to discuss the market position of the university vis-à-vis other in-state public institutions as well as local private institutions. Trend-line information by academic major is also monitored so that the university can plan for enrollments in each undergraduate program area. EPS also enables the admissions office to identify its market penetration for various academic programs, further refining the office's ability to analyze the institution's market position.

The admissions office has also analyzed the same enrollment data specifically for minority students to enhance the ability of the office to target recruitment activities to them. Not surprisingly, Georgia State faces intense competition for black students from five historically black institutions in Atlanta — Morehouse College, Spelman College, Clark Atlanta University, Morris Brown College, and Atlanta Metropolitan College.

To further hone the university's understanding of the student marketplace, the Admitted Student Questionnaire (ASQ), which has been developed by the College Board, is administered. The ASQ permits campus administrators to better understand how the institution is perceived by prospective students.

After integrating the data described above with demographic projections for the state, region, and county, the marketing plan analyzes the opportunities and threats that are on the horizon. Key opportunities include the following.

- An expanded rapid transit system will increase accessibility of Georgia State to northern and southern suburbs.
- The establishment of a new North Metro Center campus should attract more students from a heavily populated area.
- Atlanta is fast becoming a major international business center that should create more cooperative opportunities for native Georgia State students as well as make the university more attractive to international students.

Key threats for Georgia State include:

- Three of the university's primary markets and four of its secondary markets show significant declines in the number of high school graduates for the next several years.
- A steadily increasing number of remedial students makes it more difficult for Georgia State to market itself as a high-quality institution for gifted and talented students.
- Several state institutions have become more aggressive in marketing to adult students in the Atlanta market, including two former public two-year colleges that have recently become four-year schools.

In addition to identifying the threats and opportunities for Georgia State University, the marketing plan also outlines a series of institutional strengths and weaknesses. The school's key strengths are its location near a rapid transit system (the university has a station on the campus); its new college of law, which has added prestige to the university; its low tuition cost and high-quality instruction; flexible course scheduling from 7 A.M. to 10 P.M.; and a touch-tone–telephone registration system. Georgia State's key weaknesses are that it has no residential facilities, which limits the markets to which the university can expand; its perceived bad location, in a high-crime area; its inadequate scholarship funding; and that it has no obvious campus borders, which makes it hard to tell when you are on the campus.

The strengths of the admissions office include its well-trained, experienced staff, advanced computer support, and faculty and staff support. The weaknesses of the office include its poor location and small work area; its inability to capture, store, and retrieve some important student data; and that there is little opportunity to promote quality lower-level staff members.

Goals and Objectives. The situational analysis sets the stage for the specific marketing goals and objectives for Georgia State University. Administrators at the university realize that it takes time to implement enrollment changes; thus, they expect to achieve each goal by 1994. This date provides the Office of Undergraduate Admissions with time to implement the strategies and activities intended to achieve the goals. The key goals in the plan include:

1. Increase the number of newly enrolled undergraduates by 5 percent, from 3,716 to 3,905.
2. Increase the number of newly enrolled minority students by 4 percent.
3. Increase the number of newly enrolled international students by 20 percent.

Marketing Strategies and Activities. The marketing plan includes a set of strategies for each goal. For illustrative purposes, some of the strategies for three of the goals presented in the previous section are described. In the plan, the costs of each activity are also identified. The costs, however, have not been included in this case study.

The first enrollment management goal is to increase the number of newly enrolled undergraduates by 5 percent, from 3,716 to 3,905. To accomplish this goal, five strategic activities have been designed.

Strategic Activity 1 is to implement a direct mail campaign to selected targeted subpopulations of high school juniors and seniors. The advantage of this activity is that the admissions office can select the student characteristics it is seeking and send appropriate messages and materials directly to students who meet the selected criteria. In addition, since the material is sent directly to the home, parents have an opportunity to see it. It is a cost-effective and productive recruitment activity. To achieve this activity, the admissions office will

- Order from the College Board's Student Search Service Program 5,000 names of high school juniors in the greater metropolitan area (EPS market numbers 1, 2, 3, and 4) who have a combined PSAT of 100 or higher and a 3.0 GPA or higher. In late spring, freshmen will receive a brochure, a letter from the dean of admissions, a reply card, and an honors program brochure. A follow-up mailing will be sent to nonresponders in early September.
- Send packets of admissions promotional and informational materials to those prospects who have initiated contact with the school by sending official copies of SAT or ACT score reports to GSU. Personalized letters from the dean will be included. The message in the letter and the materials will be selected according to the academic qualities of the prospects. Specialized materials could include the honors program brochure, brochures from appropriate academic departments, a viewbook with application inside, and so on. The packet should be sent within five working days after receipt of score reports.
- Send letter to parents of students who have been accepted

as freshmen for the upcoming quarter. This letter is an effort to increase the yield percentage of accepted-to-enrolled students. It also serves as a public-relations tool and promotes a caring attitude. The letter will be signed by the dean of admissions and the dean of students.

Strategic Activity 2 is to initiate a high school visitation program. Actions to achieve this are: visit ninety-five high schools in the GSU primary EPS markets or in secondary EPS markets; eliminate visits where only lunchtime cafeteria contacts are permitted, unless this is evaluated as a productive contact at certain high schools; and replace cafeteria visits with meetings with school counselors.

Strategic Activity 3 is to design, produce, and utilize a GSU videotape. The interest of prospective applicants will be promoted by utilizing the twelve-minute videotape at selected high school visits, in the lobby of the admissions office, and at information sessions conducted by admissions office staff.

Strategic Activity 4 is to organize, in cooperation with the alumni office, receptions hosted by alumni volunteers. Alumni volunteers will hold informal receptions in their homes for accepted students living in their area, especially for potential honor students. Twenty-five alumni volunteers will receive a one-day orientation and training session from admissions office staff.

Strategic Activity 5 is to conduct telephone calls to accepted freshmen to help increase the yield rate of accepted-to-enrolled students. Admissions office recruitment-team staff members and selected office student assistants will call accepted students soon after receipt of acceptance letters to show interest in the students and to answer questions they may have. Selected alumni volunteers will call accepted students in their Zip code areas to show interest and to promote GSU.

The second goal is to increase the number of newly enrolled minority students by 4 percent. Six strategic activities have been designed to accomplish this goal.

Strategic Activity 1 is to utilize the computerized prospective-student contact file to follow up black student contacts made through high school visits, college fairs, and specialized programs for minority students. The contact file allows for identification of prospects for special mailings, such as the black student brochure, student newsletters, and departmental letters and brochures.

Strategic Activity 2 is to identify talented black students for scholarships. The school must attract enough qualified high school seniors to apply for the Presidential Scholarship and ensure that no less than 20 percent of these scholarships will be granted to black students.

Strategic Activity 3 is to organize a luncheon workshop or other appropriate activity for counselors from Atlanta city high schools. The workshop will reacquaint the counselors with programs, services, and personnel at Georgia State University and provide them with up-to-date information and materials about GSU to share with their students.

Strategic Activity 4 is to participate in the "adopt a high school" program with local high schools with large black enrollments. Follow up activities for students at these schools will be organized.

Strategic Activity 5 is to perform black student market analysis and recruitment planning. From information obtained through the College Board's Enrollment Planning Service, the minority recruitment office can analyze strengths and weaknesses of minority recruitment efforts. EPS data will identify GSU's primary, secondary, and fringe black student markets. Additionally, major competitors can be identified, along with market penetration and market share.

Strategic Activity 6 is to develop an early identification program for black students. To accomplish this, the admissions office will contact black eighth graders through junior high school visits and follow up by contacting their parents. The office will motivate them to begin thinking about higher education and advise them of what they can do in high school to prepare for college.

The third goal is to increase the number of newly enrolled international students by 20 percent. Five strategic activities have been devised to meet this goal.

Strategic Activity 1 is to increase the school's visibility abroad by mailing on a yearly basis well-designed international student packages and brochures to overseas educational centers, Fulbright Commissions, National Scholarship Boards, USIS posts, and international schools.

Strategic Activity 2 is to participate biennially in organized recruitment tours or college fairs overseas sponsored by the Institute of International Education, U.S. cultural centers, or U.S. organizations approved by the National Association for Foreign Student Affairs (NAFSA).

Strategic Activity 3 is to support the participation of an international admissions administrator in overseas professional development programs sponsored by foreign governments, NAFSA, and other professional organizations involved in international educational exchange.

Strategic Activity 4 is to visit foreign consulates, trade delegations, and international companies in Atlanta and provide information about university programs, such as English as a second language, business administration, and so on, that may be of interest to them and their members' families.

Strategic Activity 5 is to use out-of-state tuition waivers as merit scholarships to be awarded to superior undergraduate students accepted to the university.

The marketing plan for Georgia State University is comprehensive and realistic. It does not seek dramatic change in a short period of time. It identifies specific goals and then delineates strategies to achieve these goals. In order to succeed, marketing plans need to be based on data that enable the institution to assess its current status and then to take proactive steps to achieve the enrollment goals that campus administrators have identified as priorities.

Evaluation of marketing activities is an important part of the Georgia State plan. Although not as detailed as it will be in future iterations, evaluation is being done by the admissions office through its tracking of market yield using EPS and its own student data base. The new computerized admissions contact file has enabled the office to monitor the effectiveness of various recruitment strategies. For example, the admissions staff will be able to determine whether high school visits or targeted mailings were more effective in increasing the number of applications from traditional-age students. Furthermore, the same kinds of evaluation will be conducted on the effects of recruitment activities on minority students. As indicated in the marketing plan, the Admitted Student Questionnaire will also be administered repeatedly in order to evaluate efforts to improve the image of the university.

The return on the dollars invested in most of the marketing activities can be roughly estimated by comparing the costs of the activity with the number of leads, inquiries, applications, or matriculated students the activity generates. This, unfortunately, cannot be done for all activities. For instance, it is difficult to assess the impact of hosting a luncheon for counselors at high schools with large enrollments of minority students. It is also difficult to ascertain whether any specific strategy improved the university's image. As discussed in earlier chapters, the creation of an institutional image is complex. Nevertheless, when it makes sense and it is technically possible, marketing activities are evaluated.

Systematic marketing plans are so new to the university that it is too early to arrive at many conclusions. The university's president is very interested in marketing and has been an invaluable source of support for marketing activities. The president's interest has communicated to other senior-level administrators that marketing is important. Since the arrival of the current dean of undergraduate admissions and the president, significant marketing planning has taken place.

The scope and complexity of a university also make market planning difficult. Each school or college, and even many departments, are accustomed to operating autonomously. Many of Georgia State's publications have historically been developed by each school or department. Under the new marketing plan, the admissions office has centralized all of these activities.

At Georgia State, location and history are also difficult to overcome. In the past, students have "just come" to the school; therefore, intentional marketing efforts seem unnecessary to some faculty and administrators. Changes as simple as appropriate signs have at times been difficult to achieve. Nevertheless, the new commitment to marketing and an emerging interest in enrollment management will enable the university to exert more control over its student enrollments.

Oakton Community College

The transition of Oakton Community College from an institution whose administrators, staff, and faculty members largely rejected the concept of marketing to one that has embraced and devoted considerable resources to marketing is not easily described. Like many colleges, Oakton does not have a textbook marketing plan complete with goals, objectives, assignments of responsibility, timetables, dollar allocations, and measures of completion and success. Rather, the incorporation of marketing into the college's modus operandi has occurred more informally and erratically; as a result, because there is no formally accepted and widely distributed document spelling out annual marketing activities, this case study explaining marketing may appear at times to be rather vague. This lack of specificity is in some ways the most important lesson to be learned from the Oakton experience; that is, institutions can make significant progress in marketing without convening permanent committees or preparing formal documents or producing elaborate plans. Though useful in some places, such approaches are unnecessary or not feasible in other schools in which there is an organizational culture of informality.

Oakton Community College is located in an affluent suburban area immediately north of Chicago. Its service district includes a population of 420,000, which is aging and growing more ethnically diverse. The proportion of college-educated residents is twice the national average. District residents pride themselves on the high quality of their schools and community services; some public high schools send more than 90 percent of their graduates to college.

The college is a comprehensive, open enrollment community college that enrolls 10,500 students in credit courses and another 12,000 in adult and continuing education. It is governed by a locally elected lay board that, within broad state guidelines, has a great deal of autonomy to develop the college's culture and special emphases.

At Oakton, most (80 percent) of the students attending for credit attend school part time, and most (65 percent) are in transfer curricula. The average age of students is twenty-eight, with over 85 percent being employed. More students are experienced college students, having attended another college or university before coming to Oakton, than are first-time college students. There are 145 full-time and close to 400 part-time faculty teaching in the credit programs, 28 administrators, and nearly 300 full- and part-time staff.

The institution, whose annual operating budget is $24 million, has an exceptionally strong financial base. The college occupies a modern building set in a forest preserve at one end of the district and an older facility eight miles away, formerly used as a high school.

The Emergence of the Marketing Concept at Oakton

Oakton is in many ways an advanced college. Nevertheless, in the early 1980s the college found itself facing declining enrollment for the first time in its short history and a feeling internally that the institution was neither as good as it could be nor as highly regarded as it deserved to be. Administrators and faculty fretted a great deal about these perceptions, and gradually the word *marketing* and the concept of marketing at Oakton began to seep into their discussions. This happened despite the notion of many that Oakton was above marketing, which carried the connotation of advertising at best and crass hucksterism at worst.

People at Oakton began to read marketing literature and to attend conferences, and they came away with the understanding that marketing involves much more than advertising and promotions alone, that effective marketing could be a valuable tool for the college. Individuals from areas such as admissions, research, student affairs, public relations, and some academic departments began to talk not only to each other but to skeptics who might be converted to believe that marketing — of course appropriately shaped and constrained — could be useful to the college. What initially brought these people together was not a formal charge, but rather shared interest in improving the quality of the institution and external perceptions of it and the fact that each of them controlled some money and had some explicit responsibility for marketing activities (such as producing publications, recruiting students, researching constituency perceptions, and managing programs that were weak in enrollment).

Maturation as an institution helped to make marketing more acceptable at Oakton. Early in its history Oakton took pride in marching to its own drummer, in rejecting traditional ways of organizing an institution and teaching courses. Over time, though, key administrators and faculty members grew more comfortable and self-confident. They began to reject the "we will do it our way" rebelliousness of the early years. Faculty and administrators came to accept that achieving high quality is a demanding goal that requires energetic, committed faculty and staff members who are willing to reexamine campus programs and activities in order to make changes where needed.

With this professional maturity came a sense that the college needed to be more effective in communicating its quality and the range of programs and services to constituent groups. Campus marketing efforts sought to convey information about these points in a style appropriate to a revitalized sense of confidence and professionalism. This internal energy was an important attribute; without it, many staff and faculty members had been hesitant to promote the institution. They were, in the language of corporate marketing, reluctant to promote what they themselves feared was a low-quality product.

New leadership was also influential in prompting the college's acceptance of marketing. This leadership came from the outside, a new president and vice-president for curriculum and instruction, and from the inside, through reorganizations and key promotions. The new leaders brought a fresh sense of vision to the institution and increased support for marketing activities. The combination of new leadership, institutional maturity, and a core of individuals committed to marketing enabled the college to move into marketing activities.

In 1983, a marketing committee composed of representatives from across the institution was formed. Members included administrators from admissions, research and planning, student affairs, public relations, and academic affairs; faculty members who had experience with marketing or who claimed to have expertise; and classified staff members from offices that had large amounts of public contact. The committee issued a long report that called for a variety of coordinated activities. While the report legitimized the use of the word *marketing* and some recommended activities were implemented (such as better signs and more personal contacts with the press and community leaders), the report's major themes of coordination and boldness in marketing were largely ignored.

Soon after his arrival in 1984, the new president formed another marketing committee. Its report was similar to that of the first marketing committee; indeed, many of its members were the same. And, like the first committee, it found most of its recommendations largely ignored.

The two marketing committees and other ad hoc task forces allowed for widespread input and the generation of numerous ideas. However, many individuals resented having committees of people from outside their area telling them what to do to improve marketing, especially when many, indeed most, committee recommendations duplicated practices that were long in effect. For example, every committee recommended that members of the admissions office staff visit local high schools; in fact, numerous high school visits took place every year. Uneven support and the lack of a consistent message about which marketing activities were expected and which were not led to confusion, which was compounded by the fact that no clear definition of marketing was adopted by the college. Marketing was defined and interpreted by many different people in many different ways.

Despite the amount of time and effort being spent internally to define marketing and push for more marketing activities, several administrators, including the chair of the college's marketing program, also hired the services of marketing consultants to explain and recommend marketing activities. During this same time several college administrators who had marketing dollars in their budgets joined together to critique the college's publications. This ad hoc group concluded that the publications were characterized by too much diversity (there was no family of publications linked together through a common approach and design), too little attention to physical properties (design, paper, use of color), and too little targeting of specific audiences. Offices claimed to own their publications, while no one person or office owned them on behalf of the college and had the authority and responsibility to ensure that collegewide standards would be met.

Perhaps the best way to characterize this period is to say that lots of attention was given to marketing but that marketing was not widely understood or accepted, activities were fragmented and generated from separate offices, and marketing successes seemed to happen as much by chance as by design. Fortunately, as marketing — even in its confusing manifestations — became more salient to the institution, budgetary support for marketing expanded. Through the regular budget process, additional money was made available for publications, for the production and dissemination of videotapes and other informational materials, and for letters and postcards to be mailed to potential and matriculating students. The college allocated funds for hosting meetings and outreach activities to encourage personal contacts with the business community, civic organizations, and other groups that might provide greater visibility for Oakton. Internal marketing was also increased; for example, the school instituted employee orientations with a segment devoted to marketing, and more emphasis was placed on delivering courteous and timely service. Through one-time allocations of funds for special projects, money was made available for such marketing purposes as acquiring banners to line the college's road, improving the newsletter sent to all households, initiating a newsletter for high school juniors and seniors, and producing new color brochures for clusters of programs (such as transfer programs, career programs, and business-related programs).

Despite the marketing committees' attempts to convince college personnel that marketing involved more than just promotions, the focus of marketing at Oakton was usually on promotions. Yet, though most people did not think of these promotions under the rubric of marketing, the many forces that prompted stronger interest in promotions also prompted stronger interest in two other elements of marketing: product and place. For example, the college revamped the general education curriculum, expanded the use of computers in many disciplines, and initiated a number of short-term vocational certificate programs designed for working adults. Revised course scheduling made classes more available to students who wanted to limit their attendance to one or two days a week.

Financial considerations with respect to marketing centered on expenditures. The notion that price — the college's tuition and fees — was a marketing tool was not well understood. The college's governing board took pride in the exceptionally low tuition ($17 per credit hour). Early on, however, some individuals in the marketing committees began to suggest that the low tuition may have been sending a negative cue about the college. How could any college of high quality charge so little?

In retrospect, the most salient characteristic of the college's early marketing efforts was diversity — some would say confusion — in understanding and acceptance, in effectiveness, in organizing. In 1983, very few individuals at Oakton used the word *marketing* comfortably, and many explicitly refused to consider marketing as an appropriate activity for the institution. Over time, as people came to use the term freely, the level of understanding of marketing still differed enormously between individuals, and it still does. The dominant focus of marketing was on the use of promotions, primarily to recruit students into the college and, to a lesser extent, to build generalized community support. Though a great deal of energy began to be channeled into faculty revitalization, curriculum development, and improved teaching, few at the college considered these activities to be part of marketing.

The focus on marketing qua promotion for recruitment led to an unfortunate notion that declining enrollments were the result of poor marketing and that if only marketing were improved, enrollment would grow. This view was particularly strong in some departments that experienced disproportionate drops in enrollment. That the content and quality of the program itself might be a problem or that potential students were simply uninterested in a particular area of study were rarely seen as factors affecting enrollment. Neither was the fact that the high school population was precipitously declining in number. Some faculty, staff members, and administrators believed that good marketing was the solution to any problem. This belief was as damaging to efforts to market as the previous resistance to marketing had been because adherents of it did not understand that the quality and attractiveness of programs and services depended on much more than promotional efforts; indeed, some people were and still are unable to understand that low enrollments and participation rates in some areas of the college reflect sound consumer decisions about the quality and relevance of what the college is offering.

Although both marketing committees' reports called for greater centralization of marketing responsibilities, most people at the school resisted locating the authority and responsibility for marketing in one office. This resistance was prompted both by principle and by practice. The president and others objected in principle, arguing that for marketing to permeate the college, many offices had to have both the responsibility and the authority to plan and implement selected marketing activities. The offices needed, in other words, to own marketing. Otherwise, this group argued, marketing would be viewed as the job of "that marketing office." Those who resisted centralization based on practice argued that talented people were already successfully engaged in marketing activities and that it made no sense to remove them from this arena and vest authority and responsibility instead in an unknown and unproven officer. Issues of jurisdiction were involved in both bases of resistance but were not the only motivations for opposing centralization.

To address the need for coordination without vesting marketing authority in a central office, the president created the position of director of enrollment management to coordinate marketing functions originated by each of the areas in the college. The extent to which this coordination occurs and the salience of the coordinating responsibility to others in the institution remains unclear.

In sum, early marketing efforts at Oakton were characterized by a growing acceptance but limited understanding of the notion of marketing; a tendency to expect good marketing to solve a variety of problems, even those beyond the pale of marketing in its broadest sense; and continued tension over the degree to which marketing authority and responsibility should be centralized or decentralized. Rather than trying to resolve these tensions or to impose a master plan and force adherence to it, a less formidable route to improved marketing was taken — changes were made little by little.

The Current Status of Marketing at Oakton

Today, marketing at Oakton is more sophisticated, and more commitment to marketing exists at the college than existed in 1983. Certainly budgetary support has increased; more funds are available for publications and advertising, for outreach activities, for person-to-person contacts, and for meetings. These funds are dispersed throughout the college; it would take a careful and sophisticated reading of the budget to compile the amounts into an institutional total. Consequently, the full extent of increased support is difficult to figure.

Responsibility and authority for marketing are still decentralized — some would say fragmented. For the most part, the college seems to be comfortable with this, although periodically there are new calls for centralization, calls that presume centralization would solve perceived marketing problems. Structural decentralization of marketing has in part been offset by the assignment of general overview responsibilities to the director of enrollment management and by stronger alliances and working relationships among many people who have significant marketing responsibilities and budgets. More coordination of marketing is occurring even if this is not evident on a formal organizational chart.

The college is currently engaged in many activities and projects that enhance the quality of programs and services, accessibility and convenience of classes for students, and the institution's image in the community. Most of these programs are not seen as falling within the umbrella of marketing, even though any basic marketing textbook would so classify them. Examples of programs include a critical literacy project, involving over one-third of the faculty in vigorous professional development and teaching improvement activities; curriculum revisions that have increased general education requirements to bring the college's degrees more in line with national trends in curricula; assessment and course placement stipulations that match students' skills with the level of courses in which they are permitted to enroll; focused academic support programs for special-needs students; a more active and visible foundation that promotes the college while raising funds; touch-tone-telephone registration that has made registering for courses frighteningly easy; and acceptance of credit cards.

Substantial changes have been made in the variety and quality of written materials. Academic program brochures constitute a brochure family that uses a common design with a distinct graphic for each program. An oversized four-color brochure designed specifically for high school students confronts directly the myths about Oakton commonly held by younger students, such as the school is easy, it is not a "real" college, and only students who were not accepted elsewhere come to Oakton. The brochure is the boldest that has been developed and the most controversial. A companion brochure, neither glitzy nor controversial, is targeted to the parents of younger students. Its underlying theme is "You are a good parent to send your child to Oakton," a message that is important to convey in a community that expects students to go away to school. The college's annual report has been redesigned not only to meet legal requirements but also to provide donors with information. Postcards with four-color graphics are mailed to students to remind them of registration dates.

Some people still grumble about poor marketing at Oakton. When pressed, the complainers usually identify a particular incident or newspaper story or cite declining enrollment in a program or poor attendance at an event. Sometimes they are correct, but often they are myopic, generalizing from a particular example to the whole range of diverse marketing activities in which the college engages.

Evaluation of Marketing Efforts. Evaluating marketing efforts is not easy. Without a clear bottom line (Oakton, fortunately, does not use enrollment data alone to indicate success or failure of a marketing effort), evaluations depend on many criteria, only some of which are directly measurable. Marketing efforts at Oakton have been evaluated only informally so general observations about evaluation rather than excerpts from any evaluation report follow.

Quantitative data have been examined. For example, enrollments have risen in some programs that have received targeted marketing attention. Enrollment in materials management courses rose dramatically the semester after informational materials were mailed to company vice-presidents of manufacturing and operations and personnel directors. On the other hand, despite numerous high school and community presentations, magnificent metropolitan and local newspaper coverage, and radio and television references to Oakton's new nanny training program, enrollment has remained dismal.

Surveys of current and former students indicate that the newsletter mailed to all district households six times a year is a crucial vehicle for informing potential students about courses and programs. Telephone inquiries to faculty go up when they or their programs are featured in the local press, but enrollments may not follow. The college has spent money to advertise on the radio, but it was not possible to track whether or not radio advertising was directly connected with enrollment increases. The argument that radio advertising enhanced the overall visibility of the institution was not generally supported, and this promotional effort has been discontinued, at least for the time being.

Qualitative "data," perceptions, and anecdotes about the effectiveness of campus efforts have also been examined. Focus groups with adult women returning to college have confirmed the importance of personal contacts in keeping them at Oakton, but not in drawing them to the school in the first place. College personnel report they feel more confident and comfortable when they can distribute high-quality literature, faculty appear happy and proud when a videotape is available to promote their discipline, and everyone at the school seems to feel excitement and pride when the college is recognized for its achievements or those of its faculty, staff, or students.

Campus administrators are acutely aware that many factors impinge on the institution, only some of which are directly affected by marketing. Rising college costs at most institutions and reductions in freshman class sizes at state universities are undoubtedly contributing to Oakton's expanding enrollment of young students, marketing aside. The age of the college combined with the growing number of district residents who have been or know students of Oakton gives the college more exposure, marketing aside. An exceptional local property tax base that enables Oakton to keep tuition remarkably low makes the college much more affordable than other colleges, marketing aside.

Evaluating marketing efforts is difficult, and questions like "How many new students will we enroll as a result of this brochure?" or "To what extent will our credibility as a college increase if we host this meeting?" are frustrating. The institution has resisted justifying marketing efforts on the basis of specific returns on investment, either in terms of enrollment or dollars. Yet, campus administrators continually talk about the outcomes of marketing. Perhaps it is most accurate to say, first, that Oakton is still trying to figure out how best to evaluate marketing efforts without being caught up in burdensome evaluation activities that take more energy and time than they are worth and, second, that evaluating marketing is of less concern than doing marketing.

Lessons Learned. It is difficult to summarize themes that emerge from the loosely coupled marketing environment at Oakton Community College. Nevertheless, some closing observations are warranted. These lessons reflect the views of a number of campus administrators, but not all, who have played pivotal roles in the college's marketing efforts over the past six years.

- There is no one right way to organize for or to implement effective marketing.
- It takes three or more years for marketing to become an accepted concept at a college or university.

- Most people will always think of marketing as tantamount to promotions, publications, and advertising; they will have precious little understanding that marketing also involves product (curricula and services), price (dollars, time, and energy), and place (course location and proximity to home or work). They certainly do not include people in the marketing mix.
- Some people, especially some faculty, believe that marketing is not their concern; marketing is what others should do to increase enrollment in the faculty members' programs.
- The location of marketing authority and responsibility on the institution's organizational chart is far less relevant to marketing effectiveness than are talented and committed people willing to work together, supported by adequate resources.
- True marketing involves eliminating as well as maintaining and creating programs and services.
- Style without substance will not be effective for long, but style accompanying substance does not hurt — ever.
- Some marketing decisions will be made based on feelings and intuition, in violation of every principle of organizational design and behavior.
- Calls for a marketing expert to come in and "do things right" are fundamentally and persistently in conflict with most people's absolute confidence that they are able to judge good marketing activities and should have the right to implement their own marketing initiatives.
- Colleges and universities are typically organized messily; a certain measure of duplication and overlap is routine. Why, then, should marketing be expected to fall neatly into one office and not to duplicate any of its reporting?
- Everything takes longer than you think, and most activities take more money than you budget.

In the past six years Oakton College has channeled a great deal of cooperative effort and support into marketing, albeit in a less-organized and coherent manner than marketing textbooks suggest. There is a persistent interest in marketing at Oakton, and many employees are sensitized to its importance, though there is no single formal marketing plan. Whether the college's current health is a result of, or cause for, more and better marketing is impossible to know. What is known, however, is that effective marketing takes hard work and does not come easily. Some things have been done very well at Oakton and some things not well at all. In this respect, Oakton is like most organizations.

It is hard to imagine higher education abandoning marketing as an appropriate activity. Yet, is is easy to imagine higher education settling into a marketing routine that ignores fundamental principles of effective marketing — understand the consumer and use not only promotions, but product, price, and place as marketing tools. Using only promotions would be the path of least resistance but one that in short order would erode the benefits effective marketing can bring to an institution.

Comparison of the Two Cases

Marketing at Georgia State University and Oakton Community College look very different. Georgia State has a formal plan that includes clearly stated objectives and marketing activities. At Oakton, an ongoing dialogue about marketing has percolated through academic and nonacademic units of the campus. Marketing at GSU looks concrete and tangible, while at Oakton Community College the extent to which marketing principles have been employed is not always clear. These differences reflect the unique qualities of each institution and the number of years each place has grappled with marketing.

At Oakton marketing is more decentralized. The interplay between marketing strategies and academic departments is also more frequently mentioned in academic departments. Enrollment managers are seldom able to direct the activities of academic departments; thus it is not surprising that some aspects of the Oakton case study emphasize the need for administrators and faculty to take ownership for marketing. At Oakton, unlike at Georgia State University, senior-level administrators appear not to have created a mandate for a formal centralized marketing plan. This is not unusual. The work of Bensimon, Neumann, and Birnbaum (1989) demonstrates that college presidents have a variety of administrative styles. Not every college president believes in formalized strategic planning. Chapter Three notes that enrollment management systems emerge slowly, after an evolutionary change process. Marketing at Oakton has followed this course, and, over time, academic and nonacademic administrators have incorporated the marketing perspective into their decisions.

Georgia State University employs a textbook marketing plan. At GSU, marketing has received a strong endorsement from the president, and he expects formalized planning. It should also be noted that marketing at GSU appears to be the responsibility of the admissions office. At this point in time, individual departments do not seem to be heavily involved in the process. This is different from the process at Oakton and makes it easier to implement a formal marketing plan. The formalized nature of the marketing plan at GSU also lends itself more readily to evaluation. Clear goals and objectives can be monitored and evaluated on an ongoing basis. Nevertheless, at both institutions, information is analyzed to monitor the impact of marketing activities. Both Ernest Beals at GSU and Trudy Bers at Oakton, however, are careful to point out that not every marketing activity readily lends itself to evaluation.

At Oakton two events were behind the growing interest in marketing on the campus. First, an enrollment decline sparked the interest of some faculty and administrators in marketing. And then, a new president endorsed the importance of marketing. Similarly, at Georgia State, the arrival of a new dean of admissions and a new president was directly related to the new importance attached to marketing. External forces such as enrollment declines and support from senior-level administrators are often the impetus for the emergence of marketing plans as well as enrollment management systems.

Finally, it should be noted that marketing is newer to Georgia State University than to Oakton. Eight years from now, after more attempts to infuse the marketing perspective into the entire university, Ernest Beals's insights might reflect some of the same ambiguity that is evident in the Oakton case study. As Trudy Bers at Oakton concludes, "colleges are ordered messily," and "everything takes longer than you think."

PART THREE

STUDENT RETENTION
IN ENROLLMENT MANAGEMENT

Part Three examines the topic of student retention. Many colleges and universities have used the term *enrollment management,* but in practice they only focus on marketing and recruitment. Retaining students is an important task for enrollment managers. In Chapter Nine, Bean points out that every student who leaves an institution represents a significant loss of income for the school. Many decisions to withdraw are sound for both the student and the institution. Each year, however, on campuses throughout the country, students leave college who could benefit from staying. They leave because retention efforts were inadequate.

Chapter Nine reviews relevant research on student attrition. Theories, models, and variables that help explain why some students persist and others withdraw are discussed. This chapter provides a context for the remaining chapters, which provide practical approaches to influencing student retention.

Chapter Ten outlines methods for studying student attrition. A mistake many enrollment managers make is to assume that the general literature on student persistence provides sufficient information to design retention programs for their institutions. Retention research indicates that the most important factors associated with persistence can vary from campus to campus. Without attrition studies conducted at the local campus level, enrollment managers cannot be certain that their retention programs are targeted at the right students or problems. Most admissions officers immediately recognize the importance of conducting marketing studies for their campuses; however, enrollment managers have been much slower to recognize the

145

importance of conducting campus-based retention studies. This chapter, like the chapter on market research, is written in non-technical terms and should be read by all enrollment managers.

Chapter Eleven describes retention intervention strategies consistent with the research on student attrition presented in Chapter Nine. This chapter reviews campus retention efforts and identifies strategies that have the greatest potential for reducing student attrition.

Chapter Twelve contains case studies from two institutions that have developed some effective retention programs. One institution is a small Catholic college that has made slow but steady improvements in student persistence. The other campus is a large commuter university that has used a sophisticated data base to track students and to devise retention programs.

Chapter 9

Why Students Leave: Insights from Research

John P. Bean

One of the proverbs of marketing is that it is easier to keep an old customer than to attract a new one. If the adage holds for retention, then it should be easier to keep a student enrolled than to attract a new one. The cost of attracting students to college, that is, recruitment expenditures divided by the number of new students, is often measured in thousands of dollars. The income from the retention of a full-time student can be measured in the tens of thousands of dollars. In a baccalaureate program, students who drop out during their first year represent the loss of three (or four) years of tuition and not one. It takes four freshmen who quit after one year to equal the income of one student who stays for four years. At a community college, the student who leaves after one semester instead of four represents the same kind of loss.

For these reasons it seems foolish that colleges and universities pay less attention to retention than recruitment, but there is a simple explanation for this situation. Retention is everyone's business, while recruitment appears to be the business of an identifiable group. A college or university can organize, staff, and fund an admissions office. Its costs and successes can be identified. Factors that affect retention rates, however, occur throughout an institution. Important factors can be identified, but since attrition results from multiple causes, blame for attrition and credit for retention cannot be easily assigned. This lack of specificity makes it difficult for successful retention programs to gain high visibility and garner new resources or for unsuccessful programs to be cut. Nonetheless, an enrollment management program that lacks a strong retention component will be ineffective.

This chapter describes some underlying assumptions about attrition and retention. These terms are used interchangeably but with opposite meanings; hence, an attrition model is a retention model and vice versa—attrition and retention are in one-to-one correspondence with each other. This chapter also discusses theories of the process of attrition and the variables that affect students' decisions to remain in school or leave. These variables represent points at which institutional representatives can intervene in the attrition process.

Underlying Assumptions

Withdrawal from a college or university is a complex behavior. Neither the causes nor the cures are simple. A researcher might establish a fairly precise understanding of why an individual student left a college or university, but each student's story will be different. The statement that a student left an institution because he or she received poor grades represents only a fragment of the real issue. Some questions to consider include: Are poor grades a symptom of a problem or a cause of one? Why did the student get poor grades? Was it poor placement? Did the student have no understanding of how to use a library? Did the student want to convey a desire to leave school to his or her parents? Was the student of low ability? Was the student of high ability but bored by the classes? Was a bad admissions decision made? Did the student report that grades were the reason for leaving to save face, which would actually mislead the researcher? Researchers have identified some factors consistently related to student attrition at four-year colleges and universities. At community colleges, attrition is difficult to study because of the heterogeneity of the student body and the differences in students' purposes for attending these schools. Comparatively little is known about attrition from community colleges even though, ironically, attrition rates at such institutions are higher than at four-year schools. For either type of institution, attrition results from a web of factors influencing the decision to stay in school or leave.

Withdrawal decisions are complex, in part because they develop over time. The factors that converge to support students' staying in college or drive them to leave take effect slowly. The assumption that attrition is a longitudinal process is extremely important to enrollment managers; if attrition were spontaneous, intervention projects could not be planned and students who would benefit from such action could not be identified before they left. Since the decision to leave occurs over time, a school has an opportunity to be proactive in reducing attrition.

One fairly constant finding is that students leave school because they do not fit in. They may not fit in socially or academically or religiously or economically or for some other reasons, and they leave because the school is not a good match for their needs. Fitting in is not an all-or-nothing issue, but occurs in degrees. A student's poor match in one area can be counterbalanced by a good match in another.

Fitting in depends on the student on the one hand and the institution on the other — either can change to enhance the fit. This concept must be emphasized. Do not blame the victim: a student's leaving school is the joint responsibility of the school and the student. The student may be completely justified in withdrawal, and the college or university may be at fault. The implication of this assumption for enrollment managers is that they need to pay attention to whom they admit. Furthermore, institutions must be responsive to student needs as these evolve over time.

The research also indicates that different types of students (such as older/traditional age, commuter/residential, male/female, black/white/Hispanic, full-time/part-time) depart from institutions for different reasons. While the theories and factors described in this chapter generally hold true, in particular cases almost anything can increase attrition or retention.

Theoretical Models[1]

Theories often have a bad reputation among practitioners who view them as too abstract or not applicable to the particular case at hand. The view taken here is that nothing is more practical than a good theory because it explains why something occurs. A theory's value lies in this ability to explain and its ability to guide the selection of certain constructs (variables) to be evaluated while eliminating others. Theories can be used to guide practice.

Models are simplified versions of reality in which the minutiae and detail are stripped away, leaving what are assumed to be important factors and the relationships between these factors. Models are important because they tie theory to specific situations. The chief criterion for determining the value of a model is its usefulness. Figure 9.1, a model that shows how a sequence of variables is related to attrition, is presented because it is believed to be useful. The reasons why one variable is expected to affect another are based on several theoretical models of attrition.

The first fully developed theoretical model of student attrition was described by Spady in 1970. Spady considers dropouts to be people withdrawing from a social system and argues that this behavior is analogous to suicide — a more permanent withdrawal from a social system. Based on Durkheim's (1961) research on suicide from the previous century, Spady postulates that students withdraw from college because of a lack of shared values or normative support. *Shared values* means that students accept the importance of academic work, and *normative support* means that students have family, close friends, or significant others to support (emotionally, financially, or otherwise) their staying in school. Hence, the intellectual core of subsequent attrition models was in place nearly two decades ago. Spady (1971) was also the first to statistically estimate an attrition model using multivariate statistics.

Tinto (1975) refined and simplified Spady's model and clearly distinguished academic and social factors. Tinto emphasizes the longitudinal nature of the attrition process and indicates the importance of background factors (such as initial characteristics of the student) in affecting attrition decisions. His model guided most multivariate studies for the decade following its publication and remains very influential today.

Bean's (1980) research is compatible with the Tinto/Spady approach, but owes no intellectual debt to Durkheim. The assumption underlying this work is that student attrition is analogous to turnover in work organizations, and the model developed for this study was derived from studies of turnover in work organizations, particularly from the work of Price (1977).

Three years later, Bean's (1983) work was reflecting the psychological modeling of Fishbein and Ajzen (1975) as modified by Bentler and Speckart (1979). The latter two studies' combined models suggest that an individual's behavior is the result of a cyclical process in which beliefs affect attitudes that lead to intentions that lead to the behavior in question. Hence, students' beliefs about their experience in school lead to attitudes toward the school (such as whether or not to stay) that affect the students' intent to stay (or leave) followed by actual attrition or retention. Bean also recognizes that factors external to the school might affect retention and thus introduces environmental variables as causal factors in the attrition model. Institutions have little control over environmental factors that can contribute to decisions to remain in or leave school, such as a student's wanting to be with a friend at another college.

Bean and Metzner (1985) propose a model of nontraditional-student attrition. They define nontraditional students in part by the limited nature of their interaction with other members of the college community. The difference between this model and earlier ones is that in this model social support to remain in school is environmental; it comes from a student's family (spouse and children), friends outside of school, or people at work. This situation is in sharp contrast to traditional (residential) students, for whom faculty and peers form the most important support group. Thus, social integration was expected to be less important for nontraditional students and environmental variables more important.

Figure 9.1. A Longitudinal Model of the
Type of Factors That Affect Retention Decisions.

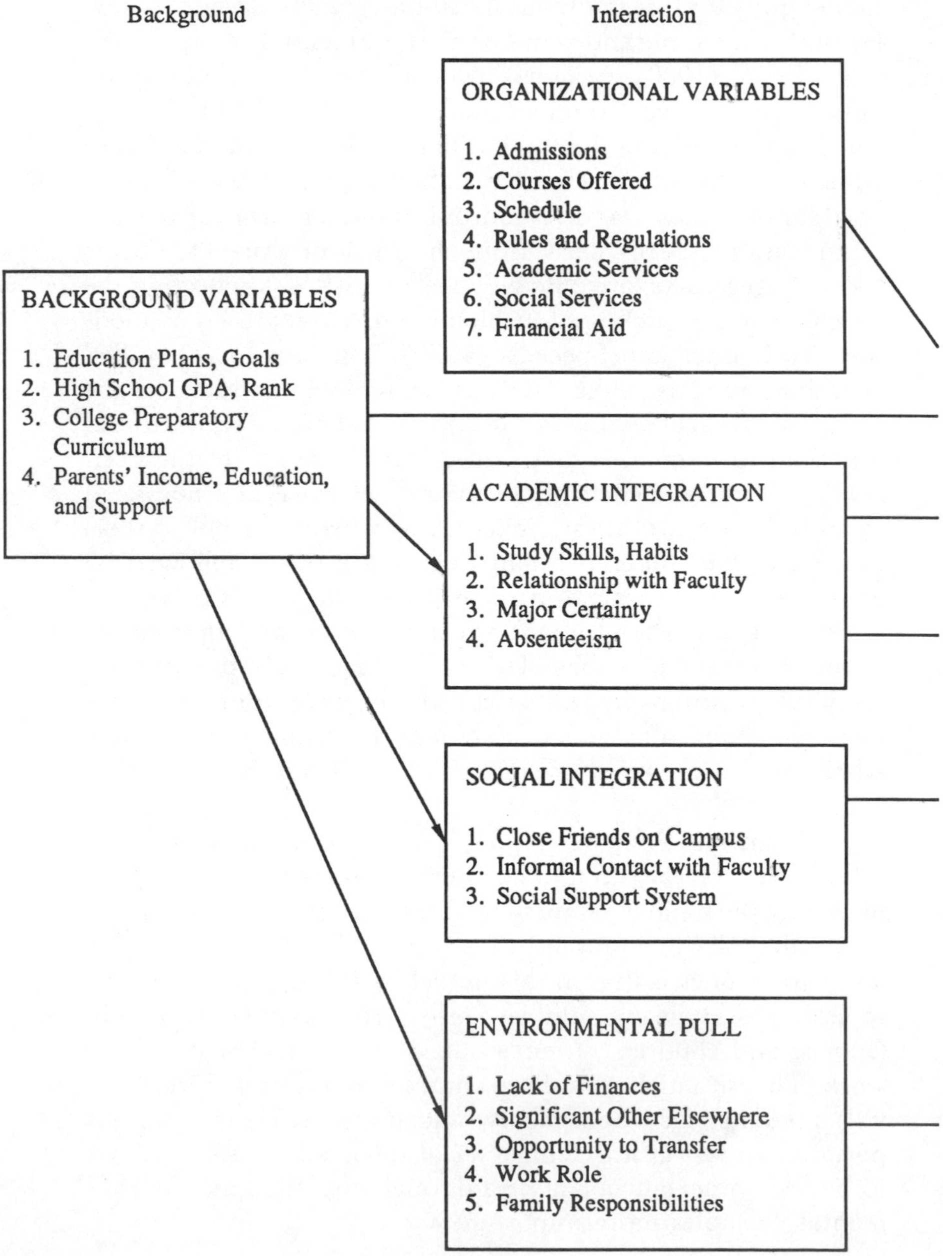

Background   Interaction

ORGANIZATIONAL VARIABLES

1. Admissions
2. Courses Offered
3. Schedule
4. Rules and Regulations
5. Academic Services
6. Social Services
7. Financial Aid

BACKGROUND VARIABLES

1. Education Plans, Goals
2. High School GPA, Rank
3. College Preparatory
   Curriculum
4. Parents' Income, Education,
   and Support

ACADEMIC INTEGRATION

1. Study Skills, Habits
2. Relationship with Faculty
3. Major Certainty
4. Absenteeism

SOCIAL INTEGRATION

1. Close Friends on Campus
2. Informal Contact with Faculty
3. Social Support System

ENVIRONMENTAL PULL

1. Lack of Finances
2. Significant Other Elsewhere
3. Opportunity to Transfer
4. Work Role
5. Family Responsibilities

Outcomes   Intent   Decision

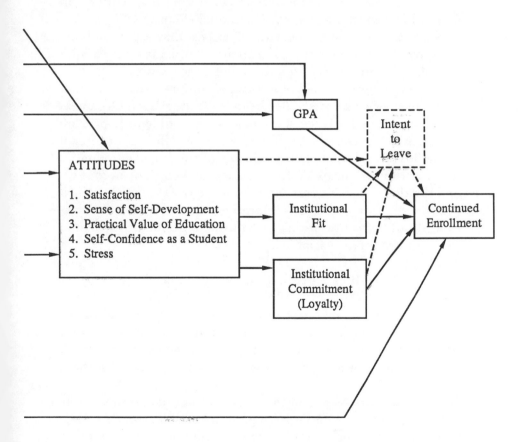

ATTITUDES

1. Satisfaction
2. Sense of Self-Development
3. Practical Value of Education
4. Self-Confidence as a Student
5. Stress

GPA

Intent
to
Leave

Institutional
Fit

Institutional
Commitment
(Loyalty)

Continued
Enrollment

The last advance in theory came from Tinto (1987), whose model was similar to the one he proposed in 1975 but with the addition of environmental variables and intentions. However, his addition of a theoretical explanation of attrition based on van Gennep's (1960) rites of passage was particularly insightful. Rites of passage occur in three stages: separation (from family and childhood support), transition (ordeals and training in new values and activities), and incorporation (adapting of a new set of values and behaviors). Tinto proposes that attrition occurs when an individual's rites of passage are incomplete.

These theoretical and empirical studies on attrition can be synthesized into a model. The model (Figure 9.1) presents attrition as a complex, longitudinal process that begins with the background characteristics of students. Students interact with the college or university organizationally, academically, and socially. The environment represents a simultaneous force that could influence students to decide to leave the school. Organizational, academic, and social interaction lead students to develop attitudes about the school. These attitudes affect institutional fit and loyalty — both potent predictors of continued enrollment. These combined attitudes directly affect students' intent to leave and the decisions students make to leave or stay. GPA, which is based on past academic performance and academic integration, should affect decisions to continue enrollment, as should the environmental variables.

Variables Affecting Retention Decisions

Several categories of variables representing experiences or beliefs, such as background and organizational variables, can affect student retention. As the effects of these variables are discussed, intervention strategies for enrollment managers are identified.

Background Variables. The characteristics of students most likely to remain in school until graduation are well known. Students most likely to remain enrolled were academically successful in high school, ranked high in their graduating class, took college preparatory courses, have high but realistic educational goals, and have college-educated parents who are well-off financially and who support their child's decision to attend college. Elite institutions attract this kind of student and usually have the highest retention rates.

Institutions should engage in adaptive strategic planning that takes background characteristics into account (Cope, 1981). Institutions need to identify their strengths and mission and then find students whose needs match the institution's strengths. Most institutions cannot compete at random for students but must attract specific types of students. In doing so, the institution can then provide the academic programs and support that these students need in order to graduate. A heterogeneous student body means that a single retention program may help only a small percentage of students. Since heterogeneity is becoming the rule rather than the exception, an increasingly wider array of retention programs will be required to meet new student needs.

The following activities related to background characteristics should enhance retention:

1. Identify the type of college or university the institution would like to be and can be given its current level of resources.
2. Identify the type of student that is likely to succeed in such an institution (that is, the model student).
3. Reach out, by letter if not in person, to the high schools that currently are or potentially are sources of this kind of student. Encourage academic excellence in these high schools. Help them develop policies that channel able students into college preparatory curricula during their last three years of high school. Help them develop career planning workshops so that those students who will need a college education for their careers can take college preparatory courses and can understand the link between the courses they take and their future work.
4. Do not ignore parents. Parental support has a major influence on how traditional-age students interact with their college environment. Students are more likely to remain

enrolled if their parents understand college life and support the student's decision to attend the college. Keeping parents informed of school requirements is a mechanism for informing students about current requirements and activities. Provide an orientation to college, ongoing on-campus programs, and monthly newsletters for parents. The support group of nontraditional students may include others more important than parents. The spouses of married students, especially first-generation students, should receive an orientation similar to that provided for parents. Employers should also be informed about the demands placed on students by college-level work as well as the benefits derived from such study.

Organizational Variables. Retention programs and other student services programs are organizational variables. Typically, single programs have little effect on the overall retention rate, either because only a small percentage of the student body takes advantage of such programs or because those students placed into the programs are selected because they are most likely to drop out. Thus, participation in the program is often associated with high dropout rates. A variety of programs designed to meet the needs of different types of students and that provide meaningful involvement for students, staff, faculty, and administrators and focus on changing student attitudes are most likely to increase retention. Student involvement has long been shown to enhance retention (Astin, 1975).

The admissions office is the interface between the client (potential student) and the product (curriculum). Admissions officers should be evaluated not only on the number of students they enroll but also on the number of students they enroll who come back to school as sophomores and eventually graduate. Administrators who decide the criteria for admission and admit students shape the student body, and if they do these things well, attrition should decline.

The courses an institution offers, when they are offered, and which courses and how many of them are required for graduation also affect the retention rate. The curriculum itself probably has more to do with attrition than any other organizational factor.

Rules and regulations cover academic conduct, such as not plagiarizing or meeting a foreign language requirement, and social conduct, such as not consuming alcohol in residence hall rooms and meeting financial obligations. Rules are intended to provide order and some degree of uniformity, both of which are necessary in colleges and universities. However, when they produce resentment and alienation and cannot be easily rationalized, they should be dropped. In any case, rules should be kept to a minimum and applied flexibly. Black students seem to be particularly alienated by the rules and regulations of majority white institutions, which results in low levels of satisfaction and higher levels of dropout.

The types of academic and social services provided for students may also influence retention. Students may drop out if they are not provided with academic support, such as academic advising, career counseling, instruction in the use of institutional resources (the library, computers, and so on), study skill development programs, and basic or remedial work in particular content areas. In addition to academic programs, cocurricular programs, such as debate or science clubs, theater, and other special interest groups; residence-life activities; intramural sports; and the student-union programs and facilities enhance the student's social integration into the institution and hence reduce attrition. Student health and counseling services are also organizational factors that can affect retention decisions.

Some of these programs and services may not be suitable for nontraditional students. Commuting students may not be able to make trips back to campus to participate in cocurricular activities. Older students may have extensive family or work responsibilities. Nonetheless, nontraditional students still need academic and social support to stay in school, and their attitudes toward the campus academic and social environment, even if they do not participate in campus activities, still affect their decision to stay in school or to leave.

The final organizational variable is financial aid. Students who do not have the funds necessary to pay for school are not (with rare exceptions) allowed to attend for free. If an institution is able to provide financial aid for these students through grants, loans, scholarships, or work-study programs, the institution changes the direct relationship between a failure to pay tuition and involuntary attrition caused by the bursar's cancelling registration. Although financial aid can help keep students enrolled, the effects of financial aid on retention are mixed. Some students who receive large amounts of financial aid drop out of school while others with no financial aid persist. Some financial aid (a modest scholarship) may symbolize to the student increased acceptance by the institution and increase the student's loyalty to the college or university. However, some students who receive extensive financial assistance come from educationally disadvantaged families and attended lower-quality high schools than other students who receive no aid. Thus, high amounts of financial assistance are not guarantees of high rates of retention.

The following organizational activities should enhance retention:

1. Admit students who match the institution's strengths. Find out what prospective students want from a college or university and consider this information when making admissions decisions. Low morale due to a high dropout rate may make students who would otherwise stay more likely to leave. If you admit an underprepared student, provide the academic and social support the student needs in order to stay enrolled. If you admit a large number of underprepared students and had not previously admitted them, recognize that the character of the school will probably change, and some excellent students may feel that they no longer fit in at the school.

2. Offer the courses students want to take at times and places convenient to the students, not the faculty. An annual poll of students, their advisers, and potential students by admissions officers can identify students' course needs. Course scheduling may be particularly important for nontraditional students and community college students; many of these students may not be able to take courses from nine to five

Monday through Friday. Also, putting the best instructors in introductory level courses is both a good way to keep students enrolled in school and a device for recruiting departmental majors.

3. Use a zero-based budgeting approach to the rules and regulations governing student academic and social life; if there is insufficient reason to keep a rule, drop it. Students who feel controlled by rules and regulations become alienated and drop out of school—and this is particularly true of minority students.

4. Provide meaningful academic support services. Students need advising, but institutions are sufficiently different so that no foolproof advising system exists. Advising is likely to reduce attrition when the advisers are concerned with and informed about the student seeking advice and are familiar with the options and regulations of the institution. Students who, through their advisers, get a positive attitude toward themselves, their institution, and how their schooling fits in with their lives and careers are more likely to remain enrolled.

    For certain nontraditional students, advising can be particularly important—in fact, older students often demand attention from faculty to a greater extent than their younger counterparts. Older students who fail to get such attention may transfer or drop out. For nontraditional students whose course goals are specified by an employer, advisers are completely irrelevant.

5. Provide a supportive social environment for students. Although this may not be a major concern for nontraditional students, it is a major concern for traditional ones. Students need the opportunity to develop friendships, interact with mentors, and have role models of how to behave as responsible students and productive members of society. Big-brother or big-sister programs, lounges, a student union, meeting places for intramural athletics and special interest groups, and advisers who are concerned with the students' academic and social development should enhance retention. The social environment is crucial in forming the

attitudes associated with fitting into and staying enrolled in a school.

Academic Integration. To succeed as a student, an individual needs both skills and attitudes appropriate for academic work. When a student develops proper academic attitudes, like integrity, delayed gratification, and valuing scholarship, the student is likely to perform well academically, which is manifest in a high or at least a rising GPA. Students who perform well are more likely to remain enrolled in a college or university, except for transfer students (who perform well in order to leave).

Few students are gifted enough to survive academic rigors without good study habits. Among the necessary study skills and habits are time-management skills and skills in reading, writing, note taking, preparing papers, critical thinking, and studying for exams. Programs that improve these skills are likely to enhance retention for students deficient in these areas.

Pascarella (1980) summarized a large body of literature indicating that informal contact by students with faculty members enhances academic integration and hence reduces attrition. Informal contact by students with faculty members who are concerned about students' cognitive and social development should result in students having positive attitudes toward the school and should increase retention. At small schools where such contact is expected, informal contact can reduce attrition by helping students develop positive attitudes toward themselves, clarify career goals, and increase their confidence in their role as students. At major research universities with large undergraduate student bodies, the faculty are often so involved in research and graduate teaching that informal contacts with freshman students are rare and hence have little effect on retention. Such contact would probably be beneficial, but it is unreasonable to assume that research-oriented faculty have the time for or interest in extensive personal contact with undergraduate students.

Similarly, at community colleges, faculty are often part time and are not on campus long enough to have informal contact with students. In other cases, faculty members have so many contact hours — thirty or more hours a week in the classroom —

that the last thing they want is more contact with students out of class. In any case, informal contact with faculty members is only beneficial to students when the meetings are viewed positively by both the students and the faculty members involved.

Students with a major have an identity, such as "journalism major," and can share values and fit in with that social group. They also have direction and should be able to link course work with later employment. On the other hand, students without a major can have a hard time seeing how the courses they take fit together into a cohesive whole. Forcing students into early decisions about their major may be unwise, but letting them delay the choice too long creates problems with unmet requirements. Ongoing discussions between students and both faculty and staff advisers that result in an academic focus should reduce attrition. By the middle of a student's sophomore year, the student should have a plan of study for completing college that can be adjusted when necessary.

Absenteeism is one of the first signs that a student is dissatisfied with school, is under stress, or is having difficulties with the course work. However, the effects of absenteeism on attrition depend on the student's GPA. For students with high GPAs, absenteeism is not related to dropout (Bean, 1982b). But students who are absent from class and also have low GPAs should meet with an academic counselor or adviser to determine if the students are considering dropping out and, if so, to see whether the institution can or should do anything to change the students' intention to leave school.

The following should help students' academic integration into an institution and enhance retention:

1. Identify entering students who are likely to need improved study skills to remain in school. Require these students to participate in academic assistance programs.
2. Require that all students take a credit course entitled something like University 101. This course would provide students with information about the campus and its services, rules and regulations, and traditions; link students with special needs to special services; help students explore career

options; provide students with informal contact with a faculty or staff member; and give students a social-support group for adjusting to life at college. A modified course might be required of nontraditional students. These courses are a method of institutionalizing informal or at least semiformal contacts with faculty members.

3. Assign groups of perhaps twenty students to the same basic courses so that they get to know each other well.
4. Help students explore career options early in their schooling and develop a program of study by the middle of their sophomore year.
5. Monitor class attendance. When students' absenteeism is high and grades are low, talk to the students and see if the institution can do anything to help.

Social Integration. Social integration into the campus — students' finding a social niche in which they share values and support each other through friendship and mutual concern for the other's well-being — is typically viewed as central to keeping students enrolled in school (Tinto, 1975). While there is good evidence for this among traditional students, for nontraditional students who have peer groups and social support outside of the institution and who may be older and have already formed a mature set of values, social integration probably plays a reduced role in enhancing retention decisions (Bean and Metzner, 1985).

Students who have close friends on campus are likely to feel satisfied with being a student and feel that they fit in at school. Social events, living arrangements, and places in which social groups can gather can foster friendships. Special interest groups can also bring students together for social as well as academic support. Programs do not make friends, but an absence of programs may prevent friendships from developing.

Just as contact with faculty may increase students' academic integration, it may also affect their social integration. Students who feel accepted by faculty members and consider faculty members as friends as well as mentors are more likely to stay enrolled in school.

It is important for students to feel that someone on the

campus cares about them as a whole person, not just a number or a source of tuition. The social support system of most traditional-age students is probably made up mostly of other students because it is with these people that students have the most contact. However, support from family, friends, faculty, residence-hall staff, counselors, staff that process student forms, secretaries, custodians, central administrators, and alumni can all influence students' attitudes toward a school and sense of fitting in there. Programs that enhance a caring attitude on campus, at academically elite and academically weak institutions alike, help keep students enrolled.

Social integration may or may not be important for nontraditional students. On-campus social integration is likely to occur to a lesser extent for them because commuter students, in particular, spend less time on campus. Social support is still necessary, but it may be the employer or spouse who provides such support.

Activities can help students become socially integrated into an institution, improving the students' attitudes toward the school and sense of fitting in and hence improving retention:

1. Provide informal gathering places on campus. For example, place faculty mailboxes next to departmental lounges so that students and faculty can meet by chance.
2. Provide social events students want to attend. These will vary depending on the student body, but try to bring students together in an environment in which they are likely to converse.
3. Publicize special interest groups, how to join them, and what they do. Consider requiring students to be members of at least one out-of-class program during their second semester at school.
4. Involve the whole campus in paying attention to the needs of students. Make the institution a flexible bureaucracy where necessary and a collegium where possible.
5. Remember to involve parents. Keep them informed and indicate that their support is valuable for keeping their child enrolled. Involve the spouses of married students.

Environmental Pull. Environmental factors are, by definition, things over which the institution has little control but that contribute to students' decisions to remain in or drop out of school. It is important to recognize that eliminating all attrition is neither possible nor desirable. Institutional resources should not be used trying to affect things that are not the fault of the college and that the college cannot affect anyway. Specific factors, such as a family crisis, serious health problems, or the closing of a local business, may result in students leaving school. It is of little use for a school to try to anticipate and counteract such events.

Elite schools should look at an attrition rate of perhaps 5–7 percent as a baseline. As the prestige of a school declines, the size of the baseline increases. The notion of a baseline may be inappropriate for a community college whose purpose is to provide certification and avocational courses for the community and that does not generate the majority of its credit hours in associate degree programs.

There are five environmental variables that seem of major importance. Students who lack or perceive that they lack finances are likely to withdraw from school. Students who want to be with a significant other elsewhere or have an opportunity to transfer to another school are also likely to leave or transfer. Students, especially nontraditional students, who have work responsibilities or family responsibilities may leave school because of these outside responsibilities. The heterogeneity of most nontraditional student populations and the variety of environmental variables at play make it difficult to demonstrate the importance of these variables statistically (see Metzner and Bean, 1987).

Although institutions can do little to counteract environmental variables, the retention rate may be improved through these activities:

1. Communicate financial aid options to students and, when relevant, to parents, spouses, and employers and do not reduce aid after the first year.
2. Provide full-time work on campus for students when reasonable and appropriate.
3. Schedule courses at times convenient for students who

must work and provide safe transportation or parking facilities.

4. Provide child care for students with family responsibilities.

If a college is really losing students due to the price of credit hours, adjust the pricing strategy. Do not automatically believe that money is the chief reason for students to leave school. It rarely is.

Attitudes and Other Outcomes. Students with positive attitudes toward the college or university they attend are likely to remain enrolled. Students enroll with a set of attitudes toward the school. When a student arrives with positive attitudes toward the school and has positive organizational, academic, and social experiences, these positive attitudes are likely to be maintained or to increase. When a student arrives with negative attitudes and has negative experiences, the student is likely to leave. Any program aimed at increasing retention should have as its first priority affecting a student's attitude toward self or school, but should not attempt to do this in a manipulative way. The service or activity provided should be evaluated in terms of its impact on student attitudes, not just on how well the service was delivered and to how many students it was delivered. A general sense of satisfaction with life at the school, feelings of self-development, a sense that the education they are receiving has a practical value for securing employment, and a sense of self-confidence as a student are a core block of attitudes positively affecting retention. Stress, on the other hand, reduces the likelihood of students remaining enrolled.

Institutional fit and loyalty are the specific attitudes toward the institution that closely affect the decision to remain enrolled in school. It is these attitudes that must be nurtured if students are to remain enrolled. These attitudes toward the self and the institution are based on the more general attitudes and experiences students have had in school.

Loyalty seems to have more of a psychological component than institutional fit, which has more of a social component. A loyal student feels attached to the particular institution, not simply to getting a degree. It is important for the student to graduate from this school, not just any school. Such loyalty is developed by anticipatory socialization. For example, family, alumni, or significant others can tell the student, "It's a great school." Such positive attitudes can also be enhanced by rites and rituals after the students arrive on campus. The campus mascot for the athletic teams may be the anathema of liberal arts faculty. But such symbols can be extremely important for incoming freshmen to identify with a college or university, to feel that they are Iowa Hawkeyes or Georgetown Hoyas or Indiana Hoosiers. When there is a deep emotional attachment to a school, a student will rarely leave by choice.

Intent to Leave. Intent to leave is included as a variable in the model because intentions are hypothesized to intervene between attitudes and behavior (Fishbein and Ajzen, 1975). The variable is content free, however, and is not an explanation of why students decide to stay or leave. The variable is valuable as a predictor of retention. Students who intend to leave are unlikely to stay enrolled, and by asking students if they intend to return to school for the next semester or year, institutions can identify very simply the students who are at highest risk for dropping out. These students can be queried as to why they intend to leave, and, when ethical and appropriate, the institution can provide programs that can increase the likelihood that the students will remain in school. The programs can be targeted toward those students who are most likely to benefit from them.

Retention of Minority Students

Fewer theoretical or empirical studies have been conducted on retention and minority students than on retention and majority students. Similar to nontraditional students, minority students are a heterogeneous and not a homogeneous group. While there is no reason to believe that the recommendations presented in this chapter would not be applicable to minority students, some factors probably are more important for minority students than for majority students.

Most research on minority students has been done with black students, with only a few studies having been done of Hispanic, Asian American, or Native American students. One study indicated that finances are particularly important for Hispanic students (Nora, 1990). Parental approval is important for continued enrollment of black students (Bean and Hull, 1984). For some students the approval of church and community is also important. When parents approved of students attending school, the students had a greater sense of academic and social integration, perceived their education to be of greater utility, and felt less alienated on campus.

Ordinarily, the higher the GPA, the greater the retention, but for some black students with high academic abilities this is not necessarily true (Bennett and Bean, 1984). If faculty members are prejudiced and assume, for example, that black students are inferior to white students, black students who are high achievers will be especially frustrated. Thus, some black students with high grades may not feel that their work is really accepted, and may withdraw from school. This problem is not as serious for black students who had poor or average grades in high school and who do better at the college or university because they see themselves as improving.

Many white students feel controlled by rules and regulations at colleges or universities, and this reduces their satisfaction (Bean and Hull, 1984). When black students feel controlled by the rules and regulations of a predominantly white institution, however, they are likely to withdraw from the school. When they perceive the rules as coming from the white faculty and administrators and as running their lives, these students can become alienated (feel an external locus of control) and leave. For white students, fitting in at college is important, but it is less important for black students (Bean and Hull, 1984).

When black students had positive interracial contacts both before and during college, they were more likely to remain enrolled (Bennett and Bean, 1984). Black students graduate from all-black institutions at higher rates than they graduate from predominantly white institutions (Green, 1989). The implication from this finding is that these institutions are not doing all they can to enhance minority-student retention.

Minority students are not a homogeneous group; neither are black students, nor Hispanics (a name that includes Mexican Americans, Puerto Rican Americans, Sephardic Jews, and black and white Spanish-surnamed Americans), nor Asians. Specific recommendations about minority retention must take into account the characteristics of the minority group in question, the characteristics of the college or university, and ultimately the characteristics of each individual student.

Summary

The purpose of this chapter was to describe some of the theories that explain the attrition process, identify key variables in the process, and identify specific types of interventions that should increase student retention. Since different factors will have greater or lesser effects on retention at different colleges, different programs will also have different effects. Programs at the same school will have different effects for different types of students.

The following are things to strive for:

1. Admit students whose abilities meet your demands and whose demands are met by your curriculum and services. Match the student and the institution from the outset.

2. Support students academically.

3. Support students socially.

4. Develop the student's loyalty to the school through the use of symbols, rites, and rituals.

5. Make sure that any services you deliver not only accomplish the intended purpose, but also give students a positive attitude toward themselves and membership in the college.

Also, recognize the way in which the external environment of the school affects attrition and retention decisions: certain students will leave no matter what you do.

All attrition is not bad. Often an individual student and the institution he or she leaves both benefit from the departure.

In thinking about overall enrollment planning, enrollment managers should track the retention rates of groups of students who enroll from important market segments.

Identifying the causes of student retention and departure decisions is an essential first step in developing sensible measures to improve retention. In the next chapter, a variety of ways to study student attrition are described and their advantages and disadvantages discussed.

Note

1. For a fuller treatment of theories of attrition, see: Bean, J. P. "Conceptual Models of Student Attrition: How Theory Can Help the Institutional Researcher." In E. T. Pascarella (ed.), *Studying Student Attrition*. New Directions for Institutional Research, no. 36. San Francisco: Jossey-Bass, 1982. Some material from this section is quoted from that chapter.

Chapter 10

Using
Retention Research
in Enrollment Management

John P. Bean

Most people view departure from a college or university, called by such pejorative terms as *dropout* and *wastage,* as a problem. Whose problem is attrition? The answer to that question will inform the design of retention research.

The three most obvious groups for whom attrition might be a problem are society, individual institutions, and individual students. For society, the loss of students from higher education means a reduction in the level of training of individuals entering the labor force and thus a loss of human capital resources. For institutions, attrition represents a direct loss of tuition income and, other things being equal, a failure to accomplish their educational mission. For individuals, departure from college before graduating can represent a personal failure to achieve educational objectives, an income about 15 percent below that of contemporaries who graduate from college, and the opportunity cost of an investment that will yield little financial benefit.

Enrollment managers are concerned primarily with attrition as an institutional problem. For them, high rates of attrition may also be a personal problem because these rates show that their attempts to increase retention have failed. Within the institution, however, some groups may view attrition as a problem while others may not. Before starting a retention study, an enrollment manager needs to find out for whom and for what purposes the study is intended. Studies can be designed to identify who is leaving college, when they leave, and why they leave; to evaluate retention programs; or to demonstrate that "things are pretty good around here" or "we are on the verge of extinction." Knowing who wants a study and why can help an enrollment manager to choose from a variety of data-gathering and data-analytical techniques.

Who is a "dropout"? From the institutional perspective, a student who enters a college or university and leaves before graduating is a dropout. Although this definition is satisfactory in terms of calculating tuition income, it leaves much to be desired. First, it does not take into account students who enter college, get from it what they want (perhaps just one course), and then go on about their lives. They have not failed and the institution has not failed, but since they did not graduate, in many studies they would be considered dropouts. Second, students who like college so much that they transfer to a better institution for their interests (for example, transferring to study oceanography) are successes to themselves and their original institution, even though they leave without graduating. Thus, for an accurate definition of attrition, the students' educational goals must be known first. Students who fail to achieve their educational goals at an institution because of either personal or institutional shortcomings represent a departure problem. It is this type of attrition that a school should study, and it is on this type of problem that an institution should expend its retention efforts.

The purpose of this chapter is to present several options for studying student retention. Retention rates are related to the interaction between the students attending the college and the characteristics of the college. The rate of retention at an institution will change when different kinds of students attend the school or when students have different experiences (social, psychological, academic) on campus. Because retention rates are not fixed and are dependent on many factors that can be changed, enrollment managers can provide direction for institutional change and thereby help an institution improve its rate of retention. Enrollment managers must understand local retention issues — the particular play of forces at an institution will not be identical to that of any other — and that the most efficient use of resources to improve retention begins by studying student departure in situ.

Chapter Nine described the theories that explain student attrition (such as Spady, 1970; Tinto, 1987) and several theoretical models of the factors that result in a student's decision to stay in or leave school (Spady, 1970; Tinto, 1975; Pascarella, 1980; Bean, 1982a; Bean and Metzner, 1985). There is a peculiar paradox in retention studies. The purpose of research is the development of theory that can be used to explain why an activity, such as attrition, occurs. The theory can be used to generate a model, and the model can be estimated using statistical or other techniques. The findings can then be applied knowledgeably to a given school. The paradox occurs because good theories are generalizable — they apply to many settings. But in being generalizable, they simplify reality and make it abstract and in the process become a less-accurate description of attrition for any given school.

The paradox creates a problem for researchers planning a study. They can strive to get an accurate picture of why an individual student drops out of school but fail to be simple and generalizable. Qualitative research often leads to this situation. Or they can strive for generalizability and fail to describe accurately or simply any particular student's departure. Quantitative models often have this problem. Finally, they can provide a simple explanation for attrition that is neither accurate nor generalizable. Simple descriptive and anecdotal studies often have this problem. (Note: Anyone wishing to conduct attrition research should read Pascarella, 1982.)

Strategies for Assessing Attrition Decisions

Six approaches to the study of student attrition will be described in this section. Each one will be evaluated in terms of its usefulness and how the results of the approach can influence institutional decision making.

Studies emphasize analysis or description or sometimes both. Analytical studies attempt to explain why attrition occurs and focus on the relationships between variables. Descriptive studies show who is leaving, when leaving occurs, and what characteristics (usually demographic) students have who leave contrasted with those who remain. A second general distinction is between studies for which data currently exist and studies for which information must be collected. New data must be collected for most of the studies described in this section. Gathering new data is the preferred approach because it allows a researcher to tailor data collection for a specific purpose; it is, however, more costly and time consuming than using existing data.

Autopsy Studies. An autopsy study takes place after a student has decided to leave or has already left school. Autopsy studies are usually descriptive. Information is gathered from the student by interview or paper-and-pencil questionnaire. The specificity of the items varies widely from open-ended questions (Why did you leave school? Were there any problems encountered here that we could have helped you with?) to specific questions about issues students in the past have indicated affected their decision to leave (Did you leave school because you couldn't find a parking place? Did you leave school because you didn't have enough money for tuition?).

The advantages of autopsy studies lie in their simplicity. The sample selects itself (those who have left), and there is maximum coverage of that sample. They follow common sense. To paraphrase Bashō, the Japanese poet, if you want to know about bamboo, go ask the bamboo. Analogously, if you want to know why people drop out of school, ask them why they left — knowledge that comes from the source is especially valuable. Autopsy studies are simple and concise, and their results can be reported in the simplest statistical terms; for instance, 25 percent of the students who dropped out of school reported that they had a financial crisis at home while 50 percent reported that they found the academic work too difficult. This kind of reporting can have a powerful impact on policy makers.

The disadvantages of autopsy studies, however, outweigh their benefits. Three weaknesses are particularly troublesome.

First, students give normatively accepted responses to questions. In the majority of cases students give three reasons for dropping out of school — academic problems, financial problems, and personal uncertainty about educational goals. These may or may not be the reasons why a student drops out, but they provide a rationale for engaging in a behavior that has often been associated with failure.

Second, students make attribution errors. They may attribute their leaving school to poor academic performance, when in fact they are leaving because they have no friends on campus or do not fit in with the social and academic ethos of the school. They report one reason for leaving when a reason they are unaware of was the real reason.

Third, students who stay and leave can have the same problems. If a study only looks at people who leave, the researcher has no idea whether or not the same problem exists for people who stay. For example, all the students who drop out of a college one semester may say they did so in part because they hated the residence-hall food. But all the students who remained at the school may hate the food also. Thus, what is consistently reported to be a reason for leaving school may be a problem for those who remain, but it cannot be pointed to as a cause of attrition.

Autopsy studies are easy to conduct, easy to understand, and easy to use in policy making, but they are the least reliable in terms of their conclusions. They function best as descriptive studies (who leaves) and are to be viewed with extreme caution as analytical studies.

Cross-Sectional Studies. In a cross-sectional study, information is gathered from a number of students at one time as opposed to longitudinally, that is, gathered at several different times. Typically, cross-sectional studies use existing student records or data gathered by questionnaires. Researchers can obtain information on a variety of demographic variables, facts about what the students did (academically, socially, and with people outside of the college), attitudes, and intentions and then track the students to see which ones remain in and which drop out of school. These data are then analyzed to see whether the characteristics of students who leave the school systematically differ from the characteristics of those who remain. The data can also be treated descriptively, comparing the characteristics of the two groups.

In a true cross-sectional study, intent to leave can be substituted for actual departure, and thus an institution can gather data all at once that can be used to analyze and describe the attrition patterns of students. This approach works well with traditional students but less well with commuter, part-time, and older students, whose intentions to stay in school are not as closely related to staying in school as are those of traditional students. The advantages of this approach lie in the relative ease with which a great variety of data can be gathered from representative groups of students.

Data gathered from institutional sources, such as entry-level demographic data from the admissions office and academic performance data from the registrar's office, can be collected unobtrusively. These data can give a snapshot of attrition that indicates who drops out, when dropout occurs, and the differences between students who stay and leave in terms of grades, majors, age, gender, race, ethnicity, full- and part-time status, or other descriptive statistics. These data answer the question "Who drops out and when?" but do not answer the question "Why do students leave?"

Cross-sectional data can be used to determine why one group of students at one point in time leaves. Data are gathered from students about their background (such as high school grades), current activities (such as informal contact with faculty, and if they are taking the courses they want to take), external environmental variables (such as if they have a job or want to be with a significant other elsewhere), attitudes (such as satisfaction with being a student and feeling their education is leading to a better job), and finally intentions (does the student intend to re-enroll next year?). This information can be put in a statistical model, the parameters (links between variables) estimated, and the important factors affecting attrition decisions identified. This kind of data can be used with regression or path analytical techniques that attempt to explain the longitudinal process of attrition.

The problem with cross-sectional studies is that they are subject to several types of error.

1. Measurement error—the reliability or validity of measures such as the number of close friends a student has on campus can be low, resulting in erroneous conclusions.
2. One set of students—for a particular group of students, some unique factor, like intramural sports, may be so important that students who do poorly in this activity may feel that they do not fit in and therefore leave school. However, this factor may be of little or no importance to another group of students.
3. One time—a particular one-time event, like the firing of a popular professor, may cause a dramatic negative shift in attitudes toward the school, and students may leave because of these negative attitudes. Although an important reason for departure at this time, the event does not recur and thus is not important for students in the future.
4. Random error—since statistics deal with probabilities, some improbable associations occur in one data set and not in subsequent studies. For instance, there may be a statistically significant relationship between distance home and the helpfulness of an adviser in one study, but only because of chance.
5. Complexity—a final problem is that the statistical modeling can become quite complex. It requires the use of a trained methodologist to analyze the data in model estimation. While the study may appear elegant to the methodologist, the decision maker can be completely lost and, not understanding what the study means, not act in concert with the findings.

Cross-sectional studies can be fairly easy to conduct in terms of data gathering, descriptive statistics, and quick turnaround. They can also provide data for complex statistical analyses, which, if properly used, give the fastest and cheapest insight into the attrition process at a college or university. Some of their limitations can be overcome by longitudinal designs.

Longitudinal Studies. Longitudinal studies involve collecting data at more than one time from the same group of students or from different groups at the same time in their academic careers. Descriptive longitudinal retention studies involve collecting data about students at least twice. Often, students' entry-level characteristics are compared to these same characteristics at a later date. For example, if the freshman class is 60 percent male and 40 percent female, but this same group less dropouts is 40 percent male and 60 percent female when seniors, dropout is more frequent for men than women. If the gender difference between a class as freshmen and as seniors is used to track dropout rates, then transfer students (who could be predominantly male or female) would obscure what happens to the class.

Cohort studies track incoming students at critical points during their schooling, often at the beginning of each term for five or more years. In this way, the patterns of attrition for different types of students in the group can be described. By partitioning the freshman class into several subgroups based on such variables as gender, race, 3.0 or higher GPA, number of semester hours enrolled, or other meaningful factors, a researcher can discern both when and for what groups the highest and lowest rates of attrition occur. Such information can be very useful not only for planning retention programs but in marketing and overall strategic planning as well.

Panel analyses involve gathering two or more "panels" of data so that a researcher can examine how the relationships between the variables change over time. For example, panel data might be used to decide if student GPAs one year are a function of the previous year's GPAs or of some other factor, like participation in a time-management seminar. Panel data can be used in sophisticated statistical modeling of student behavior and are highly esteemed by researchers. The weakness of most panel studies comes from the decay of the sample — as students drop out or fail to complete later questionnaires, the sample containing complete data becomes smaller and smaller, and the validity of the conclusions from the data becomes more and more suspect.

On the one hand, longitudinal studies provide the best quantitative, descriptive, and analytical data for the study of attrition. On the other hand, the analyses can become very complex, requiring methodological specialists to conduct the study and communication specialists to present the findings in a meaningful way (a rare combination in a single individual). Data from students are difficult to get for this kind of study, and the results from the study may not be available for years. Researchers will need to be skilled at describing findings in lay terms in order to make either cross-sectional or longitudinal analyses usable for most senior-level policy makers.

Qualitative Studies. The traditional approach to attrition research has been the quantitative study. Quantitative studies and the models or descriptions they produce are limited to variables previously identified by the researchers. These studies can be very useful for examining the relationships between known variables and identifying those variables most directly associated with attrition. They are of little use in discovering new variables.

Qualitative studies are designed for discovery and an accurate description in a limited context. In these studies, the researcher looks at attrition without a preconceived notion of what is important to students and the institution and what affects retention. Important factors emerge through observation, document analysis, and open-ended interviews with students, faculty, staff, parents, and any other group found to be relevant to departure decisions. Such findings can be corroborated through triangulation — reference to other institutional data such as admissions information — and confirmed by reinterviewing students.

The clear advantage of this kind of research is that it leads to surprises. By understanding a problem in its context, a researcher gains insights that are not possible through closed-ended questions. For example, through interviews, researchers have found that commuter students who interact with other students between classes are less likely to drop out of school. Thus, the unexpected conclusion is that advisers should not schedule classes consecutively for commuter students because the short-term gain in time is a long-term liability in terms of the students' being attached to the institution. The effects of class scheduling on attrition can be tested quantitatively. Discovering that this variable should be examined is the result of qualitative research.

Qualitative research gives the clearest picture of the attrition process for those students included in the study. It differs from autopsy studies by being of longer duration, using open-ended questions, checking findings by triangulation, and focusing on accurate descriptions that make discovery of new influences on attrition likely. Qualitative studies take longer than cross-sectional studies and less time than longitudinal studies. Weeks or months are generally required. Full-blown ethnographies take years.

The chief drawback of qualitative research is that gathering the data is labor intensive; there is no substitute for spending time with participants in the study. Data transcription and analysis can also be a protracted process. The second drawback is that while researchers discover factors that might affect attrition decisions and gain a better understanding of attrition for the participants, participation in such studies is limited. A total of ten to thirty participants is not unusual. The generalizability of the results is questionable: Is what the researcher found for this group typical of all the institution's students? Should policy making for the entire campus be based on this type of study? Such questions must be answered at the local level. Qualitative studies seem very appropriate for unique populations — students who for demographic or other reasons can be assigned to a group, such as single working women with children. Good policies can probably be made for particular groups of students based on qualitative research on those groups.

Quantitative Analytical Approaches. Autopsy, cross-sectional, longitudinal, and qualitative studies have been identified on the basis of data collection. Quantitative analytical approaches concern issues of data analysis. These approaches assume that an institution has quantitative data, which would come from any of the data-gathering techniques, that can be used to predict attrition (or length of time enrolled). Four approaches will be considered: correlation, multiple regression, ordinary least squares path analysis, and LISREL (maximum likelihood) path analysis.

Correlation indicates the extent to which one variable is related to another. When correlations are high, two variables have a high degree of association. If one of these variables precedes the other, a change in its level might cause (*cause* is used loosely) the level of the second variable to change. Thus, if college GPA is negatively correlated with attrition, an increase in GPA might lead to a decrease in attrition.

In multiple regression, more than one variable is used to predict attrition. For example, high school grades, college grades, and absenteeism might be used to predict attrition. In the regression (that is, multiple correlation) equation, each variable is allowed to predict attrition while holding levels of the other variables constant. In this case, high school grades may have no effect on attrition, college grades a negative effect, and absenteeism a positive effect. In multiple regression, one statistic generated (standardized regression coefficients) indicates which variable has the largest effect on attrition, while the squared multiple correlation coefficient (R^2) indicates how well these variables explain the changes in attrition rates. Thus, a researcher can find out which variables are most important and how well they work in explaining changes in dropout.

Through ordinary least squares path analysis, a researcher can examine a sequence of effects on attrition. A variable can have a direct effect on attrition or indirect effects, acting through other variables. For example, high school grades could have a substantial effect on college GPA, and college GPA could have a substantial effect on attrition. Thus, high school GPA would have an indirect effect on attrition, making attrition less likely by increasing college GPA. Using multiple regression, a researcher might have concluded that high school grades had no effect on attrition; however, through path analysis the researcher could see that high school GPA has important effects on attrition and could also have a model to help explain how the effects work. At the same time, the researcher could see whether absenteeism or college GPA has larger effects on attrition, just as in multiple regression. Path analysis requires that a model of attrition be developed ahead of time and that the data be in an appropriate form for the statistics used to estimate the model.

LISREL stands for linear structural relationships and is an even more sophisticated statistical tool for estimating the relationships between variables in path models. This method has the added advantage of taking error in measurement into account when estimating the parameters of the model, whereas in ordinary least squares path analysis, error is assumed to be zero. Properly used, LISREL can provide the most sophisticated statistical look at the attrition process. This technology for analysis, however, may outstrip most people's ability to theorize about attrition. Few administrators may be able to understand how the study arrived at its outcomes and, therefore, may ignore the results of the study.

These four quantitative techniques can be used to give progressively greater insight into theoretical models of the factors that affect attrition decisions. But because of their complexity, they may or may not provide fruitful input for decision making.

Program Evaluation. A different approach to research related to retention focuses on the effects of interventions on retention rates. In program evaluation, participants in a program are compared to similar students who did not participate to see if they leave at different rates. If fewer program participants than nonparticipants leave, the program was effective.

The chief drawback to such an evaluation process is that other positive benefits from the program would go unnoticed in an outcomes evaluation. For instance, a study skills program may not have demonstrable effects on retention but may improve the quality of student performance. Any evaluation system chosen must be sensitive to what actually occurs because of the presence or absence of the program on campus.

The issue of program evaluation is one of extreme complexity. The timing of the evaluation is one problem. For example, retention program A was started at W College. At the end of one year, the dropout rate for students involved in program A was identical to a control group, so the program was dropped. However, 100 percent of the students who participated in program A and did not drop out after the first year graduated from W College while only 80 percent of the students in the control group graduated. Had the program been evaluated at a later date, it would have been kept.

The criteria for evaluation pose another problem. For example, retention program B was started at X College. At the end of the year the attrition rate was unchanged and the program was dropped. However, the program inspired the faculty so that the students who remained in school learned more than previous graduates. Had the program been evaluated on the basis of either faculty morale or value added to students' education, it would have been retained. Since the only criterion used was retention rate, it was dropped.

The source of evaluation data is also a problem. For example, retention program C was intended to improve academic performance and thus reduce attrition. Students who participated in the program were asked what they thought about it, and 75 percent said it was a waste of time so the program was dropped. However, 50 percent of those who said they liked the program went on to graduate school, but only 5 percent of those who disliked the program went on to graduate school. Since the future commitment to higher education of the 25 percent of participants who liked the program could not be judged during the evaluation period, additional weighting could not be given to their responses and program C was dropped.

Programs have unanticipated consequences, some of which are often quite good. Unless the evaluation procedure is flexible enough to identify these consequences, which might not appear until years later, evaluation of the true worth of a program cannot be calculated. When change in the rate of retention is the only criterion used to establish the value of a retention program, indirect or delayed benefits to the college or its students are ignored.

Programs can be evaluated according to a variety of criteria: overall retention, retention for one type of student, academic achievement, institutional status, graduation rates, faculty morale, faculty retention, and so on. These approaches will not be described in detail but are presented to indicate that retention research can focus on program evaluation.

Recommendations. It is difficult to recommend one research procedure for all enrollment managers since many local circumstances might dictate that one method is preferable to another. Some general statements, however, might be helpful.

1. When seeking immediate information, use descriptive data taken from existing institutional records. Many excellent data go unanalyzed because no one takes the time to use them or knows how to perform the analysis.
2. Avoid autopsy studies.
3. When seeking explanations for attrition for a large number of students, use path analysis.
4. When confirming hypotheses, use multiple regression and/or path analysis.
5. When in a hurry, use cross-sectional data.
6. When seeking discoveries, use qualitative methods.
7. When seeking detailed understanding of particular groups of students, use qualitative methods.
8. Use longitudinal data if available, retesting hypotheses with each group or at each time period.
9. When possible, use a combination of methodologies. Establish a data base and maintain it. Update analyses annually. Evaluate new retention programs as they develop. Look for long-term trends. Reconfirm past findings.

Implementation of Findings

Retention studies are only valuable in enrollment management if they are used by the institution that conducts them. There are several difficulties in implementing new programs based on research findings. New programs will be easier to implement if retention research that supports their implementation is easy to understand and relevant to a particular issue and has reliable and valid results.

Enrollment managers may wish to use the following suggestions for organizational development based on retention research. The relevance of each suggestion depends upon the particular circumstances of the institution.

1. Translate your findings into understandable forms. When decision makers have no idea how you reached your conclusions and no idea what the statistics mean, they are less likely to support retention program development. Do not give complicated statistics to nonstatisticians.

2. Give different presentations to different target groups. Retention studies are likely to be complex because decisions to remain in school are based on many factors. Presentations should be tailored to the specific needs and level of understanding of different groups interested in retention. To give the same presentation to everyone would reduce the effectiveness of the change stimulus (retention research report). Enrollment managers presenting research findings must recognize that different groups are concerned with different aspects of the attrition process. Both internal and external target groups, such as central administrators, advisers, admissions officers, registrar's office staff, counselors, financial affairs officers, housing staff, faculty members, students, and parents, should be presented information in differing formats. Make sure your reports speak to their concerns.

3. Structural change is easy; behavioral change is hard. It is often easy to change someone's title or create a new enrollment management office but beyond the symbolic impact, the creation of a new office may not lead to behavioral changes. To change retention rates, group behaviors need to be changed. The group affecting retention can include the entire staff and faculty of a college, plus students. This is not a trivial amount of change. A study indicating that a caring attitude on campus is important for retention is impossible to implement if no one takes the time to care. Effective implementation yields slow but steady gains.

4. Since changing retention rates requires a change in behavior and change is threatening, resistance to change must be overcome. One nice thing about student retention is that, in fact, everyone in the institution can benefit from increased retention rates. These increases can often be translated into tangible material gains for programs and academic departments. Use these probable gains to overcome resistance to change.

5. Various groups on campus will perceive that they are winners when a retention program based on an institutional study is implemented, while others will perceive that they are losers. Be sensitive to these perceptions. Since everyone can play a part in retention efforts, it makes sense to distrib-

ute resources for retention programs widely. Enrollment management should be used to coordinate diverse efforts.

6. Use your retention study as the rationale for resource allocation decisions. If people see the logic behind decisions, and if they are logical people, they are more likely to accept the decisions. If they are logical people and do not see the logic, they will not accept the decisions. If they are illogical, persuade them on subjective grounds; logic will not make any difference.

7. Market retention programs within the college or university. Just as an institution needs to market its product to the public, retention programs must be sold to administrators, faculty members, and students. Identify the needs of particular groups (for example, those mentioned earlier), and provide them with information they feel they need so that retention programs can work.

8. Use your successes to generate more resources. Demonstrate that a single retention effort yields tangible results. Based on this success, ask for more resources to reduce attrition even more. Get testimonials from retained students. Remember that a single student who remains enrolled for four years generates the same amount of tuition income as four students who remain for only one year. Retention programs are cost effective.

9. Start at the top. If you can convince the chief executive and chief academic officers of the soundness of your study and implementation program, you have a chance to succeed. Without this support, even the best retention study can be ignored, and your chances of successfully implementing a broad retention program based on this study are very slim.

An enrollment manager's decision about the type of retention study to conduct should come with a full understanding of what each approach to the study of student attrition has to offer, what changes are possible at an institution, and how organizational change takes place. Retention programs can help an entire institution. They are not just a staff activity. It is truly a win-win situation — everyone benefits from improved retention, and everyone should be involved in retention efforts.

Chapter 11

Programs and Activities
for Improved Retention

Robert O. Thomas

This chapter links existing research on student retention to institutional intervention strategies. Such strategies range from activities that can begin during the admissions and recruitment process to activities that focus upon career planning and placement. It should be emphasized at the outset that each retention strategy will almost certainly have a different impact in each school, depending upon the prevailing circumstances at the institution prior to the implementation of the strategy. Furthermore, the effects of implementing a retention strategy will be different for different kinds of students: male and female, minority and majority, full time and part time, commuter and residential, and older and traditional age.

The theories of Spady (1970), Tinto (1975, 1987), and Bean (1983, 1985) attempt to explain how student characteristics and attitudes and institutional variables affect a student's decision to remain in college. They focus on why a particular student leaves a particular school, rather than trying to understand why the attrition rate differs at different colleges or universities. By explicating the complex interactions that lead to student withdrawal, the theories suggest many institutional practices that can promote student persistence.

The Spady, Tinto, and Bean theories differ in their explanations of student retention, but share an emphasis on the importance of student academic and social integration as precursors to student persistence. The three theorists each state that the likelihood of student retention is increased by the degree to which students become involved in the academic and social systems of the school they attend. Therefore, the more an institution facilitates student interactions within its academic and social systems, the more likely students are to remain at that school.

One theoretical model of student retention uses the institution rather than the student as the unit of analysis (Thomas, 1988). Thomas explains how institutional characteristics, policies, programs, practices, and so on affect the retention rate at small liberal arts colleges. His model also includes institutional financial viability because in theory this trait would affect the school's ability to finance retention-enhancing activities and foster student confidence in the college's quality and stability. Thomas expects well-funded retention programs and student confidence in the institution to increase the likelihood of student persistence.

Taken together, the models of Spady, Tinto, Bean, and Thomas identify three student outcomes that can increase the likelihood of student persistence: student academic integration, student social integration, and student confidence in the quality and stability of the institution.

Institutional Activities Designed to Promote Student Retention

Institutional activities that promote student retention can be divided into three categories: admissions/recruiting activities and practices; activities promoting student academic integration; and activities promoting student social integration.

Admissions/Recruiting Activities. Spady (1971), Tinto (1975), Terenzini and Pascarella (1978), and Pascarella and Terenzini (1983) all found that students who were committed to getting a college education and graduating from a particular institution were more likely to persist in college than those who lacked such commitments. Bean (1983) found that students' intentions were the strongest predictors of students' decisions to remain in or withdraw from school. It follows that recruiting students

who are committed to getting a college education will increase
the chances of enrolling students who will become integrated
into the academic and social systems of the institution and persist in school. Recruiting activities that can serve this end include concentrating on prospective students who list the institution as their first choice, say they intend to earn at least a
bachelor's degree, indicate they plan to graduate from the school,
and have parents who are committed to seeing their children
graduate from college or university.

Carleton College, a private liberal arts college in Minnesota, has developed an elaborate data system on prospective students that enables the admissions staff to target their most intensive recruiting efforts on students who are likely to persist
(Litten and others, 1983). Bowling Green State University in
Ohio has offered a special summer program that concentrates
on building the academic skills and aspirations of conditionally
accepted students (Scherer and Wright, 1982). Summer study
opportunities on campus for high school students can initiate
early academic integration for the participants. Campus visits
that include meetings with faculty and attending classes can serve
the same purpose. Involving upper-class students in the recruiting process can also facilitate the first stages of social integration for prospective students. DePauw University in Indiana
carefully plans prospective-student campus visits that include
attending a class, personal appointments with faculty members,
and overnight stays hosted by "DePauw Ambassadors," upper-
class students selected and trained by the admissions staff (Hossler, 1986).

Starr, Betz, and Menne (1972) pose the theory that the
congruence between the needs, interests, and abilities of students and the expectations, rewards, and values of the schools
they attend contributes to retention. Other researchers (Pantages and Creedon, 1978; Ramist, 1981) also offer support for
the theory that the fit between student and institution can have
an effect on retention. Institutional research that identifies not
only the students who are most likely to attend an institution
but also those who are most likely to persist there thus becomes
an important instrument in promoting retention. Comprehensive and accurate written and verbal communications to prospec-

tive students about the school's climate and values are also important methods of creating a good fit between an institution and its student body (Lenning and Cooper, 1978).

Alumni can draw upon their knowledge of the school and help in identifying and recruiting prospective students who are likely to fit into its environment. For example, Westminster College in New Wilmington, Pennsylvania, organizes "Operation Impact," a program in which alumni make telephone calls and host receptions for prospective students. However, institutions that enroll students with varied cultural, racial, or academic backgrounds may not have a homogeneous, dominant collegiate culture into which all students can fit. Students may have to fit into one of several subcultures on campus. These institutions have to balance diversity, desirable in its own right, with homogeneity, which promotes (for the majority group) fitting in and hence retention.

An institution that builds student confidence in its quality and stability ultimately promotes retention. The school can begin to build this confidence by showing evidence of its quality and strengths during the recruiting process. For example, Denison University in Granville, Ohio, works to make prospective students aware of the scholarly achievements of its faculty and the high job and graduate and professional school placement record of its graduates. Showing students outstanding and well-maintained physical facilities can also help to build their confidence in a school's stability and quality.

Faculty participation in recruiting and admissions activities can also promote retention. Faculty interest in improving the academic qualifications of incoming students at the University of Wisconsin, Oshkosh, led the school to raise the academic standards for continuing students, create an honors program for outstanding students, and enlarge the list of academic subjects required of students for admission. These measures contributed to strengthening of the academic potential of incoming students, which in turn helped to raise the university's retention rate (Hossler, 1986).

Activities That Promote Academic Integration. Student-faculty interaction in and out of the classroom can promote student academic integration and ultimately persistence (Spady, 1971; Tinto, 1975; Pascarella and Terenzini, 1978, 1979, 1983). Such interaction may take many forms. In the classroom, for example, faculty can provide students with course performance feedback in addition to grades. They may also frequently engage students in class discussions or provide extra assistance to students who are having difficulty with the course work. They may even seek out students who are having problems in the course or missing classes. In other instances, faculty members may involve students in research projects, employ them part time in academic departments, or involve them in a student advisory committee for a department.

Several institutions have taken special measures to improve the quality of student-faculty interaction in the classroom. Faculty at Central Oregon Community College in Bend, Oregon, for example, take the initiative to contact students the first time they miss a class (Saluri, 1985). At Johnson County Community College in Kansas City, Kansas, selected faculty members were given release time to research and design the best course programs for their departments. Master teachers also visit classes in order to observe the teaching effectiveness of other faculty. Faculty at the University of Wisconsin, Oshkosh, established a special honors program for the most academically talented freshmen in an effort to engage these students in the university's academic program (Hossler, 1986).

Faculty may also advise student organizations, participate in new-student orientation activities, or host small groups of students in their homes for social occasions. They may also extend their office hours, eat meals in the cafeteria with students, or serve on committees with students. At Biola University, a private institution in La Mirada, California, faculty are given free meals in the cafeteria at least once a month if they eat their meals with students. Smith College in Northampton, Massachusetts, provides money to faculty for entertaining students in their homes. Faculty at Brandeis University in Waltham, Massachusetts, teach informal noncredit courses in their hobbies and thus provide students with a chance to become better acquainted with them outside of the classroom (Saluri, 1985).

Institutions can promote student-faculty interaction by rewarding faculty who devote time to such student contact with promotions, extra compensation, increased professional travel funds, or reduced teaching loads. However, student-faculty interaction may serve to increase a school's retention rate only if there has been a lack of such interaction in the past.

Institutional emphasis on teaching effectiveness can enhance the quality of instruction, which can, in turn, promote student academic integration and ultimately retention. Beal and Noel (1980) found that college and university officials identified effective teaching as the second most important institutional variable related to student retention. Louis, Colten, and Demeke (1984) found in an empirical study of freshman retention at the University of Massachusetts, Amherst, that student perceptions of the quality of teaching were strongly related to persistence. Saluri (1985) found in case studies at thirteen institutions that school officials reported that the use of their most effective instructors for freshman classes increased freshman-to-sophomore retention. Strong consideration of teaching effectiveness in faculty promotion, tenure, and salary decisions; comprehensive teaching evaluation systems; grants for teaching and curricular innovations; faculty development programs on instructional effectiveness; awards for excellent teaching; and the use of the best instructors for freshman classes are examples of institutional practices that promote effective teaching. Enrollment managers must evaluate the effectiveness of the teaching at their institution before assuming an improvement in this area will increase retention. Schools that do not emphasize instructional effectiveness may benefit more from renewed emphasis on teaching than institutions already strong in this area.

Faculty scholarly and professional activities such as publishing, attending professional meetings, and so on are frequently seen as taking too much faculty time away from teaching (Beal and Noel, 1980). However, Thomas (1988) found that these activities were a significant predictor of retention at liberal arts colleges. He theorizes that faculty scholarly activity can engender student confidence in the quality of an institution's education, and that this confidence promotes persistence. Moreover, faculty may promote student academic integration by discussing their research with students or perhaps even involving them in it. For example, advanced undergraduate students at Denison University participate in the research of some faculty.

The positive effect of faculty scholarship on retention may be greatest at institutions where expectations for faculty professional activity are not particularly high. In such an environment, professionally active faculty can build student confidence in the academic quality of the school. Making students aware of this activity in classes and through publicity on and off campus is an important practice on such campuses. At Westminster College, the campus newsletter regularly features the notable scholarly and professional achievements of faculty. On the other hand, students attending an institution where faculty are expected to publish may find such activity ordinary, and it is therefore less likely to attract their attention.

Institutional services that help students improve their academic skills (reading, writing, study skills, and so on) promote student persistence (Beal and Noel, 1980; Lenning, 1982). Such services include diagnostic testing in academic skills, developmental instruction in these skills, institutionally organized tutoring programs and study groups, and skill-building programs that precede a student's first enrollment.

At the University of Missouri, Kansas City, the Learning Skills Center provides staff who attend classes in which a large number of students are having difficulty with the course content. These staff members then offer special help sessions for students needing extra assistance in the course. At the University of Hartford's College of Basic Studies, students are required to take a study skills course that is directly tied to other courses required of the college's students. Peer tutors, selected and trained by staff at the University of Alabama, Huntsville, accompany students needing assistance to their classes and then offer assistance with the course content (Noel and Levitz, 1982). Faculty at Jefferson Community College in Louisville, Kentucky, prepared a publication for students entitled *Full Classrooms: 95 Practical Suggestions to Guarantee Student and Teacher Success*. At the University of Arkansas, Little Rock, conditionally

admitted students take reading and math placement exams and
are then required to take appropriate developmental classes in
these areas (Saluri, 1985).

Enrollment managers should consider two things when
viewing academic skill-building services as an antidote to attrition. First, such services are more likely to reduce attrition
among less academically able students than among stronger students. Although the latter group may benefit from this type of
assistance, they are already more likely to become academically
integrated at the school. They are also more likely to earn better grades than their less-able counterparts, and academic success has consistently been found to be strongly related to retention (Pantages and Creedon, 1978). Second, academic skill-
building services are more likely to reduce attrition if the participation of students who need them is required. Effective skill-
building programs tend to share the following characteristics:
they are formal classes that are taught by specially trained professionals; they enroll students for a full term; and students are
systematically identified, placed, and required by the institution to complete the courses. These programs are much more
likely to promote persistence than services that are poorly staffed
and used voluntarily and sporadically by those students who
need them the most.

No student service is mentioned in retention research
more often as a means of promoting student persistence than
academic advising (Beal and Noel, 1980; Ramist, 1981; Lenning, 1982). In fact, two empirical studies (Rose, 1965; Frank
and Kirk, 1975) found that student use of counseling and advising services was related to retention. Morehead and Johnson (1964) found that the extent of contact between advisers and
their advisees was related to persistence.

There are numerous ways for institutions to strengthen
their academic advising systems. They can appoint full-time
coordinators who are able to devote all of their time to overseeing advising and centralizing the system. Advisers can be carefully selected for the advising responsibilities rather than all
faculty members drafted for the assignment, regardless of their
ability or motivation for the task. Advisers can receive special

training, resource handbooks, and extensive background information on their advisees. Faculty who advise students can be given extra compensation, reduced teaching loads, and consideration of their advising work in promotion, tenure, and salary decisions. Schools can encourage frequent adviser-advisee contact and advisers taking the initiative to contact students who are having academic problems or who have not recently seen the adviser. Institutions may also maintain low adviser-advisee ratios as a way of facilitating extensive contact between advisers and students. They may employ peer advisers to work with faculty advisers and have both types of advisers participate extensively in new-student orientation programs. Identifying students whose academic or personal background indicates they may be less likely than other students to persist in school and then providing these students with additional advising services (diagnostic testing of academic skills, academic skills workshops, frequent adviser-advisee contact, and so on) is also a measure schools can take to promote persistence.

A common feature of advising programs that appear to have contributed to retention is that advisers in these programs draw students into the advising process (Saluri, 1985). The advisers seek out students, persist in maintaining contact with them, and engage them in significant conversations about their academic progress, career planning, and personal adjustment.

Duke University in Durham, North Carolina, offers an effective advising program in which university admissions staff identify, prior to enrollment, students they consider to be exit prone because of their academic background. Professional advisers take the initiative to schedule frequent meetings with these students in order to monitor their academic progress and identify early any difficulties they are having. South Dakota State University in Brookings has an advising center for students who are uncertain of their major that is staffed by a full-time coordinator. Faculty who advise undecided students are selected and trained through the center and maintain regular contact with their advisees. Faculty advisers working in the Academic Assistance Program at Central Michigan University in Mount Pleasant have only three advisees each and participate in ongoing in-service training programs. Faculty at Grinnell College, a private institution in Grinnell, Iowa, turn in progress reports on all of the students in their classes each month. Students having difficulties are referred to the college's advising center (Saluri, 1985).

It is important for enrollment managers to note that extensive advising programs may not necessarily increase retention on campuses where students are likely to interact frequently with and receive help from faculty and college staff in other campus sites (classrooms, residence halls, student organizations, counseling centers, and so on). To be sure, comprehensive advising programs can be of significant assistance to students regardless of how much other contact they may have with faculty and institutional staff. Nevertheless, advising programs in such circumstances may not necessarily increase retention.

Researchers have consistently found that students with career plans are more likely to persist in college (Spady, 1970; Tinto, 1975; Pantages and Creedon, 1978). Terenzini and Pascarella (1976) also found that students who believe their education will lead to a job (or graduate or professional school if that is their wish) are more likely to persist in school. Institutions can provide career planning and placement assistance to students by offering career counseling and testing, courses in career exploration, career and graduate and professional school information in libraries, career exploration and job placement workshops, internships and other forms of practical experience, and on-campus interviews with representatives of prospective employers and graduate and professional schools. Faculty can assist students by maintaining contact with professionals off campus in careers related to their disciplines and sharing information received from these people with students. They can also discuss the relevance of the skills and content associated with their courses to career skills and maintain current information about careers for people with degrees in their discipline. South Dakota State University requires a career planning course for students undecided about their major. Wartburg College, a private liberal arts college in Waverly, Iowa, trains students to be peer advisers who contact all freshmen and urge them to use the college's career planning service. Washington University, a private institution in St. Louis, published a booklet for students that outlined possible careers, employment outlook, and graduate school information for each of the academic majors offered at the university (Saluri, 1985). Westminster College's "Lunch Bunch Program" regularly brings alumni from varying careers to the campus so that students can meet with them and obtain information and insights into their respective careers.

Career planning and placement services that contribute the most to student persistence are likely to involve students in internships and other practical experiences they find especially rewarding and interesting. Such involvement can become central to students' undergraduate experience, give their academic study sharper focus, and motivate them to remain in school. Moreover, the mere presence of prospective employer and graduate and professional school representatives on campus can contribute to student persistence. Thomas (1988) found that students may view the presence of these recruiters on campus as evidence that people outside the school believe that their education is of high quality. This perception can enhance students' confidence in the school and strengthen their commitment to remain.

Activities Promoting Social Integration. Astin (1975), Fetters (1977), Terenzini, Pascarella, and Lorang (1982), and Louis, Colten, and Demeke (1984) all found that measures of student social integration into an institution were related to rates of persistence. Institutionally sponsored activities that can promote social integration include social activities during orientation, a broad range of extracurricular student organizations, recruiting campaigns to involve freshmen in student organizations, on-campus sites for social activity, and weekend social activities. Upper-class students at Denison University, for example, work very hard to recruit freshmen into student organizations. The student staff for new-student orientation at Westminster College maintain regular social contact with freshmen after the formal orientation program ends by inviting them to social gatherings.

Institutions that succeed in retaining students in part because of their ability to socially integrate them are most likely to have a strong sense of campus community and tradition to which students feel affection and loyalty. In fact, Bean (1986) recommends that institutions use rituals, traditions, and symbols as a way of enhancing a sense of campus community and students' loyalty to the institution. For example, students at Phillips University, a private institution in Enid, Oklahoma, conduct "Friendship Fire" at the beginning and the end of each academic year. At this ceremony, students gather at a campus bonfire, sing the university's alma mater, and listen to brief testimonial speeches from student leaders.

Meyers (1981) found that freshmen who made a significant contact with an adviser, faculty member, or residence-hall staff member during their first three weeks of classes were more likely to remain in school than those who did not. Three studies have found that making a friend during the first month of school increases the chances for retention (Simpson, Baker, and Mellinger, 1980; Fiedler and Vance, 1981; Billson and Terry, 1982). Such findings emphasize the potential importance of orientation programs to retention efforts. These programs can include workshops on issues related to college academic and social life, social-recreational activities, meetings with academic advisers, courses on adjustment to college, and so on. Although orientation programs typically precede the beginning of the academic year and often end with the start of classes, such programs that continue throughout the first term, frequently in the form of classes, are the ones most likely to promote retention (Forrest, 1982). By meeting regularly and continuing the process of addressing important academic and social issues in students' adjustment, these programs extend the institution's efforts to promote the social and academic integration of their freshmen. The University of Notre Dame in Indiana, for example, plans social opportunities for freshmen throughout their first semester. The University of South Carolina offers University 101, a course for first-semester freshmen that covers a wide range of topics including study skills, career planning, and adjustment to university life (Saluri, 1985).

Sexton (1965) reports that parental support of completing college promotes retention. Pantages and Creedon (1978) and Saluri (1985) also found that institutional contact with students' parents was related to persistence. Institutionally initiated communication with parents is thus considered a useful measure to promote retention. The contact can be in the form of admissions materials, interviews, and campus tours designed for prospective students' parents; parent orientation programs; opportunities for parents to meet faculty and administrators; parents' days; newsletters for parents that include information about student services, institutional activities, and so on; and parent associations. For example, faculty advisers at McPherson College, a private institution in McPherson, Kansas, send personalized letters of introduction to the parents of their newly assigned advisees. The dean of freshmen at the University of Notre Dame sends a newsletter containing information about university news and student services to the parents of freshmen. Eastern Michigan University prepares a special handbook for the parents of its students and organizes a program for parents during orientation that focuses on ways in which they can help their children adjust to the school.

It is important to note, however, that engendering a sense of campus community and institutional loyalty is accomplished more easily at traditional residential institutions. Campuses enrolling significant numbers of nontraditional or commuting students will probably have more success in retaining them through other institutional measures.

The results of five empirical studies (Astin, 1973, 1975, 1977; Kuznik, 1975; Forrest, 1982) all indicate that students' living on campus promotes retention by increasing student social integration. Schools with residence halls may, therefore, want to maximize their on-campus populations, even if a policy requiring students to live on campus is necessary to accomplish the task. Social integration in residence halls may also be enhanced by having housing officials thoughtfully match freshmen with roommates on selected criteria. No such matching scheme is perfect, and some trial and error might be required before discovering what criteria work for each kind of residential student.

Finally, Astin (1975) and Beal and Noel (1980) report that students who have part-time jobs on campus are more likely to become acquainted with faculty, administrators, and other students and thus become socially integrated more readily. Campuses with a large number of commuting students and limited opportunities on campus for social integration may want to consider maximizing opportunities for students to have on-campus jobs.

Common Features of Successful Retention Efforts

Programs that succeed in raising retention rates tend to share common characteristics. First, they are likely to be both comprehensive and coordinated (Saluri, 1985). Retention results from a complex interaction of many student and institutional variables. Efforts to improve retention rates are therefore not likely to be successful if they involve only isolated student or institutional variables. For example, the positive effect on persistence of a strong academic advising program may be undermined if classroom teaching is poor or if extracurricular activities are inadequate. An effective program to reduce attrition must almost always address several areas of students' involvement with the academic and social systems of the institution. For example, the Freshman Year Program at the University of Notre Dame includes a curriculum designed especially for freshmen, a guidance team consisting of a faculty adviser and peer advisers for each freshman, a learning resource center that assists students in developing academic skills, and social activities planned for the freshmen throughout their first semester at the university.

Focusing on multiple dimensions of students' interaction with an institution requires that a broad range of college personnel (faculty, academic and student affairs administrators, administrative staff) work cooperatively. For example, the academic adviser-advisee relationship can be emphasized if admissions personnel organize opportunities for advisers and their prospective advisees to meet prior to enrollment. The relationship can be enhanced even further if the institutional staff responsible for organizing new-student orientation provide extensive time during the program for advisers and advisees to meet and get better acquainted. Institutions should, therefore, establish coordinating groups for their retention programs that include representatives of areas that will play a role in the effort.

Second, effective retention efforts usually involve faculty and administrative staff who consistently take the initiative to establish and maintain contact with students. They are particularly conscientious in reaching out to freshmen — they do not simply make themselves available to students; they seek them out. Faculty members invite students to discuss issues with them, talk with students outside the classroom, seek out students who are having difficulty in their classes, participate in orientation programs, and even involve students in their research projects. Advisers contact students they have not seen recently and those who are having academic difficulty. Student affairs staff recruit students to become involved in extracurricular activities. In effective retention efforts, such faculty and administrative behavior is the rule rather than the exception.

Third, successful programs usually use data and information extensively that help faculty and administrative staff understand more about the students and attrition at their school. Advisers have and make use of information about their advisees (high school courses and grades, SAT/ACT scores, academic and career interests, expressed need for assistance with academic skills or career or personal counseling, interests in extracurricular activities). Institutional research personnel gather descriptive data (class, sex, major, age, grade point average) on students who persist in school and those who withdraw prior to graduation. Administrative staff or faculty interview students who leave school before graduating to determine the cause of their withdrawal. They also regularly gather data on student perceptions of the school's academic programs and instruction, student services, campus facilities, campus environment, and institutional policies. All of these data are shared with personnel who are responsible for planning and implementing retention programs. They, in turn, use the data to improve the teaching and advising of students as well as the retention programs' effectiveness.

Well-coordinated retention programs can influence student success, satisfaction, and persistence. To ensure the development of well-coordinated programs, many campuses have found it necessary to appoint a retention officer who monitors retention rates and coordinates retention efforts. Effective retention programs must be designed to meet the local needs of students at individual institutions. Programs designed for students at four-year colleges are unlikely to succeed at two-year colleges. As Bean pointed out in Chapter Nine, black students interact with institutions differently than white students do, and different factors might influence retention for different types of students.

A recent summary of the problems related to minority student retention at predominantly white campuses identified nine minority student concerns that might lead to dropping out: adjustment to college; academic performance; financial resources; feelings of loneliness and isolation; racial/ethnic identity development; racial hostility in the form of harassment; feelings of alienation or not belonging; feelings of not deserving to be in college; and lack of a fit with the college environment (Ponce, 1988). From among these, only racial/ethnic identity issues and racial hostility could be said to be unique to minority students. However, the programs to remedy racial issues can differ for different minority groups and need to be designed with a target group of students in mind. Programs to serve all students may end up serving no individual student well.

Chapter 12

Successful
Retention Programs
at Two Institutions

Faye D. Plascak-Craig
Frances K. Stage
L. Sandy MacLean
John P. Bean

Retention programs, just like the institutions they serve, are very diverse. Retention issues are complex, understanding retention is difficult, and it is hard to tell beforehand which students will be helped by a retention program. This chapter presents case studies of the retention efforts at an urban university and an urban liberal arts college. These schools were chosen because they represent categories of institutions that tend to have serious retention problems and because each acted in a carefully considered manner to improve student retention. Each case unfolds as a school's struggle to understand and cope with a decline in enrollments, and in each case the struggle is rewarded.

The first institution is the University of Missouri, St. Louis, a relatively new commuter campus enrolling about 10,000 students. The second, Marian College, is located in Indianapolis and enrolls only about 1,250 students. It has a long history and is about equally divided between nontraditional commuter and traditional residential students. While the institutions and their approaches to retention are dissimilar, modest but significant gains that accrued to each school indicate that their retention efforts are worthwhile.

Some important similarities exist between the two cases. Each institution

1. Perceived that it had a serious attrition problem
2. Had top-level endorsement of the retention program
3. Combined academic and administrative (largely student affairs) staff in the program
4. Researched the problem using literature, consultants, and self-study
5. Developed a data base that takes student demographic differences into account
6. Made strategic decisions
7. Planned and implemented a variety of programs
8. Met with a few surprises
9. Had only limited success

The differences between the cases were also striking. At the University of Missouri, St. Louis, widespread concern about attrition allowed the new chancellor to declare retention a top priority and get a sympathetic response from the faculty. At Marian College, retention efforts were met with a surprising amount of resistance among faculty members. At UM-St. Louis seven task forces were involved in retention efforts while at Marian College a single task force was put in place and five staff and three faculty members carried out most of the interventions.

UM-St. Louis used existing (largely descriptive) data in analyzing student attrition. At Marian College, interview data and questionnaire data on a variety of attitudes were gathered for an analysis of the causes of attrition and the identification of potential dropouts. The UM-St. Louis task forces focused on retention programs to be run by student affairs staff (for example, marketing, career planning) and faculty programs centered around academic advising. At Marian College, faculty development and awareness of the importance of faculty roles in retention were emphasized.

Four questions are useful to keep in mind while reading these case studies.

1. Are the proposed activities consistent with what is known about student attrition summarized in Chapter Nine and with other programs summarized in Chapter Eleven?
2. Are the methods of research used at each institution con-

sistent with the recommendations for attrition research presented in Chapter Ten?
3.   Was the planning of these retention efforts consistent with strategic planning?
4.   Which proposed programs and recommendations are relevant for developing retention efforts at other institutions?

The University of Missouri, St. Louis

The University of Missouri, St. Louis, is an urban commuter institution that was founded in 1963. Currently, the university enrolls approximately 10,100 undergraduate and 2,100 professional and graduate students in academic programs. UM-St. Louis awards approximately 1,300 bachelor's and 400 graduate and professional degrees annually.

Like most urban commuter institutions, UM-St. Louis faces sharp declines in the number of college age students in its metropolitan area. A 35 percent decline is predicted in the group of students from fifteen to twenty-seven years old between 1985 and 1995.

Additionally, retention rates of undergraduates were typical of a four-year commuter institution. Only 58 percent of new students were returning to campus following their first year. And after seven years, only 26 percent of first-time students graduated from UM-St. Louis. An 8.7 percent drop from 1981 to 1985 in the number of students enrolled brought home the reality of the problem to faculty and staff alike.

Widespread concern at the school about retention of students as well as recruitment provided an opportunity for a campuswide initiative to reverse the decline. Gradually, a comprehensive and flexible retention program was created. Staff and faculty continue, in the fourth year of the program, to try out ideas, discard those that do not work or are unfeasible, and reevaluate retention programs. Their aim is to be flexible in their attempts to meet the needs of a diverse student body. This case study presents an overview of the development of a retention program, its successes and failures, and its plans for the future and offers suggestions for others who wish to improve retention and graduation rates.

Setting the Agenda. A new chancellor for the UM-St. Louis campus provided an impetus for change. Following her appointment on June 1, 1986, she identified student recruitment and student retention as two of her six priorities for the university and placed responsibility for both with the vice-chancellor for student affairs. In announcing these priorities, she also moved the organizational reporting functions of admissions, financial aid, and registration from the academic affairs area to student affairs (Barnett, 1986).

During the summer months of 1986, the vice-chancellor for student affairs conducted a review of the literature on enrollment management and collected data on the school's student retention. The vice-chancellor proposed educational programs and the involvement of faculty, staff, and students in a campuswide effort to improve the persistence and success rate for students enrolled at UM-St. Louis (MacLean, 1986).

The proposal incorporated the practical advice of enrollment and retention studies. Beal and Noel's (1980) campuswide retention committee structure, Smith, Lippitt, Noel, and Sprandel's (1980) model for mobilizing the campus for retention, and Hossler's (1984) enrollment management systems were all evident in the proposal.

The first part of the proposal involved educating those who would plan and implement the program. Participants were given the proposal and familiarized in workshops with the literature on recruitment and retention. In the workshops, the literature was related to the unique problems of UM-St. Louis.

The workshops focused on the importance of students' involvement on campus, the pull of outside influences on a commuter campus, and the importance of both academic and social dimensions of campus life. They provided a basic understanding of multiple factors that influence students' decisions to leave or remain enrolled in the university.

A second part of the proposal involved faculty, staff from clerks to vice-presidents, and students in the development of a university plan. The widespread involvement was intended to ensure that the eventual implementers—everyone at the university, including students—would have a stake in the outcome.

A critical element of the project was the grouping of seven planning task forces around two themes, recruitment and retention. Two recruitment task forces, marketing and ongoing recruitment, focused on reaching potential students and attracting them to UM-St. Louis. Four task forces dealt specifically with retention planning—career counseling, academic advising, involvement activities, and support services. Finally, one task force on faculty and staff participation developed plans that integrated recruitment and retention.

The Data. A frequently mentioned key element in any enrollment management program is a system for effective and efficient data collection and analysis. At UM-St. Louis, new first-year students enrolled each fall were tracked throughout their enrollment at the institution. The data base included enrollment and graduation data on every such student since 1975.

In addition, a comprehensive retention study completed in 1985 (Kulage, 1985) provided retention and graduation data on students enrolled between 1977 and 1984. Considerable longitudinal data were also available on recruitment practices; enrollments by type of student (new first-year students, continuing, new transfer, readmits, and graduate); enrollment by school, college, and class; and graduation numbers by years.

The goals of the retention project were to increase the first-to second-year retention rate, increase the percentage of first-year students who graduate within seven years, increase overall numbers of students who graduate, and increase overall enrollment.

Achieving Consensus and Gaining Credibility. Achieving consensus and gaining credibility on campus for this enrollment management project were key factors in its success. The first step was to gain the support of the Student Affairs Department directors. After reviewing the proposal, they supported it. Since the proposal emanated from the vice-chancellor for student affairs, the critical endorsement was from academic affairs. The vice-chancellor for academic affairs took the proposal to the Academic Council, which included academic deans and other key academic officers. This body amended the proposal and then endorsed it, and it was eventually endorsed by the chancellor and her cabinet. The chancellor named the vice-chancellor for

student affairs and the vice-chancellor for academic affairs cochairs of the Student Recruitment and Retention Project. The
cochairs consulted with each academic dean for suggestions on
faculty and academic staff to serve on the task forces.

Since a longitudinal retention study indicated that the loss
of students between the first and second years was the major
campus retention problem, the chancellor established a Student
Retention Program office to increase the retention of first-year
students. The program was experimental, and the director of
it became an integral part of planning and implementing the
overall campus retention effort.

The Work of the Task Forces. A year after the initial impera-
tive, the task forces were ready to begin planning for the creation of a campus that was responsive to its unique clientele, the
urban student. A consultant was brought in to help launch the
undertaking. He reinforced the informational effort that had
already begun on the major issues related to student recruitment and retention. Additionally, he focused members of individual task forces on some salient issues in their area of responsibility.

The task forces met frequently through the summer and
into the fall as individual groups. Task force chairs and campus
administrators (heads of admissions, counseling, academic advising units, and academic support staff) also met regularly as
an operational group to share information and coordinate activities. The task forces delivered their recommendations by De-
cember of year two.

Task Force Reports. Each task force delivered a group of recommendations to the vice-chancellor for academic affairs and the
vice-chancellor for student affairs. Some of the most viable suggestions are listed here, along with the name of the task force.

1. Conduct a campuswide survey of academic services provided by individual schools and colleges (academic advising).
2. Utilize the campus computer system to implement an early
   warning system (academic advising, information systems).

3. Provide first-year students attending new-student orientation a free catalogue and course description (academic advising).

4. Conduct a campuswide retention awareness program, "Freshmen Forecast," to predict the number of returning first-year students. Winner receives a one-year reserved parking space (involvement).

5. Make presentations throughout campus on the decline in enrollment, the importance of student retention, and what faculty and staff can do to increase student retention (faculty/staff awareness).

6. Provide more information during orientation on student academic and support services — especially on the Women's Center and campus child-care services (support services).

7. Provide evening hours in the counseling service (counseling).

8. Schedule quarterly meetings between counseling services and academic advising staffs (counseling).

9. Develop a coordinated, targeted direct mail and telemarketing program to recruit former students as well as traditional and nontradional students (marketing).

10. Conduct a campuswide University Center needs survey and, from the data collected, develop a plan to increase the size and services of the present student center (involvement).

11. Conduct a survey of support service programs at other, comparable urban institutions in order to compare UM-St. Louis programs with other urban universities (involvement).

12. Develop a sophisticated institutional marketing plan capitalizing on the school's twenty-fifth anniversary celebration (marketing).

Many other suggestions were rejected because they were too expensive, too difficult to implement, or too narrowly focused. Some of these included building an informational center on campus that would be staffed seventy hours per week; adding administrative staff to the admissions office, all academic advising offices, and the cooperative education program; and requiring all new students to participate in a summer or fall orientation program.

After all task forces presented their reports, only the academic advising task force agreed to continue meeting. By continuing to meet, they thought they could improve communication among schools' and colleges' academic advising offices and help implement their recommendations. The other task forces elected to dissolve (as originally planned), except for the operational group. It agreed to continue to meet regularly and monitor ongoing recruitment and retention programs. The operations group expanded to include interested faculty members, other student affairs offices (such as student activities, recreation, the Women's Center, and placement), and representatives from university relations and administrative services.

Implementation. Toward the end of the second year and beginning the third, the twelve initiatives mentioned and others were put into place. The third year began on a particularly positive note. Enrollment had increased by 10 percent over the previous two years. For the first time in a decade, new first-year student enrollment did not decline but increased slightly. However, most of the initiatives probably had not been in place a sufficient length of time to explain the increase. Perhaps a heightened awareness resulting from the planning year had some positive effects on the general campus atmosphere.

Successes and Failures. Some of the initiatives were particularly successful. For example, the targeted direct mail and telemarketing campaigns produced significant increases in enrollment of former (readmitted) students who had not registered for several semesters. It seemed that some former students needed only a reminder to reenroll. These same techniques produced more applications and campus visits from prospective first-year students and transfers that eventually may produce enrollment increases. The twenty-fifth anniversary marketing plan was so successful that plans are under way to launch another campaign stressing UM-St. Louis as "The New First Choice" for students in the St. Louis area. Plans for enlarging the University Center were undertaken. Staff members are prioritizing information about the center gathered in the campuswide need survey. The University Center is scheduled to become a part of the school's long-range building plan.

After a year of study and preparation, the Student Retention Program initiated an innovative retention program for 100 new first-year students called "Path to Success." It includes extensive academic advising; block scheduling; study skills and career counseling workshops; a faculty/staff mentoring program; a first-year student noncredit seminar; and a follow-up of all students after midterms, finals, and preregistration. The students were also encouraged to become involved in one or more extracurricular programs. After only the first semester, Path to Success students had statistically significantly higher grade point averages and hours completed than a similar control group.

Enrollment continued to grow. In fact, enrollment has increased each successive semester or term over the previous year by 1.0 to 5.8 percent. Applications and preenrollments indicate that this growth will continue for the fall semester of the fourth year. Between fall 1986 and fall 1988, the largest percentage of enrollment increases by category were former students (stopouts), with a 13 percent increase (n = 137), and continuing students, with an 8 percent increase (n = 586). These two categories of students accounted for 723 additional student enrollments, nearly all of the increase between these two years. These data indicate that the campuswide student retention program has had a positive impact on enrollments.

Since many former students are returning to complete their degrees, the graduating class of UM-St. Louis increased by 9.5 percent over the past two years. It is expected that in the third year of this program, the university will graduate more than 2,000 students, the highest number in its history.

Some of the initiatives were not successful; either they failed to produce results that contributed to retention or they were too costly. The Freshmen Forecast contest resulted in over 250 entrees but seemed not to effect student retention. In addition, establishing a reserved parking space for a staff member and then attempting to enforce that reserved space throughout the year created several administrative problems. The early warning system was much more difficult to implement on the computer than anticipated and, after it was implemented, following up all the students on the early warning list required so much time that the academic advising staff had to drop the idea.

Presentations on the importance of student enrollment and student retention were made to nine groups on campus, but after a few months no further invitations were received. Some members of the faculty and staff complained that they were tired of seeing the presentations more than once. Several student service areas were underfunded compared to other urban universities, but given other campus priorities, it is unlikely that these services will receive additional funding in the near future.

Continuing Programs. The operations group will continue to meet and monitor ongoing student recruitment and retention efforts. During the past two years, this group has become interested in the availability of child-care services on campus, retention of minority students, and the welfare of foreign students. Also, the operations group recommends funding priorities for student retention programs to the vice-chancellors for student affairs and academic affairs — their top priorities have been submitted annually to the UM-St. Louis budget planning program. Additionally, the operations group is planning a daylong workshop in the fall in which they intend to provide a student retention program and establish retention goals for the future. The Path to Success program will enter its second year by tracking the 100 students who participated in the first-year program, and it will initiate a second-year program for an additional 100 new students. After this year, a comprehensive two-year evaluation will be completed that will provide longitudinal data on the impact of this program on first-year-student retention.

Conclusion. This comprehensive and flexible retention program achieved only part of its objectives. To date, the UM-St. Louis longitudinal retention study does not indicate an increased student retention rate above 58 percent for the first-to-second-year retention for any recent new class. On the other hand, more former students are returning to campus and continuing their enrollment, and more students are graduating. These trends have produced a 10 percent cumulative enrollment increase since fall 1986. Enrollments for the second semester and the summer session as well as applications and preregistrations for fall 1989 indicate that the enrollment increases should continue into the fourth year of the program. It is too early to evaluate the first-to-second-year retention rate of the Path to Success program or the seven-year graduation rate of new first-year students who have enrolled at UM-St. Louis since fall 1986. The school's administrators are confident, however, that short-term achievements will help meet the long-term goals of the project.

The changes at UM-St. Louis were dramatic. As an urban campus that had faced steady declines in enrollments, the school had plenty of room for change. The strategies used at UM-St. Louis might not produce such dramatic results at an institution that is not in an extreme state of decline. Nevertheless, these suggestions should prove useful for any campus striving to maintain or make more modest gains in enrollment.

This program provides empirical support for the campuswide retention models recommended by Beal and Noel (1980) and Smith, Lippitt, Noel, and Sprandel (1980) and the enrollment management model of Hossler (1984). These authors point out that campuswide efforts produce awareness, commitment, and concern, which frequently lead to enrollment increases. Clearly, retention is everyone's responsibility, and unless there is campuswide interest and commitment, the best planned programs probably will fail.

The school's ongoing approach to student retention continues to evolve as new initiatives are started and others are discarded. As a result of this experience, several suggestions can be made for other schools that plan to adopt this approach.

1.   Include faculty, staff, and students in planning and implementing a retention program. Anticipate that planning,

consensus building, and gaining credibility may take at least
a year.

2. Develop data bases and utilize campus data on recruitment,
   admissions, enrollment, and graduation when establishing
   retention goals and evaluating the program. Today, many
   offices of admissions, registration, and institutional research have large computer data bases that can be pro-
   grammed quickly to generate valuable reports on the retention program.

3. Try many different retention activities and evaluate each
   one. If nothing else, a multitude of activities builds awareness, interest, and concern that may have an indirect effect
   on enrollment.

4. Establish an ongoing operations group that monitors and
   coordinates retention activities. Its membership should include representatives from all university divisions and areas.
   It needs to be chaired by the chief academic affairs or student affairs officer and should meet often. A small budget
   to pay for meeting refreshments, workshops, or unique initiatives should be provided.

Marian College

Colleges and universities have used a number of techniques to
achieve academic and financial success; for example, admissions
strategies, unique academic programs, unique institutional services and facilities, aggressive marketing and recruitment of
freshmen and transfers, and combinations of these techniques.
Administrators and faculty are now aware that previous techniques of recruiting from an enlarging applicant pool are no
longer sufficient for dealing with present student constraints.
Fewer academically prepared applicants and fewer transfers are
available to replace students who drop out before program completion. Management efforts at schools have recently been en-
larged to include the retention of an institution's matriculated
share of an ever-changing student pool. Marian College is no
exception in this regard.

Marian College's executive officers commissioned Faye D. Plascak-Craig, working with John P. Bean, to study student attrition at Marian. The data gathered by these researchers were used to create and implement empirically based retention interventions and to set up longitudinal data-collection procedures and data bases for strategic planning purposes. The research was designed and implemented over an eighteen-month period. An intervention task force of interested faculty and professional staff was set up to use the research data in proactively addressing the attrition factors specific to the institution.

The purpose of this case study is to show how research was used at Marian College to guide the implementation of retention programs and to present the results of the implementation. The case study will describe the institution, its specific management problems, and the methodology of the research component; present the findings; emphasize the development of retention strategy and interventions; discuss the outcomes of the changes made; and present conclusions and observations for the future.

Marian College is a private, independent four-year liberal arts college, with a student body of 1,250. The Carnegie Commission would place the school in the Liberal Arts College II category. This Catholic school's religious affiliation is with the Sisters of Saint Francis, Oldenburg, some of whom serve on the board of trustees, in key administrative positions, and as faculty and professional staff. In keeping with current Catholic educational trends, however, less than 15 percent of the employees of the school are religious. The Catholic church does not provide financial assistance beyond the contributed services of the sisters.

The school is located in a large urban area in which three other liberal arts colleges and one commuter university operate. These predominantly secular, somewhat larger liberal arts colleges compete with Marian College for residential students, particularly for the nonprofessional studies majors, in that their liberal arts programs are similar; all of the schools compete for commuter students. Cross-registration is offered by three of the four schools, and transferring from Marian College to one of these institutions is relatively simple in many program majors.

The size of the freshman class at Marian College has increased annually since 1980; in 1982, 174 first-time freshmen enrolled full time, and in 1988, 246 enrolled. An additional 200 nontraditional students were also classed as freshmen in 1988. Approximately one half of the students are traditional-age residential students and half are commuters of all ages. Two-thirds of the students are females, and 54 percent are Catholic. A sizable proportion of the residential students are from rural areas of Indiana.

Both liberal arts and professional programs are offered at Marian College, and four two-year degree programs were established during the last fifteen years. The overall program completion rates from 1983 to 1988 differ by length of program: the two-year program attrition rate averages 26 percent; the four-year program attrition rate averages 62 percent. The average attrition rate from 1982 to 1987 for the freshman-to-sophomore years was 27 percent. In general, one-third of the freshman class (traditional and nontraditional students) leaves after the first year; an additional one-third leaves across the succeeding three years.

Liberal arts colleges have been described as homogeneous residential institutions that benefit from a shared institutional identification, increasing in direct relation to the elite nature of the school's academic standards and indirectly with size (Baldridge, Curtis, Ecker, and Riley, 1978; Clark, 1983). Marian College, although small enough to sustain shared institutional identification, is neither elite nor wholly a liberal arts college. Marian College's well-enrolled professional studies programs and its increasing number of nontraditional commuter students tend to interfere with a unified focus of action, academically and administratively. Although heterogeneous subgroups contribute many valuable, diverse perspectives to the classroom, to student government, and to campus life, heterogeneity presents special problems for an institution trying to develop programs that respond to individual students' needs and expectations. Marian College's consumers are numerous, varied, and not consensus bound. How does a small, financially modest, individually oriented college deal with an ethically, financially, and institutionally unacceptable attrition rate?

The Study. A questionnaire, based on the theoretical and empirical models of Bean (1983) and Metzner and Bean (1987), was used to collect freshman survey data in 1985, 1986, and 1987. The data were analyzed using multiple regression and path analysis. Interview data were also gathered and these data supported the statistical analyses.

For residential students (n = 396), the most important factors affecting dropout were intent to persist and family approval, followed by loyalty to the institution, perceived practical value of education, taking desired courses, and clear educational goals. Loyalty was most related to peer friendships and practical value of education.

For commuter students (n = 381), the best persistence predictors were GPA and number of hours enrolled, followed by loyalty, institutional fit, clear educational goals, and peer friendships. College GPA was positively related to high school GPA, clear educational goals, and less than twenty hours per week work commitment.

The model was much more successful in describing residential student departure (accounting for about a third of the variance) than in describing commuter student departure (about 7 percent of the variance). The findings suggested that, to be effective, interventions should be tailored to the needs of each student subgroup.

In interviews, residential students who persisted at the college reported selecting Marian for its small size and deciding to pursue higher education for its practical value in career development. They believed they persisted because of their peer relationships and the programs offered in their majors. Residential dropouts reported leaving because they did not meet minimum GPA requirements and wanted to transfer to other schools to be with significant others.

Commuter students who persisted did so because they valued the personal development they experienced at Marian

College and their relationships with faculty. Commuter dropouts had low GPAs and financial problems.

The interviews indicated that first-generation students (25 percent of the entering freshman class) had unrealistically optimistic expectations for their social life at college. Some were dismayed because such inflated expectations remained unfulfilled in the first six weeks on campus.

Development of the Interventions. The first step in developing interventions was to assess the school's matriculants. All incoming freshmen now fill out a forty-item survey during orientation. Some items are used to develop demographic data bases, and some are used to identify students at high risk to drop out. Incoming freshmen are also given a battery of tests: reading speed and comprehension, writing sample for idea development, learning style indicator, and study skills inventory. Files containing results and interpretations for students are sent to their faculty academic advisers.

Given the complex profile of retention factors and the heterogeneous student body at Marian College, the researchers recommended and the administrators implemented multiple strategies to reduce attrition among at-risk students. The strategies, paralleling theoretical models, were divided into three types: academic, social, and institutional.

The academic strategy was to increase student perceptions of the practical value of education, of personal development, and of faculty competence and to offer the academically underprepared students, those without certain college-level skills, an equitable chance to persist. The social strategy was to increase the number of opportunities for curricular and cocurricular bonding between students, to increase communication between families and the college, and to facilitate greater faculty-student contact in and out of the classroom. The institutional strategy was to financially support proactive retention interventions, to staff and fund academic and personal counseling, to encourage faculty and professional staff development, and to better educate the college community about college programs and procedures.

The names of those freshmen who answered survey items in such a way as to indicate that they were at high risk to drop out were compiled and grouped by retention factors. For example, respondents who circled on the survey that their families were "not very supportive" or "not at all supportive" of their educational plans were placed on the "Family Support Risk" list. Those students whose names appeared on three or more lists were interviewed immediately and at length by one of three college counselors. Three faculty and five professional staff members formed a proactive task force, doing intrusive advising and counseling with the remaining students who appeared to be at high risk to drop out. Each student at risk in one or more areas was asked by a member of the task force to come by for a talk. If needed, the student was referred elsewhere for help. If no additional help was warranted, the student was, at least, made aware of the opportunity for help and familiarized with campus personnel and facilities.

Academic Interventions. An individually focused program for the professional development of faculty, previously organized by the incoming dean for academic affairs, was used to clarify and to increase students' perceptions of faculty competence. Faculty were made aware of their roles in students' perceptions of personal development during presentations at open college forums. An annual adviser training program for faculty was established to improve advising in the major fields of study and in practical career preparation. Each department was encouraged to create practicum and internship opportunities for majors.

Academically underprepared students were identified by their levels of performance on writing samples, verbal SATs, and high school GPAs. These students were enrolled in developmental English composition and in basic study skills classes. The Transition Center, established the previous year as a support services facility, was utilized as a peer-tutoring center for nineteen different courses.

Social Interventions. First-generation students and those with undeveloped social skills were particularly prone to report during the interviews that they perceived few or no social opportunities or that they felt left out and isolated from the college's current social activities. More cocurricular activities were planned for the beginning of the year to increase formation of peer relationships. Also, under the direction of the residence-hall directors, student resident assistants in the dormitories made unscheduled weekly visits to first-generation students to discuss problems, clarify perceptions, and monitor the students' adjustment to their college environment.

The Transition Center was used more extensively as a personal and group counseling facility. Those new students reporting shyness, social anxiety, and nonassertiveness were offered services as needed.

Institutional Interventions. Programs such as orientations for freshmen and their families and "Bring a Friend to Campus" weekends were established to create realistic expectations of campus life for students. The focus of marketing and recruitment efforts was changed to include a greater number of mailings to families and more active alumni involvement in practicums, internships, and social events.

Restructuring of admissions procedures was necessary to accommodate pretesting and developmental course assignments. The honors program was redesigned and funded to offer richer opportunities for the academically "overprepared." Evaluations of faculty were redesigned to include peer and chair reviews and classroom observations. Faculty now prepare professional development plans annually.

Retention Intervention Outcomes. According to evaluation data, approximately 93 percent of the students at high risk to drop out were seen by the task force members; 23 percent were referred on for more help, and 77 percent did not require further interaction. (The 7 percent who were not seen were those who withdrew during the first week of classes or those who repeatedly broke appointments.) Resident assistants visited virtually all of the targeted first-generation dormitory students at least three times during the first month of the three fall semesters.

Participation rates for group therapy sessions and personal counseling were greater and peaked earlier in the academic year after the retention strategy was put in place. Implementation of the interventions occurred as designed.

The overall retention rate from freshman to sophomore year increased 4 percent during 1987 and 5 percent during 1988. The annual gains appear modest, but when separated into subgroups of students the retention rates were more distinctive. For those students who entered with clearly defined educational goals, a high school GPA greater than 2.0, SAT verbal scores above 370, and a writing sample at or above the average rating, retention had increased by 11 percent. For the group not meeting those criteria, retention had actually decreased.

Conclusions. The retention of students in today's educational environment is exceedingly complex. For some academically underprepared students, little could be done with one semester of developmental courses and other interventions to mediate the negative effect of poor grades. Many of Marian College's faculty, professional staff members, and administrators now believe that multiple, individually tailored contacts with freshmen will be more effective in increasing retention. Today's students are more variable — in group composition, in experiences, in academic preparation, and in the types of problems that influence persistence across four years of school, even for small liberal arts schools.

Some staff and faculty found the changes inherent in such a retention effort threatening. The program planners were surprised and at times discouraged by the variability in support for the research findings and the retention efforts. Program planners must expect some opposition to changes.

The program planners at Marian College began this project highly optimistic about the changes they could make in the retention rates — they are now more cognizant that change takes time and are gratified by the small improvements accomplished thus far for some subgroups. It is impossible to eliminate attrition; some is even healthy. The level of acceptable dropout must be established by each institution as a part of total enrollment management, and then strategies must be designed with that management in mind.

To plan future strategies, Marian College is asking itself several questions related to academic, social, and institutional issues. Marian will be taking a hard look at its admissions criteria by asking: Is it ethical to admit students sufficiently underprepared so that they have only a 10 percent chance of graduating? Should the school place proportionally more financial and administrative emphasis on programs and opportunities for those students with good credentials who matriculate?

The school is concerned about meeting the different social needs of its two student groups. The older students desire more faculty contact; the younger students are concerned with peers. Do the standard student-union-type activities suffice for this campus? Will busy nontraditional students, who are oriented toward their job and family, participate in on-campus activities if they are available?

Institutionally, Marian College is torn between habit and innovation. For the last fifty years, the school has served traditional-age students who resided on campus. How does the school best shift gears to accommodate the other 50 percent of its student body? The information that emerged from the research and evaluation components of this project will be used as part of a major strategic planning project to address many of these questions.

As a result of this four-year study, administrators at Marian College are less naive, less optimistic, and less routinized in their thinking about student persistence. But they are also more knowledgeable, more tolerant, and more confident about their abilities to make a difference, however modest. A great deal of work remains — in keeping with the pattern of careful investigation, the research at Marian College uncovered more questions than it answered.

Comparison of the Two Programs

At the University of Missouri, St. Louis, a new chancellor placed a high priority on student recruitment and retention. Faculty were mobilized in task forces, but the task forces emphasized staff approaches to rectifying enrollment problems. The extent to which faculty actually changed their behavior in or out of the classroom is not clear.

What is interesting at UM-St. Louis is that retention actually improved before several programs were implemented. Perhaps students noticed faculty enthusiasm for improving the situation at UM-St. Louis, and that was enough to increase retention. Four findings seem clear: Sophisticated marketing practices are worth their cost; personalized attention (the Path to Success program) produces results; retention programs often produce unanticipated beneficial consequences, for example, the increase in the number of stopouts returning to UM-St. Louis and graduating; data are essential for understanding attrition and retention; and looking at the retention of important groups of students is more meaningful than looking at overall rates of enrollment.

While demographic data and sophisticated marketing were most important at UM-St. Louis, at Marian College the sophisticated analysis of attitudinal information and a proactive personalized approach to retention were most important. Ironically, this personalized approach was the result of centralized planning by staff and faculty experts. Perhaps because the programming was centralized, more faculty resistance to retention programming was encountered than at UM-St. Louis. But the emphasis at Marian College on developing faculty members' understanding of their own role in student retention seemed particularly appropriate. The identification of at-risk students followed by proactive intervention was one of the strongest points of the Marian approach. Another clear strength was the continued analysis of student retention data. The later analysis uncovered the interesting finding that while below-average students continued to drop out of school at the same pace as before, students who met certain academic criteria increased their retention rate by 11 percent.

At both UM-St. Louis and Marian College, several intervention strategies were suggested. Regardless of how different an institution is from these two, it is worth considering whether their programs, perhaps modified slightly, might succeed at another institution.

The complexity of retention problems usually precludes simple solutions. As was the case at Marian, new research often raises more questions than it answers. While knowledge of the exact effectiveness of any one retention program is imperfect, each program probably helps some students stay in school and should be tried. Every program has some costs, but the mathematics of retention suggest a bias for action. If retention programs cause 1 percent of a class of 1,000 (10 students) to stay in school for four years instead of one, thirty student-years of tuition are produced. If tuition is $10,000 a year, $300,000 in revenue is taken in, a tidy sum to pay for retention programming.

Unfortunately, retention issues will probably get cloudier before they get clearer. What is best known about retention is known about traditional students. In these two institutions, and for the majority of colleges, community colleges, and universities in this country, nontraditional students will soon be in the majority. As student populations become more heterogeneous, global explanations of student attrition and the identification of specific programs to reduce attrition across the board will become more and more difficult.

PART FOUR

BUILDING
COMPREHENSIVE
ENROLLMENT MANAGEMENT
SYSTEMS

This last part moves from the individual aspects of enrollment management to a broader institutional focus. Chapters Thirteen and Fourteen describe the issues that should be considered when developing a management information system that is computer-based. It is impossible for all but the smallest institutions to succeed without some kind of management information system. These chapters have been placed in the last section because student data bases serve the planning, policy making, marketing, and retention activities of enrollment management. Management information systems should be particularly useful in integrating marketing and retention strategies. Chapter Thirteen examines the issues that enrollment managers should consider when they develop or refine a student information system. Chapter Fourteen describes the development of a student information system and how it helped to improve student enrollments at one university.

Chapter Fifteen presents case studies from two universities that developed successful enrollment management systems. In keeping with a theme of this book, both institutions have utilized different approaches in creating their systems. In both cases, however, the enrollment management system is a centralized approach.

The final chapter synthesizes key points from each of the chapters in this book. Its purpose is to integrate theory and local information to design effective local practices. It offers a series of suggestions for staffing an enrollment management system. It also suggests some general guidelines for marketing and retention activities.

Comprehensive enrollment management strategies and programs represent new concepts that appear to be here to stay. Properly executed, enrollment management should grow because it is beneficial to both the student and the institution. The final section of Chapter Sixteen looks at the future of enrollment management and some issues enrollment managers must confront.

Chapter 13

Understanding and Designing Information Systems

Nick Vesper

At Harvard I learned that facts are facts. In Italy I learned
that facts are the way you look at them.
                          — Sean O'Faolain

This chapter provides an overview of the issues campus administrators should consider when developing or evaluating a management information system (MIS) or a decision support system (DSS) to aid enrollment management efforts. Although the
acronyms MIS and DSS are often used interchangeably, they
refer to two different approaches to managing information, either
of which can aid the efforts of enrollment managers. MIS is intended to make current and accurate data available to campus
decision makers, while DSS is a future-looking ad hoc procedure that uses MIS data and modeling techniques to enhance
strategic executive decision making (Masland, 1985; Mills,
Linger, and Hevner, 1986). Modeling will be only indirectly
discussed in this chapter, and the distinction between MIS and
DSS will not be emphasized. As Sean O'Faolain might note,
the facts about information systems come from perceptions of
a technology and process that are constantly changing.

The distinction between MIS and DSS is often arbitrary
and based more on a business than an educational perspective of

information use (Mills, Linger, and Hevner, 1986). In a simple hierarchical model of a business, the MIS department would play a central role in information collection, distribution, and use across the entire organization. DSS in this context would be used only by a handful of senior executives making strategic decisions. In a college or university, however, each unit, such as the admissions office or the liberal arts college, may have exactly the same information needs as the entire institution. When the same information needs arise between units and within units, the distinction between MIS and DSS is blurred. Information will not only be distributed widely, but also used for different purposes. Retention data, for example, can be used to plan effective retention strategies for individual students on the one hand and in strategic calculations about resources on the other.

A traditional approach to enrollment management is to consider it as a complex set of processes that needs to be fit into an organizational structure. From this perspective, information related to enrollment management is designed primarily to meet the needs of senior administrators. This places information in an important but adjunct position to the functioning of enrollment management offices (Graff, 1986; Hossler, Braxton, and Coopersmith, 1989). By blurring the MIS-DSS distinction, it is easier to think of enrollment management as a part of an information system rather than the other way around. Information can be the unifying concept around which enrollment management processes are constructed.

MIS and DSS distinctions are also often based on the false dichotomy of executive decisions versus everyone else's decisions (implicit in Jones, 1982; and McDade, 1987). A few individuals may be ultimately responsible for strategic decisions, but the choice process has both local characteristics, such as the admissions office, and global characteristics, such as the entire college. The power of information is not limited to its use at the top of the organization.

Taking a broad systems approach does not mean that administrators should play fast and loose with terminology. The words *management information systems* that make up MIS should probably be reordered as "ISM": *information, systems, and manage-*

ment. This order more clearly reflects the theory and practice of information use in colleges and universities.

Five assumptions set the context for the discussions that follow. First, this chapter is written primarily for the directors or deans who form the bridge between operational and strategic activities. They understand with equal clarity what is going on now and what needs to be done for the future. Second, there is no one best information system for enrollment management. Third, information systems continually evolve. Fourth, system development and use is a collaborative effort. Fifth, computers are necessary for information systems, but they are only a tool and not an end in themselves. Although this may seem obvious, it is easy to mistake the acquisition of computers for the development of an effective information system. These assumptions were derived from several areas: the history of computing in higher education (Masland, 1985; Green and Gilbert, 1988); descriptions of the growth of electronic data processing into information systems technology (Andriole, 1989; Somogyi and Galliers, 1987); recent approaches in systems development theory (Hurtubise, 1984; Land, 1987b); and the growth in communications technology.

Most people believe that the technology of MIS/DSS is difficult to understand, while the conceptual framework is easy to understand. Just the reverse is true. For example, people get glassy eyed when discussions turn to LANs, data switches, data structures, logical and physical records, or VGA or RGB monitors. Once technical issues are defined, however, they are relatively easy to deal with because they have clear-cut answers. The real problems arise from a misunderstanding of the concepts of information systems. Designers and users of an information system should keep at least three things in mind when interacting with technical support staff:

1. Be prepared to explain any managerial jargon to people outside of your area of expertise. Ask the technical staff to explain their jargon. Be both a teacher and a learner. It is ironic but true that many information systems fail because users and designers do not communicate well.

2. Do not be afraid to say, "What does that mean and how does it affect me?" Be prepared to listen, take notes, think, and ask questions.
3. Recognize and act upon the fact that both you and the specialist will often display the "mathematician's syndrome": "He wrote A, said B, and meant C." Without clear communication between managers and specialists, a good information system is unlikely to emerge.

Data and Information

It is usual to take the statistical approach and describe data as deriving from observation or measurement and quantify them (Jones, 1982). Thus 3.459 is a student's cumulative GPA, 427 is the number of graduating seniors, and 12 is the code for enrollment in a college or for the geographical region where an applicant lives; these are all data.

To obtain or use a piece of data, one must know to what it refers: for example, students, books, or classrooms. Then one has to have in mind a particular descriptor: a student's GPA, a mathematics book, or a room number. One then writes a code: 3.459, LC124.59, or WH108. One might also consider a student's gender, the size of a book, or the number of chairs in the room and write F, 9×6, or 127. However, anything cannot be read into the data—if a student's GPA suggests to an observer that the student might be eligible to graduate cum laude, the observer is overstepping the bounds of data and entering, ever so slightly, into the realm of information, because the observer is bringing a set of assumptions and inferences to bear on the numbers.

Might there be other things besides numbers or codes that qualify as data? Would the statement "Fifty-five undergraduates assembled on the sidewalk outside of the president's office last night" be a piece of data? It would be as long as nothing was read into the statement. If someone's reaction was, "Were the police called to disperse them?" then he or she is assuming more than might be intended. A thorough discussion here about quantitative and qualitative data, objective and subjective data, or normative references to data is unnecessary (see, for example, Jones, 1982; Lincoln and Guba, 1985). The point is that as managers begin to design an information system, they must consider what basic objects are to constitute data and what are to be considered information.

The essence of information as opposed to data is this: information is intended to eliminate uncertainty whereas data are not (Ricker, 1979; Hurtubise, 1984). In fact, from a coding theory view, the most important ingredient of information is "surprise," or the appropriate exchange of knowledge for uncertainty (Hamming, 1980). Information can be defined as "a formatted object (endowed with identifiable forms) artificially created by the human being to represent a type of event which he can perceive and identify in the real world" (J. L. Lemoigne, as cited in Hurtubise, 1984, p. 23). Information, then, is what decision makers need in order to decide. Since knowing what is uncertain and what is needed to remove that uncertainty is a process, rather than a static structure, the MIS/DSS context must be dynamic and emphasize the roles that information processing plays with the managers who must make sense of their environments (Earl and Hopwood, 1987).

If these different perspectives are combined, information can be defined as data + context + purpose + surprise. That we need data is clear enough. As for context, why were those fifty-five students outside the president's home — to protest or to sing "Happy Birthday"? Are the students on a GPA = 4.0 list part-time or full-time? Is the student with a GPA of 2.0 an undergraduate or a graduate student? Obviously, context is the framework that distinguishes one piece of data from another.

If context is always associated with the data, what about purpose? Purpose differs because it is relative to the user. The registrar's purpose in sending a department chair a list of graduate students with 2.0 GPAs might be to suggest that they be dropped from the department. The chair's purpose might be to design interventions in order to raise their GPAs. The purpose of gathering information about protesting students might be to show them support or to discipline them.

Jones (1982) has written that in order for information to

be accurate in the way that data are supposed to be accurate, it must be interpreted by the receiver in the way intended by the provider. This is clearly not always the case. Indeed, in a strategic mode, a person might seek or receive data + context and use them in ways not intended by the sender. For much operational communication, especially within an institution, managers should first take the data + context message as intended, and then, if needed, turn it to their purposes.

Surprise, as with the removal of uncertainty, is difficult to deal with because it is different not only from data and context, but from purpose as well. A full discussion would require addressing the modes and roles of decision making. Suffice it to say, to eliminate surprise one must design an information system containing data, context, and purpose, but there is no easy way to decide on the precise forms of these three elements.

Systems

There are no generally accepted definitions of a system, whether we are talking about an economy as a system, a university as a system, the Enrollment Management Office as a system, or a system of six PCs networked together. What most definitions have in common is that the systems view must be global and include the dynamic relationships and links between parts, and that the system as a whole must have a purpose (Hurtubise, 1984). At various levels in a college or university, a system's purpose might be identified with a mission, goals, or objectives, as described in Chapter Two.

The systems approach to information management is global and macroscopic and must have at the same time the decompositional properties of analysis and the compositional properties of synthesis. To consider a phenomenon from both of these views is not easy because people want information that is *systematic:* detailed, sequential, certain, and complete. Trying to develop an information system using the systematic approach, however, is wrong.

An information system has three principal information

sources: the real world, or a portion of it of interest to the user; the designed information system, such as a computer system that tries to model the real world in a one-to-one fashion; and the informal undesigned system of people who provide evaluative or supplementary information to the designed model (Land, 1987a). Hence, an information system is a bridge between the real world system, the designed model system, and the human system of roles, relationships, and needs that forms the unit using the system. All three systems must be analyzed separately and also considered as parts of a whole to design and implement an information system.

Seven design systems for computers have been identified by Andriole (1989) as satisfying the operational or the tactical and strategic needs of an office or institution. In the strict sense, only the last three might be considered systems as discussed here. These seven systems are:

File drawer systems, in which the aim is immediate access to data (such as displaying a student admissions application)

Data analysis systems, in which data can be manipulated according to a set collection of operations (such as computing a GPA or creating a standard report on applicants by region)

Analysis information systems, which provide access to a number of data bases (such as comparing financial aid data with registration data or ad hoc reports)

Accounting systems, which can model planned actions based on standard well-defined accounting or routinized definitions (such as budget forecasting or recruiter contact scheduling)

Representational systems, which can estimate consequences of planned actions based on models that have parameters that are not well-defined (such as enrollment forecasting or market projections)

Optimization systems, which provide guidelines for action by providing optimal solutions subject to constraints

(such as finding out the number of students to recruit given budget needs, residence-hall space, and availability of instructors for a required English course)

Suggestion systems, which can provide specific decisions for well-defined and well-structured but mechanically difficult tasks (such as a decision to build or not build a new residence hall based on a complicated series of financial investment calculations, enrollment projections, and availability and costs of staff).

Data-oriented systems, the first three in the list, can solve most operational, transactional, and some tactical needs of a user by supporting data retrieval and basic forms of analysis. Model-oriented systems, the last three, rely on simulations and prescriptive practices, and can solve most tactical and strategic problems. The accounting system is a step between the data-oriented and model-oriented systems. It should be remembered that the accounting system uses routine procedures, but is not limited to what business offices do.

The order of these systems is evolutionary, from simple to complex, and they might be implemented in that sequence rather than all at once. If the statement "You must crawl before you can walk" has any meaning here, it would suggest that enrollment managers and their staffs concentrate on the first three or four computer systems first. Then, as their experience and needs change, they can expand their systems. A designed information system should certainly stretch the users and their imagination, but it should not be so far ahead of how they are currently doing their work that it alienates them (Land, Le Quesne, and Wijegunaratne, 1989).

Management and Design

The users of an information system are its managers. Management includes system design, but design of a special kind done in a special way, consistent with modern management theories such as contingency theory.

A traditional approach to designing a system, especially a computer system, can be thought of as a triangle sitting on a wide base. The inside of the triangle is empty. On the left leg is a team of users; on the right is a team of technical specialists. A decision is made at the apex to design and install a system. The specialists meet with the users, review procedural manuals, and start detailing a system. As time progresses, each team moves down the legs of the triangle, getting farther apart as the specialists grow frustrated with the users, and the users receive information that increases their uncertainty. Eventually, a system is *presented* to the users — the broad base of the triangle — which has only one characteristic of an information system: it is on a computer. This approach almost always fails except for the simplest of systems (see, for example, Land, 1987a; Hurtubise, 1984; Davies, 1987; Land, LeQuesne, and Wijegunaratne, 1989).

This approach usually fails because the specialists' model of the world and the users' model of the world are different. The systematic approach, besides wrongly assuming a sequential, ordered, and known world, fails to consider the human system within the office and the gulf between the world of the specialist and the professional consumer of the information.

What is needed is a shared, participatory approach. It can be illustrated by a triangle resting on its apex (rather than its base), and in which there is an "S" that represents the interactive and iterative actions between the teams as time goes by. The end of the process is the single point at the bottom of the triangle where the users and specialists merge their worlds. Although this may seem to be a precarious way to balance a triangle, it can be done, and it is required to develop effective information systems.

Two kinds of participation are important in the design of the system. The first is participation in decision making, whereby the user is permitted to choose among alternatives presented by the designer — creating the first model. The second is participation by the user in the analysis, design, and implementation of the system — creating the second model. In the creation of the second model, the strongest form of responsible participation allows the users full authority to make decisions, involve other user groups, consult with specialists as needed, and generally be an essential part of the building of their own information system. Their action is constrained only by a few issues related to management coordination and the compatibility of hardware and software systems.

How might this approach be accomplished? A possible model is a systems approach known as prototyping (Boar, 1984). The primary assumption of prototypers is that systems cannot be developed easily, quickly, or without substantial input from the users (Andriole, 1989). As the system is being developed, the users will be learning parts of it and making suggestions for improvement in an interactive way that becomes progressively complex. Overall, prototyping will produce an accepted and useful model of the organization and frequently do so in less time than the systematic approach. Such an iterative process does not mean prototyping is haphazard. In fact, it is highly structured and methodical as a systems approach (Andriole, 1989).

Boar (1984) lists three principles for this approach:

- *Capture* an initial set of needs, implement them quickly, and clearly convey to the users that the process is iterative and the model will be expanded and refined as mutual user and specialist understanding of the problem grows. Note that the users themselves might not fully understand what they want and need.
- *Define* the system through gradual and evolutionary discovery and understanding rather than the systematic approach of all-certainty and all-knowledge. This applies to both the user and specialist, since often enough the user is unsure why a particular function is done and how they do it might not be as rational as they first think.
- *Control* and minimize risk by accepting gradual learning, incremental change, and revisions as normal, required, and desired.

Boar's principles can be expanded as follows. First, the users' and the specialists' basic needs must be identified. Only initial or core needs must be identified, not all needs. Both users and specialists have to understand this point. If either has an all-or-nothing mentality, the design will fail.

Second, the specialists should quickly develop and deliver a working model of the system. They should teach the users good systems practices as the process continues. The specialists should also learn the importance the users put on their work and its role in the institution.

Third, the specialists should present and explain the prototype to all the users, not just to senior administrators, at their site and under working conditions and should ask about requirements, improvements, and extensions. All involved must recognize that the process is evolutionary and requires active participation.

Fourth, the specialists must demonstrate and revise the system again and again, until the system is satisfactory and understood by everyone involved.

Computer Models

For the purpose of illustration, this section will focus on the information systems needs of a newly created enrollment management office. The office's first task will be to design an information system. How can the ideas in the first part of this chapter be applied? What issues need to be faced in this process?

Information and Records. How can a system be designed to remove as much uncertainty as possible? First, the staff of the office should write down everything they want to know, think they ought to know, and, in a perfect world, would be able to find out about all the elements of concern to the office. This material should be written in general terms. For example, its elements might include possible students, current students, economic conditions, market conditions, student services, new programs, things that affect retention, or changes in financial aid. Each of the elements should be rated as a piece of information: What is its uncertainty? What is its purpose? What is its context? And what data are required? What referents, descriptors, and codes do or might the data have?

This technique is a "top-down" approach, in which the office starts with the most general descriptions and then refines them, increasing their detail but all the time rating the elements as information. This process is best done in a relaxed setting, over many days, with a large blackboard or lots of paper and with the understanding that the task is difficult and might have to be repeated several times. It is not a systematic task and the participants will quickly find that they are not all-certain nor all-knowing.

If an element of this new system cannot be sensibly classified, it should be thrown out. It may be unnecessary, impossible to identify, or too uncertain to define. Next, the links and the relationships between the data elements must be identified to determine whether certain data belong in a different informational set than was first believed or whether such information should be in the system at all. Diagrams are helpful at this step.

Finally, the office should finish with an idea of what constitutes data for the new system under the many different global elements. Writing record descriptions of these elements is the easy part, and a specialist must help here. For any software system being used (such as a relational data base; see, for example, Lin, 1988; "Review of Data Management," 1990), room must be left for future record expansion. For example, if an applicant record is described, where can data elements be added when they are identified in the future? The system is evolutionary even after it is in place and being used.

Hardware and Software. After the preliminary work on systems design has been done and campus specialists contacted, the office must decide whether to use the university's centralized computer facilities with terminals, rely on some form of distributed system, or get their own stand-alone microcomputers (PCs). A full discussion of this topic would lead too far afield from enrollment management (see, for example, Ryland, 1988, for an overview and McCredie, 1983, for case studies describing different approaches to campus computing). In keeping with the information systems view, the users should have maximum control over both the design and use of the system. This suggests using PCs. PCs can increase communication in offices and enhance productivity (Ryland, 1988). With a PC and a mainframe, a user could, for example, compose a letter with a word processor and send it by electronic mail to a colleague down the street or across the world. PCs also give users the flexibility to analyze data and write reports exactly to individual specifications in a short time.

Gattiker, Gutek, and Berger (1988) report that PCs lessen users' alienation from technological change and enhance the quality of work life. PC users can learn by doing and by correcting errors as they occur. PCs are also fun and have a leveling effect: a staff member can become more proficient on one than the department head.

With the wide availability of communications software, the PC can function as a terminal to the institution's mainframe data bases, or the enrollment manager can purchase time on commercial data bases to seek external data. This software can be used to "upload" or "download" data to or from a mainframe in straightforward and easy ways.

Technical questions of speed of transfer of data and compatibility between machines do arise, but they are usually easy to solve, especially if the download mode is the routine and the users are not requesting that the transcripts of every student be loaded onto their PC. The upload mode raises serious issues about data ownership and responsibility, which will be discussed later.

The PC can be used by itself to do local work. The availability and diversity of software are astonishing. Choosing software, however, does not have to be overwhelming. The campus should have preferred products that will be supported, frequently determined by their function, local fit, and market survivability. Enrollment managers should rely on specialists, but also ask their peers at other institutions what they use and why.

A major issue is whether the office should use an existing commercial product or write its own software in collaboration with a specialist. An existing product for data base management and report generation, for example, might fit well with the information systems ideas formulated in an office, but it might require modification of what the users want the system to do. The key is flexibility. Approaching the question inflexibly, demanding information so special that no existing product can provide it, is a symptom of systematic thinking. If the users and the specialists can both agree that a standard product will not meet the office's needs, prototyping should be started.

Hardware systems should be straightforward, "take out of the box and set up" PC systems that are either IBM-like or Macintosh-like. However, some PCs designed to be like other systems do not actually run all the software designed for those systems. If a system requires the vendor to send in a team of experts to install it, it is probably unnecessarily complicated (unless the office purchased a very fancy network along with the basic systems).

The office must also decide on storage devices and printers. The basic guide is easy: Consult with specialists and rely on systems from reputable vendors that have "in the box" configurations. Designing a system that is larger than is currently necessary but not so large that its potential is wasted is the best strategy.

If users have doubts about either hardware or software, they can, first, let the market guide them. Over time, technology for microcomputers has become more or less stable. Second, they can ask what peers use and why. Third, they can ask for demonstrations of hardware on the local site using the office's versions of the compatible software and not the vendor's. Software can be demonstrated using in-house data and a simple prototype. Fourth, they can get the names and telephone numbers of users of the hardware or software and call them.

Networking. Networks connect PCs to allow, for example, electronic mail and the sharing of software, files, and devices such as disks and printers (a local area network, or LAN). Networks have human as well as technical advantages: they can create positive, nonthreatening environments and a climate of peer support (Pliskin, 1989). Usually, networks are either essential or unnecessary (Seymour and Dvorak, 1990). They are sometimes expensive, and it is easy to "overnetwork" a system; that is, to use networks because of their "bells and whistles" rather than because of need.

O'Malley (1990) suggests alternatives to networks, one of which is a number of PCs that share a single printer by using a simple switch. Another alternative is a dedicated PC with a modem that can be quickly accessed and from which a user can download files or check electronic mail. Small offices with a few PCs can use a simple and friendly device: users can put the file on a diskette and go for a visit.

Management Support and Training. In any design situation, it is absolutely essential that the director of enrollment management or another top officer support the decision and efforts to design the system at every step of the way (Land, 1987a; Land, Le Quesne, and Wijegunaratne, 1989; Pliskin, 1989). Also, a single person in the office should be designated as the go-between with technical specialists. This designation does not invalidate the user participatory approach, but it recognizes a simple reality: the office must function as the system is being developed, and it is not practical to always meet as a group to discuss the system. However, this go-between is the office representative and not the owner of the system. Office participation in the system design is still essential.

A training plan to use the system is essential to strategic management (Rothwell and Kazanas, 1989). The office representative can play a key role in the training plan. As the person closest to the system and its development, the go-between must act as a resource person and trainer during and after development. As a natural outgrowth of the participatory design approach, most users feel a sense of ownership in the system and would enjoy teaching office newcomers.

Security and Ownership. Who owns the data on the system and who is responsible for security? In the participatory system the answer to the first question is "no one" and to the second, "each person."

Viewing the college or university as the owner of the data and each office as the trustee of its data is preferred. Trusteeship confers some rights, but it also has responsibilities. Letting another office use the data for which the enrollment management office is responsible should involve negotiation so that some but not all of an individual's responsibilities can be transferred to others along with the rights to use the data. For example, if an office has the authority to publicize enrollment figures and another office needs the data, the authority to publicize does not go along with the data. Similarly, attempting to upload from a PC to the mainframe data base without due regard for the integrity of the data and the way they effect the data base is a violation of others' rights to use those data.

A few simple rules can keep data secure. First, if a PC can be locked when not in use, it should be. Second, confidential data should be kept on a removable diskette that can be made as secure as a file folder. Third, if the system has password protection for file access, the password should be changed frequently. The password should not be a family name and should not be posted on the monitor as a memory aid. Fourth, erase sensitive material in the "zero-over" mode as soon as it is no longer being used — do not leave it on a general access hard disk. It might be tedious, but large files can be transferred to a secure account on the mainframe, erased on the PC, and then downloaded in the morning. The trusteeship of the data should be taken seriously.

Almost certainly, the needs and mission of the office will change over time. The advantage of the systems approach is that such change is manageable, especially if the prototyping strategy (or its variants) is used to constantly refine and improve the system. Of course, some day it might be necessary, due to fundamental changes in the conceptual system or the usual advances in technology, to start all over. But the second time should be much easier.

Chapter 14

Case Study:
How Information Systems
Support
Enrollment Management

Mariea T. Noblitt

This chapter presents a detailed look at the issues involved in developing a sound student data base for a graduate school at Cornell University in Ithaca, New York. Although the chapter looks at a graduate school, the principles behind the creation of a useful student data base are similar for both undergraduate and graduate programs.

Student information systems must be enabling. That is, they must create and then sustain an environment that supports the people who are using them. Data bases are created around the need to store, retrieve, and interpret data. Enrollment managers, however, must always remember that the primary purpose of manipulating data is to enable them to deal with individual prospective students. A school may attract a large group of applicants, but it must enroll them one at a time.

Data base management systems can be designed with personal attention to students as the most important function. For example, applicants who are by name instantly recognized by staff members become more interested in a school. A data base system can be designed to access data rapidly so staff can quickly respond to calls from applicants and call applicants by their first names. Another form of personal attention is to ensure that system users feel they function in accord with their own beliefs

243

and are convinced of the importance of what they are doing within the organization. A system that gives each admissions counselor and support staff member feedback on specific functions he or she is performing and how these functions impact enrollment encourages these feelings.

Admissions staff members provide a service, and the information system should be designed with this function in mind. The single most important point here is not what the system can do, but what the staff members can do with the system. The system should enable them to meet their own standards of job performance. One result of such a design is that applicants will become familiar with staff who are open and personal and, during the admissions process, get to know them as individuals as well. Often, applicants will begin asking for staff members by name. This kind of interaction is often cited as decisive in an applicant's enrollment decision. The impact this staff behavior is having on enrollment can then be shared with the support staff so they know that staff members are using the system in an effective way and are having a positive impact on enrollment. The personal validation admissions staff members receive invests them in the process, and they perform their jobs knowing that they are contributing to enrollment management functions. Too often, systems are viewed as producing numbers of matriculants rather than contributing to a process that supports institutional goals. Creating an environment that places a priority on people, both those within the organization and prospective students, results in support for the administrative functions of a particular division and the educational goals of an institution. The technology supports an atmosphere in which everybody wins.

This chapter will not examine the highly technical aspects of designing systems. Instead, it will focus on how the process of system design can be an organizing event for an institution and an exercise in institutional planning. The chapter will include a discussion on how an institution can use a student data base management system to interpret the organization and the information it uses to determine its effectiveness and efficiency. Organizational structure, departmental procedures, data format, and system design will be discussed and shown within the context of enrollment management strategy. Discussions of recruitment and retention will be focused around data storage, retrieval, and interpretation techniques. Finally, a case study of the process, implementation, and evaluation of a student data base system at the Johnson Graduate School of Management at Cornell University will be used to illustrate in detail each of these areas.

The Need for Communication

Only recently has the design of student data base systems involved division managers. Before this shift, managers were reluctant to take the responsibility for organizing and designing information or to take the initiative to communicate what was needed to programmers. This was a fundamental mistake. Systems designed without the input of the division manager and staff are doomed to inefficiency or failure. Without the participation of the users, programmers produce systems that are operationally correct but do not meet the users' needs. This problem is complicated further by faulty communication between managers and programmers. The manager begins by trying to explain what is needed, and the programmer projects back what is heard in what sounds like a foreign language. This can be very intimidating for the manager and frustrating for the programmer.

Many institutions use a mainframe computer to house information on applicants, but these systems were designed primarily to perform specific functions like registration and billing and were put in place as a response to an administrative directive rather than as part of a cohesive enrollment management strategy. Managers who must use systems they did not help to design either must compromise on how they want to do their jobs or give up certain functions they want to perform. Moreover, users of the system become alienated because they feel that their input was not wanted or was ignored. Users of a system are the experts in how functions need to be designed; they are highly motivated to have a system that is responsive because they want what they need to do their job, gain recognition, and advance professionally. The best way to design a student data base management system is to have the users of it participate. Often, the problem is one of vocabulary rather than knowledge and is easily corrected with some study by managers and staff. This new dialogue between users and programmers eliminates intimidation that delays or deters the development of needed systems.

Functional Audits

An institution can use the design and installation of a student data base management system as an opportunity to reevaluate how well it is responding to the demands of enrollment management. By taking a comprehensive look at all departments and activities that support enrollment (like admissions, financial aid, marketing, recruitment, registration, retention, and placement), an institution can better understand how information, people, and skills should be organized to support each department and activity individually and collectively.

A functional audit is one way to pursue such a reevaluation. An audit helps managers understand what the problems are, which ones can be solved, and what has to be done to solve them. Simply stated, a functional audit helps uncover what is working to support the institution and what is not working. Although this strategy sounds easy, it is often overlooked in the haste to simply install a system.

Functional audits take many forms and look at such things as the procedures followed for handling the mail, individual staff members and the jobs they perform, procedures for processing and tracking applications, and paper flow in the office. For example, by knowing how the phone is being answered by the staff, a manager knows how staff members are responding and interacting with the public and if this interaction needs to be improved. Through looking at this kind of activity managers gain the best understanding of how well their people and procedures are functioning and what information and support systems are needed to support their division.

The application and the design of student data base systems play a critical role in enrollment management. It is difficult, for example, to create an environment of service when the design does not include specifications that enable the staff to give service. This audit process, in effect, is the beginning of a planning exercise for the institution.

Many institutions do planning. Unfortunately, they are often forced to be reactive rather than proactive in admissions because of system limitations and a lack of accurate data. Operational audits are a great help in carefully evaluating what is needed to support enrollment and developing strategic plans of action. Each office, by carefully assessing what it needs to support the overall enrollment plan, becomes invested in succeeding and is prepared when problems surface. Planning brings offices together and creates the communication links by which institutions thrive. Student data base management systems can then be designed and implemented around a factual basis that is widely shared.

Personnel, eager to solve problems, sometimes approach system design by proposing to solve every problem identified with a single comprehensive system. This attempt often fails because there is no one student data base management system that will address the uniqueness of both all office functions and the people who have developed procedures. A single system cannot be all things to all people.

A functional audit prevents an institution from trying to fit all administrative functions onto the main campus computer. Too often, attempts to merge all functions on one computer force admissions to eliminate the personal elements so important to making a student information system useful. Audits can also identify the costs of maintaining an old system or implementing a new one. It is not unusual for an institution to avoid implementing a new student information system and dismantling an existing one. This can be disruptive to the institution and very time consuming. However, the costs of maintaining an old system can exceed those of implementing new systems. Audits make evident whether or not current technology meets managers' needs and whether or not new technology is needed. An audit provides the basis for obtaining needed equipment, staff, and support by projecting what benefits the institution will gain with the ability to be responsive to the problems that have been identified.

Brief mention should be made here regarding the expense of installing systems. Student data base management systems require funding that can ensure that they are designed, documented, and installed properly. It is of no use to invest the time to design something only to find it cannot be funded. Money, time, and staff must be committed and a realistic timetable established for installation before any new system is designed and installed.

The Need for Tracking Information

As the sophistication of the admissions process has changed, so have the requirements to do the job. It sounds like a catch 22, but if information management skills are not learned, then information and data cannot be obtained that make the case for the kinds of support needed to do a job well. Many routine tasks are easily performed by a microcomputer, making the learning investment well worthwhile. Moreover, the fundamentals of data base management are easily learned and there are currently many tutorials available that make this process quite painless. These new concepts allow for information tracking, which enables staff to use information more effectively in each division of an institution. Since enrollment management systems are at their best when designed with the ability to track outcomes, tracking programs are some of the first things that must be put in place whenever any system is being proposed.

Tracking information provides the foundation for strategic planning. With the ability to organize, store, and retrieve accurate data, managers can be sure that they are succeeding at improving areas identified as needing attention during the functional audit. Tracking allows the institution to evaluate whether a new marketing, recruitment, or enrollment plan is effective and efficient. It directs the limited resources of the institution toward those activities that ensure the school is getting the most value for its money.

Admissions is an integral and critical office for an institution. Almost all institutions are tuition driven. Information obtained through the admissions process is the basis upon which

an institution plans growth or reductions in enrollment so that
it is not caught with empty or overcrowded residence halls and
classrooms. When data collection can be shown to support the
institution in substantial ways, managers can make a powerful
argument for obtaining the support needed to continue data collection. But how many institutions are capable of looking at how
cost effective their data collection is?

Each year hundreds of admissions counselors take to the
highways to recruit students for their institutions. They take
with them thousands of brochures produced at relatively high
cost. They also are paid a per diem for their travel expenses.
While out recruiting, each counselor sees hundreds of prospective students. The counselors return to their institutions with
prospect cards and give them to support staff. The support staff
types mailing labels and the information that has been requested
is sent.

What happens to the information on those prospect cards?
Without a tracking system it is thrown away without any attempt to assess how these trips are contributing to enrollment.
Through tracking, institutions can learn who is expressing interest, how many students contacted actually apply, and how
many admitted actually enroll. This information is invaluable
for enrollment management as it helps in planning for operating
expenses. If information on prospects is not being tracked, the
number of catalogues and viewbooks to produce each year will
be based solely on the greatest number previously distributed,
that is, an arbitrary figure. The cost of producing these publications will be higher than necessary because many more than
are needed will be produced each year. Postage costs are like-
wise inflated by lack of information. With tracking, duplicate
or triplicate requests for materials can be prevented. Costs of
postage, materials, and labor can be controlled. If the volume
of requests increases, tracking that is in place can identify the
reasons for the increase and affect managers' ability to anticipate enrollment. Recruitment budgets can be reduced because
managers know how attendance at recruitment programs is influencing enrollment and can send staff only to those programs
that have an impact on enrollment. A simple program that could

track this kind of information can save thousands of dollars in operating costs because hard data are available to back up proposals for office support. There is no question as to whether or not additional computers or staff are needed because managers document their proposals with outcomes using figures for money saved and figures for increases in application fee revenues resulting from better marketing strategies.

Tracking also affects the professional growth of the admissions and support staff. Admissions counselors do a difficult job and receive little feedback. How do they know what impact all their effort is having on their ability to enroll students? Without the ability to track each program they attended and the students they saw, they cannot know if what they are doing is making a difference. They move on to professions that give them a better measure of the impact they are having on the organization. Expertise becomes rare in a profession with high turnover. Searching for and training staff on a regular basis can be a significant drain on an institution's resources. The ability to track the impact of staff participation supports not just marketing and enrollment management but also the individual whose efforts account for success in these areas.

Symptoms of the Need for a
Student Information System

Institutions rely on the distribution, gathering, and interpretation of information. If, for example, an institution has a problem with name recognition, it needs a way of communicating with inquirers and a distribution channel so that it can get the name of the school and information to prospective students by using direct mail. Without a student data base and tracking capability, this task is difficult, if not impossible, because there is no way to produce the mailings or track their results. An institution may find that it has adequate facilities and faculty but that its inquirers do not become applicants. If inquirers do apply and are admitted, they may regularly attend other schools or those schools judged to be weaker than the institution. Diagnosing what is happening here can be as simple as having the ability to mail a questionnaire with acceptance letters asking applicants to tell why they are enrolling at the institution and why not if they are enrolling elsewhere. Any student data base system has this capability. The institution can then store, retrieve, and interpret this information and be sure it has mechanisms in place to deal with the problems that have been identified. Good information directs marketing and recruiting strategies and provides the basis for a plan of action to address enrollment concerns.

A constant fluctuation of enrollment figures is a serious symptom. Since most institutions are tuition driven, they must enroll a certain number of applicants each year. An effective system for tracking makes it possible to project enrollments accurately to reduce serious stresses on facilities such as laboratories, counseling services, and residence halls. The institution can plan and execute a realistic operating budget, and student morale is enhanced by a stable learning and working environment.

Another symptom is that information cannot be obtained during the admissions process. This means that managers are unable to identify potential problems in meeting targets set by the campus administration. With tracking, managers are able to get a summary of ongoing admissions activity and know what to correct. Faculty complaints about the size of classes or the quality of the enrolled students can be adjusted for, if necessary, by going to standby lists. Managers are no longer in a constant state of crisis management, and the institution is less at risk.

An additional symptom, often overlooked in the decision to implement a system, is chronic complaining about customer service. Admissions work comes in large volumes and is inherently a deadline business. With a system that allows frontline staff members to be responsive to the needs of applicants, the staff members' jobs do not become punishing. A student information system makes it easy for staff to answer routine questions regarding application or decision status. They do not get frustrated and do not pass their frustration on to the applicant. Since applicants usually develop a view of the institution by how well they are treated by support staff, a strong case can be made for systems that support people trying to give service.

Ineffective publications can benefit from a student data base and tracking system. Admissions offices utilize publications to educate prospective students about the benefits of attending their institutions. Having an efficient way to store, retrieve, and interpret data on the institution's clientele reduces the risk of an institution's marketing only to itself. The information being distributed may be seriously out of touch with what the clientele want to know. Market research yields valuable information on how an institution is perceived. If, for example, prospective students feel that the institution does not place its graduates well, the institution can enter information on graduates into the data base and summarize it in future publications. Tracking this information allows for evaluation of its impact on targeted applicants and prospective students who reflect the profile of the institution's graduates. The tracking program can reveal problems with what the institution is or is not communicating about itself, and enables the school to reorganize or rewrite brochures to address these concerns, improve publication design and content, and sharpen its marketing segmentation.

Problems Addressed by a Data Base System

Up to now, the discussion has centered around why a data base and information management system should be implemented and ways of identifying when one is needed. The following sections examine what an institution needs to consider before, during, and after a system is implemented. Student information systems can address a variety of problems. The designs that have the most impact are those that address a specific goal or target for improvement. For example, if an institution has a problem with attracting enough high-quality applicants, one goal of the system may be to contain functions that will increase applications.

Student data base management systems are the most useful when they enable the institution to perform specific functions and to answer straightforward questions. Some of these questions include: Have applications increased or their quality improved over the past admissions cycle? Is the institution trying to increase applications? By what percentage? What kind of information is needed to monitor the process? How often will the information need to be extracted? What format does the information need to be in so it can be interpreted intelligently? Does the institution have a problem with retention and, if so, why? Starting out with a list of questions is one of the most effective ways to begin the design of a system.

Student information systems have a less than obvious effect on an organization. Not only are they the beginning of clearly stated objectives for effective operation, but they also have a significant impact on the expertise required of staff hired to support them. It is not unusual to hear stories about staff who have been loyal to an institution but who lack the skills needed for enrollment management. The introduction of new technology may force managers to ask a series of questions about staff training. If this is the case, additional questions must be answered. Who will supply training? What will happen if current staff are not eager or willing to learn new skills? The implementation of student data base management systems has a way of causing organizations to ask tough questions that can result in benefits for both individuals and the institution, if professional development is supported.

After a commitment to a systems approach is reached, institutions face more questions concerning the technology to be used for its implementation. Should microcomputer or mainframe technology be used? Does the institution have the commitment of resources? Is the time frame for installation realistic? Can someone from the staff oversee the installation? Will the department support this technology on its own or depend on the computer services department? Unless the managers of departments have a clear idea of what they are trying to accomplish, they will be second-guessed by others. These questions are a good starting place for an institution that is seriously considering designing and installing its own system. If answers to the questions are not readily available, it would be inadvisable to undertake such an activity. It would be better to return to the original audit and reevaluate desired outcomes.

Technical Considerations for Installing a System

What issues an institution decides to address will have implications for the technical specifications, the structure of the data base, the content and design of application materials, and how information is organized. For the purpose of example, this discussion will focus on the issues that relate to the functions of an admissions office.

One of the first questions that must be answered is whether the data base is being designed to support transactional processing, or daily operations of the office. Transactional processing includes such activities as producing folder and mailing labels, sending letters, and marketing through direct mail. To support these activities, operating procedures for the processing of applications must be in place. The outcomes of the system must be stated in operational terms, such as "Lower the lag time between the request for information and when it is mailed from three weeks to one day." The system can then be designed to supply the proper technical capabilities for storage of data and fast retrieval. If the office is going to develop a tracking system to help increase applications, it must decide whether to start tracking from the inquiry or the applicant stage. Applications may number in the hundreds, but inquiries may number in the thousands. The tracking system chosen has technical implications for both the design of the data base and the size of the machine that will be used to store the data. The data to be tracked on each inquirer or applicant must also be decided. If information entered into the system is being obtained from application materials, the design should include the ability to follow the flow of information as it is being extracted from the forms. Information in the data base should also be clearly presented on the screen so that it can be updated and accessed easily by staff answering the phone. Security of the data, especially if machines are in a public area, is also a concern.

A data base can also be designed as a decision support system of the office. Information to support enrollment management decisions should include such activities as analysis of recruitment, admissions offers, and financial aid awards and information on matriculation, retention, attrition, and demographic variables. This information is the basis of planning and enrollment management. Student information systems do not have to be developed separately for transactional processing and decision support. To support both, however, a design must be in place that outlines the data to be tracked, the format of the data, the frequency of use, the output specifications, and the format and frequency of reporting capabilities.

Up to now, discussions have centered on the types of activities that must be conducted and concerns that must be addressed to develop a student data base management system. The next section of this chapter offers a case study of the admissions audit and the design and installation of a student data base management system at the Johnson Graduate School of Management at Cornell University.

Johnson Graduate School of Management

In 1984, the author was hired as director of admissions at the Johnson Graduate School of Management at Cornell University. What follows is the process used to develop a student data base management system at the school and the results of this effort.

Problem Definition. Between 1980 and 1984, the Johnson Graduate School of Management at Cornell University had experienced three name changes in a span of four years. The program in public health had been discontinued and the name was changed from the School of Business and Public Administration to simply the Cornell Graduate School of Management. That same year, the school received a gift of $20 million and changed its name again to the Samuel Curtis Johnson Graduate School of Management. The frequent changes caused a problem with name recognition.

The school was posting acceptance rates that were as high as 48 percent. This meant the school had to admit almost half of its applicant pool because it was able to enroll only 33 percent of those offered admissions. Neither of these rates was competitive with the school's peer institutions.

The school had no historical data base that had integrity. A manual system was in place using a Rolodex and a Magcard typewriter. No direct mail marketing could be done because no word processor was in use. The school did not track information at the inquiry stage and did not know what percentage of inquirers became applicants or from what area of the country most inquiries came. The school had no accurate data that could be used for planning purposes. One computer terminal was in the admissions office, and it allowed one staff person to enter, but not to extract, data.

Publications had not been revised for several years and had content and distribution problems. High costs for repetitive mailings occurred because applicants were making multiple requests for information due to lag time in excess of forty-five days between the initial request for and the mailing of that information.

Admissions personnel attended many recruitment programs, but the impact of their efforts could not be assessed and the school continued to support high budgets for travel. Volunteer alumni were used to interview applicants, but there was no feedback to them on this activity regarding the applicants, admissions decisions, or the impact of the interviewing on enrollment.

These problems may seem severe, but they are similar to the difficulties evident at most institutions. What follows is the strategy used to address these problems.

Operational Audit and Findings. The audit began by looking for and reviewing any information found on applicants and how the school was perceived by prospective students. It also reviewed every procedure, operation, and staff function in the admissions office and all materials being distributed to applicants.

Fortunately, a questionnaire had been included with every admissions letter for several years. This questionnaire requested information on what school applicants were going to attend and the reasons for their choice. It also contained comparative information in a variety of areas, such as curriculum, perceived reputation, and location. Although this information was available prior to the beginning of the audit, little use had been made of it. The questionnaires revealed that there was a perceived weakness in the school's ability to place applicants in careers like investment banking. Applicants also reported that they found it difficult to understand the school's curriculum or course offerings because of unclear presentation in the catalogue.

The operational audit revealed that there was a compartmentalization of staff functions. Certain staff members only did certain things. If the person who typed mailing labels was ill, no one else felt responsible for producing mailing labels. In addition, inquiry names and addresses, once put on a label, were not retained, so there was no accurate record of demand for materials. This made it hard to project the number of catalogues or other promotional materials to be printed each year or to determine in which areas of the country the school had good institutional representation.

Responsibility for mailing catalogues and applications was divided between university and business school offices. This expense was unusually high given the volume of requests for information at the time of this audit. A high rate of duplicate mailings resulted from the school's not having a mechanism to track what materials had been sent and by which office or if materials were being requested repeatedly by the same person.

Desired Outcomes. The audit took approximately one month. During this time, the staff outlined operating procedures and how to implement them and determined what information was to be tracked and what goals and outcomes were desired. The staff determined that the plan could be implemented by designing a student data base system and using microcomputer technology. The following goals were identified:

1. Increase the school's ability to enroll more of the applicants it was admitting. To be competitive with peer institutions, the school needed to lower the percentage of those admitted from 48 percent to 25 percent of applicants. The school needed to track better information on its inquiry and applicant pool.

2.   Eliminate enrollment fluctuations that the school had experienced and stabilize tuition revenue.
3.   Meet enrollment targets for tuition revenue by increasing the percentage of the students enrolled from 35 percent to 47 percent of those admitted.
4.   Improve customer service in order to make a more positive impression on inquirers.
5.   Design recruitment and marketing strategies around what applicants were reporting in order to communicate the correct perceptions about the school.

During the audit, information was listed that would be important to have for planning. This is where the initial design of the student information system began. A data base design was created that gave both transactional ability (to respond faster to inquirers and applicants) and decision support (to obtain accurate data to store, retrieve, study, and interpret outcomes).

Actions Taken. Catalogue and application materials were reorganized, redesigned, and rewritten. This forced the school to review its mission statement, as it was to be included in the new catalogue being designed. Computer data entry screens were designed to reflect the order of input of the information that was being requested. This proved to keep data entry time to a minimum.

Data were organized so they could be extracted whenever needed to give immediate feedback during and after the admissions cycle. Information retrieval was menu driven and did not require the user to be a sophisticated computer operator. Data to support the alumni volunteer groups who did admissions interviews were included in the design so these individuals would receive feedback and the school would learn what impact this activity was having on enrollment.

The data base was designed to report accurate profiles on applicants at any time during the admissions process. Information requested by the dean, faculty, recruiters, or any other administrative offices was to be available on the spot and admissions would not be dependent for it on any other office. In addition, the data base design gave instant feedback on enrollment goals that had been set by the faculty on an ongoing basis so any discrepancies could be corrected for during, and not after, the admissions process.

Customer service was improved by expanding the functions and services performed by support staff and introducing needed computers and staff willing to learn how to use them. The decision to introduce computers and the effect on support and professional staff was noticeable. Those who decided they did not want to invest the time to learn new skills pursued employment outside admissions, and those more eager and capable of learning new skills were hired. Many of the mundane tasks being performed by staff were now assigned to the computer, making admissions less oriented to paperwork and more oriented to contact with applicants. The emphasis of the admissions office was expanded from simply processing applications to identifying and recruiting the prospective students who were most likely to be successful at the school, admitting them, and then enrolling them. For example, admissions could now identify those applicants who had a higher chance of being admitted, get their applications to the admissions committee, process the decisions, and communicate the decisions within days of receiving application materials. The office could then solicit the help of alumni and staff to recruit those applicants. It could also track the impact of quicker decisions and see if the strategy and programs the school was implementing were, in fact, having the desired outcomes.

Problems in Implementation of the System. The normal admissions office routine was disrupted. The manual system, though tedious, had to be maintained in tandem with the new one. Data being entered into the new system had to be compared to the records being kept manually to ensure accuracy. This increased work load in the short term. Some staff members, not eager to learn the technology, were not using the system properly. This caused some initial inefficiency and morale problems.

There were difficulties in communication with the office of computer services. Admissions chose to purchase a microcomputer because of its low cost, but decentralized computing was not supported by the existing technical environment. These difficulties continued because central computing preferred to develop an admissions system compatible with its administrative software, without incorporating local admissions requirements.

A programmer who worked independently had to be hired. (To write a cohesive system, the programmer must have the system implementation as a full-time priority.) Each new module had to be tested for reliability and performance on a regular basis. The staff had to provide instant feedback so that the programmer could make the system perform according to functions needs. The system code had to be documented so that if the programmer left, another programmer could interpret it without having to spend large amounts of time. Staff wrote the user's manual while installing the system.

The first version of the student data base tracking system was installed in November 1985 and used to enroll the incoming class. The programmer spent fifty hours on this first version at a cost of $1,500. The school further invested $4,000 in the purchase of a microcomputer with a hard disk and a printer.

Evaluation. The system made an immediate and noticeable contribution to the admissions function. Applications increased 5 percent in the first year and continued to increase due to direct mail marketing and improved capability for market research.

The school's new image, presented through publications, attracted a higher quality of applicants. The mean GPA and GMAT scores rose for both attracted applicants and those that were enrolled. Applicants commented during interviews and on the questionnaires that the school's publications were among the best they had seen.

Admissions tracked participation in recruitment activities, maintaining those that worked and eliminating those that did not affect enrollment. This resulted in a $7,000 reduction in the travel budget. The school began admissions receptions, in which accepted applicants were invited to campus to meet with faculty. Eighty-five percent of those who attended the receptions enrolled. Activities such as these helped the school to increase yield by 15 percent in the first year. This tracking ability further assisted the establishment of consistent yield figures, and this eliminated enrollment fluctuations. It also helped in developing an operating budget that did not have to be adjusted midyear because of unforeseen problems or shortfalls.

With the continuing ability to track and interpret admissions activities and address concerns, the school lowered the percentage rate of those it had to admit to enroll a class from 48 percent to 17 percent. The school began posting acceptance rates that were competitive with its peer institutions.

The school was able to obtain accurate information on demographics and to implement better and more effective institutional planning. The school did not lose students because it was able to identify, admit, and then enroll those applicants who resembled the profile of its successful graduates.

The operating costs of the admissions office were decreased by $10,000. Postage expenses were decreased by $17,000. The size of the support staff was reduced by 50 percent, from four to two, for a savings of $34,000, including salaries and benefits.

The school was now able to correspond with inquirers and applicants on a regular basis. The time between requests and mailing of information dropped from forty-five days to one day. The school could also personalize those mailings. The image of the school changed as customer service was improved. The school was now being perceived differently by clientele interacting with support staff more interested in giving service.

The school was able to better identify its competition for matriculants and understand the criteria used by students in making comparisons. Strategies were planned that directed resources toward concerns noted by applicants. Financial aid award packages could be studied to see the impact they were having on matriculation.

The Johnson School was ranked fifth in the country as a business school in the November 1989 issue of *Business Week*. The criterion used to determine this rating was a survey of the students in attendance and company recruiters who hire them. Both administrators and faculty believe that the marketing and recruitment activities implemented by the school have contributed to this achievement. The school was able to identify and then enroll more highly qualified applicants. Recruiters, happy with the quality of students they were seeing, hired more of them, and the school got high ratings among this group of reviewers.

One primary reason that this system was so successful was that time was spent identifying the right problems to solve, implementing a system that had specific outcomes, and then tracking and interpreting the results. The time and effort were well worth it. This new technology allowed the school to hire and promote staff more eager to learn new skills. Annual salary increments have been high. Applicants now ask for members of the staff by name and cite the treatment they received during the admissions process as one of the primary reasons they decided to enroll.

The system installed is currently in use at ten other business schools. Savings to the school in the first year of implementation were $77,000. The savings included $17,216 on postage, $15,000 from staff reductions, $5,000 in travel expenses, $10,000 on overhead, and $30,000 on revenues (fees) for a total of $77,216.

The school experienced a 47 percent increase in applications in 1989. From 1984 to 1989, applications increased by 66 percent and yield improved by 25 percent. Table 14.1 shows improvement in admissions figures.

Table 14.1. Changes in Admissions Figures.

	1985	1986	1987	1988	1989
Total Inquiries	10,565	13,768	15,780	16,952	16,900
Total Applications	1,500	1,565	1,920	1,700	2,438
Total Offers	717	437	466	467	435
Total Enrolled	269	244	229	220	215
Acceptance Rates	48%	28%	24%	27%	17%
Yield	41%	47%	49%	47%	49%
GMAT	624	631	618	623	635
GPA	3.12	3.26	3.16	3.25	3.20

Chapter 15

Enrollment Management
in Action

Barry Abrams
Marsha Krotseng
Don Hossler

In this chapter, the enrollment management activities of two institutions, St. Mary's University in San Antonio, Texas, and the University of Hartford in West Hartford, Connecticut, will serve as case studies of enrollment management. These case studies provide a framework for integrating many of the organizational concepts and activities that have been discussed throughout this book. This chapter is not intended to suggest that these case studies present the best models; rather, the case studies should be viewed as providing readers with an opportunity to think through how enrollment management can be implemented or enhanced on their campuses. Questions that readers should consider are:

1. How did the enrollment management systems discussed in this chapter come into being? Are the histories of any of these examples similar to what is happening on your campus? What can you learn from comparing your campus to these examples?
2. Did key events or changes in personnel precipitate the emergence of these enrollment management systems?
3. What support was necessary from the president and senior-level administrators?
4. What key resources, either personnel or support systems (computer hardware, software, budget), will be essential for you to accomplish your enrollment management goals?

5. What are the strengths and the weaknesses of your current enrollment management system?

This chapter looks at St. Mary's University and the University of Hartford in detail, beginning with a brief description of the institution. Following the description, other areas will be discussed: development of enrollment management, attributes of enrollment management on each campus, results of enrollment management, problems encountered on each campus, and concluding observations about each institution.

St. Mary's University

St. Mary's is an independent Catholic university that was founded in 1852 by the priests, brothers, and sisters of the Society of Mary, the Marianists. The institution has been largely devoted to meeting the career development needs of the south Texas population. Its 3,900 students are divided into roughly equal proportions among five schools: business and administration; humanities and social studies; science, engineering, and technology; graduate studies; and law. Originally an institution for men only, St. Mary's undergraduate population now is more than half female and more than half minority (mostly Hispanic).

Several years of severe budget deficits in the late 1970s caused a change of administration and of administrative philosophy at St. Mary's as the school entered the 1980s. Undergraduate enrollment had declined steadily by more than 1,000 from the university's highest enrollment, which came at the height of the Vietnam era. Declining numbers of veterans had combined with the rapid development of the new two-year and four-year public college and university systems in San Antonio to deliver a substantial blow to St. Mary's enrollments and tuition revenue. The senior administration that took office beginning in 1981 recognized the need for effective enrollment planning, improved admissions marketing, and better student retention.

Awareness of the need to improve programs, services, and facilities preceded St. Mary's decision to embrace enrollment management. To the university's credit, several significant improvements were begun even before the introduction of an enrollment management organization.

In 1981, the Retention Task Force (RTF) was created to advise the president directly on the need for improvements in any aspect of retention management. Upon the arrival of the enrollment manager in 1983, he and the vice-president for student services were asked to cochair the committee. The partnership that was formed by asking them to share the leadership responsibility served St. Mary's well. In addition to the symbolic demonstration of administrative unity, active participation of two campus leaders gave valuable weight to the task force's recommendations.

The scope of the Retention Task Force's inquiries touched virtually all areas of student life from curriculum and instruction through student development opportunities to physical facilities. The group also dealt with the general treatment of students and the array of administrative procedures with which students are required to comply.

The task force can claim responsibility for improved service to students on many levels. The committee played a variety of helpful roles in the quest for improved retention, including proposer, supporter, facilitator, informer, educator, and catalyst. Substantial amounts of institutional resources have been reallocated because of RTF influence and persuasion. In other cases, RTF ideas and enthusiasm inspired successful grant proposals, which are bringing better service to St. Mary's students.

Development of Enrollment Management. St. Mary's University, like many two- and four-year colleges, developed an enrollment management system as the result of concerns about budgets and student enrollments. At St. Mary's, an actual decline in student enrollment precipitated the interest in enrollment management. Enrollment declines also led to the creation of many other enrollment management systems, such as those at DePaul University in Chicago; Drake University in Des Moines, Iowa; Humboldt State University in Arcata, California; Johnson County Community College in Kansas City, Kansas; Suffolk

County Community College in Selden, New York; and the University of Wisconsin, Oshkosh.

Unlike many institutions, however, St. Mary's University was able to use external funds to engage in the planning process that resulted in the establishment of an enrollment management system. Both the president and the academic vice-president at St. Mary's were committed to developing a more systematic approach to guide their marketing and recruitment efforts and to increasing the rate of student persistence.

A federal grant provided funds for a comprehensive market study in 1982 and seed money for the start of an enrollment management function in 1983. A staff assistant to the president for enrollment management was hired to develop an undergraduate market plan and to coordinate and supervise undergraduate admissions and all institutional financial aid activities. This new "enrollment manager" was appointed to St. Mary's two chief policy-making councils, the Executive Council (president and vice-presidents) and the Academic Council (vice-president for academic affairs and deans) and was cochair of the Retention Task Force. When the enrollment management position was institutionalized in 1985 at the end of the grant period, it was given the title vice-president for enrollment management.

Currently, St. Mary's enrollment manager continues to supervise undergraduate admissions and financial assistance. He is a full participant in the Executive and Academic Councils and chairs two university-wide standing committees: the Admissions Marketing and Student Retention Councils. Currently, the organizational structure of enrollment management activities at St. Mary's University is an example of both the enrollment management division and the enrollment management matrix. The enrollment manager has direct responsibilities only for admissions and financial aid. In other areas, he functions more like a coordinator, relying more on informal influences.

The informal nature of enrollment management at St. Mary's is an important attribute of the system that has evolved. As noted in Chapter Three, small institutions lend themselves more readily to this approach. However, there are several characteristics of the St. Mary's system that merit discussion.

St. Mary's, like other colleges and universities, organizes enrollment management planning, activities, and influence around four conceptual viewpoints: market theory, student-institution fit, educational excellence, and pricing and financial aid. The principles of each viewpoint are applicable to issues of both recruitment and retention. The role and responsibilities of the enrollment manager and his staff may vary according to the issues, but education and collaboration are essential and ongoing. In practice, enrollment management facilitates, focuses, and interprets important conversations between prospective and current students, university staff and faculty, and administrators.

The primary marketing objective of any institution is to identify and, as much as possible, satisfy legitimate student-consumer needs. The availability and effectiveness of academic programs and support services are significant influences in recruiting and retaining students. Marketing must inform the institution and its future and current students about needs and the means to satisfy student needs.

Colleges and universities typically define themselves according to the student constituencies that they intend to serve. Recruitment is enhanced by identifying and attracting those students who best fit the particular design of the learning environment. Retention is improved by ensuring that the learning environment satisfies the essential needs of the enrolled students and those the institution wants to enroll.

The character and quality of the learning environment also influence recruitment and retention. The distinctiveness of the institution's educational program should be clearly described to student consumers and carefully crafted by faculty and support staff. The institution's definition of excellence must be explained in meaningful detail in terms of expectations for both students and educators and implemented in a comprehensive and consistent manner. These factors give direction to programs and services as well as enrollment goals. The value, benefits, and rewards that accrue constitute the bases for recruitment and retention and enrich communication.

The perceived balance between cost and value may be the single greatest influence on recruiting and retaining most students. But financial aid strategies at independent colleges and universities must be much more than carefully orchestrated programs of selective discounting in support of enrollment objectives. Independent schools, like St. Mary's, need to demonstrate both the affordability and superior value of an alternative to public education that is available to many purchasers only at a premium. An even more fundamental challenge is just getting the attention of many potential students who never consider independent higher education because they assume it is not affordable.

A substantial overlap exists between the issues related to the four conceptual viewpoints of enrollment management. Even the seemingly different concerns of cost and financial assistance share common ground with the other views when value and quality are considered.

The enrollment manager can perform a vital role in the campus community by educating and informing colleagues about the need to deliver consistent messages to their students and by helping colleagues become aware when they are not consistent. This is a significant function of enrollment management at St. Mary's. It requires knowledge of the issues and processes related to curriculum, instruction, student development, and learning, as well as of market strategies. It also necessitates some skill in the collegial process.

The organizational structure at St. Mary's includes both tightly and loosely coupled units. The Enrollment Management Council, chaired by the enrollment manager, meets monthly to share information and coordinate joint activities, review unit procedures and policy, and recommend procedural or policy changes to appropriate councils and individuals in other administrative units. As a result of its small size and clearly delineated reporting relationships, this council is tightly coupled.

The Enrollment Management Council is a significant source for ideas and issues that are considered by the Admissions Marketing Council and the Student Retention Council. Both groups include faculty or deans from the five schools of the university, staff and administrators from support functions that significantly influence student recruitment or retention, current students, and, when appropriate, alumni. Agenda items are solicited from St. Mary's various constituencies. Both of these councils are more loosely structured, and as a result, tangible outcomes require more time to develop.

The councils were early products of a strategic planning process that was recently initiated by the university's current president, who took office in 1988. They were authorized as part of a renewed commitment to the support of enrollment planning.

The four recruitment functions serve distinctly different audiences. The faculty, for example, are most interested in enhancing educational excellence. The student affairs division is committed to enhancing the student-institution fit. Nevertheless, the administration believes that several common needs are served by the Admissions Marketing Committee: (1) sharing and discussing of ideas, concerns, and plans; (2) planning for more comprehensive and effective promotion; (3) assisting individual units with ongoing development, evaluation, and refinement of marketing plan components; and (4) supplementing production and research capability of individual units.

The Student Retention Council is a reborn version of St. Mary's Retention Task Force, which was discontinued in 1986 after a five-year life span. As was the case with the original retention committee, the vice-presidents for enrollment management and for student services again share the task of chairing the new council. The new retention committee is charged with (1) developing and refining an operating philosophy regarding university goals as related to student retention; (2) raising consciousness in the campus community about attrition problems; (3) generating ideas, promoting awareness, and developing proposals for referral to appropriate individuals and councils; and (4) pooling campus research resources (faculty and staff) for retention related activities.

The network of resources for advice and assistance that has been assembled at St. Mary's provides for representative participation of all the school's constituencies in the enrollment planning process. The work of the Admissions Marketing Committee is supplemented by a monthly report from the enrollment manager to campus leaders and others. In addition, several members of the enrollment management unit are assigned to work on a grass-roots level with faculty and staff, students, and alumni in planning, coordinating, and conducting joint recruitment activities. At a small institution like St. Mary's, these structures seem to work effectively.

Virtually everything that is included in a definition of enrollment management is related to the recruitment or retention of students. However, the notion that an enrollment manager might participate actively in traditional faculty matters is sufficiently controversial (or at least potentially so) to warrant special mention.

There are four roles in academic affairs in which the enrollment manager participates at St. Mary's. They are: (1) informing faculty members and deans of comparative student characteristics; (2) acting as a source of ideas for new academic programs and services, as well as for innovation in curriculum and instruction; (3) working on committees with faculty members formulating or revising academic programs, services, curriculum, and teaching/learning methods; and (4) deliberating on academic policy questions as a member of the Academic Council and the Executive Council.

The enrollment manager has provided relevant demographic trends and academic profiles of students that St. Mary's faculty can use to redesign general education requirements to focus on particular student needs. These same kinds of data have helped faculty make decisions regarding developmental and remedial problems. They have enabled faculty to become more sensitive to students' socioeconomic and cultural differences in classroom situations and to become better forecasters of needs pertinent to students' personal, civic, and professional lives.

The enrollment manager has played a significant role in conceptualizing and advocating the development of several additions to St. Mary's academic programs. Among the ideas that have been adopted are an honors program, several interdisciplinary majors, and an academic internship program. In addition, the enrollment manager was an early advocate of curriculum reform in writing, instructional innovation in team teaching and assessment, and the upgrade of academic support services available through advising and the university's Learning Assistance Center.

As an appointee to faculty committees, the enrollment manager has participated in the development of several academic program proposals. These include St. Mary's Honors Program, Academic Internship Program, and Semester Abroad Program. In that role, he has contributed to program content as well as through a more traditional mode as a resource to help justify the need and market for such innovation.

Strategy and Results. The primary function of the enrollment management organization at St. Mary's, as on many other campuses, is the development and implementation of admissions marketing strategy. Since the scope of student recruitment responsibility in the school was limited to traditional undergraduate students from the outset, the enrollment manager's first task was to prepare and institute an undergraduate marketing plan.

The plan was based largely on the results of a comprehensive market study of St. Mary's undergraduate population and market potential, which had been completed by an independent consultant just prior to the enrollment manager's arrival in 1983. Some aspects of the marketing plan were implemented as they were formulated during the 1983–84 recruiting year. However, the plan did not become fully operational until the following year.

The marketing plan established both quantitative and qualitative enrollment objectives. In spite of a moderately declining population of high school graduates in Texas during the early and mid eighties, the plan ambitiously sought to increase new-student populations, while contributing to retention. Enrollment growth was anticipated as a consequence of recruiting and retaining more students who were better prepared and otherwise better suited for the learning environment that St. Mary's offers. The plan was based upon market themes and strategies that evolved from specific consumer needs. Most important, however, it was (and continues to be) shaped in the context of St. Mary's essential character and purpose.

The plan also assumes that prospective students and parents are concerned about programs and services and that they typically require considerable information about one or more areas of concern. Faculty, deans, administrators, current students, and alumni play significant roles in student recruitment activities.

The quality of newly enrolling undergraduates has been improving at St. Mary's. Admission standards have been upgraded. Broader college preparatory course completion now is mandatory. Writing samples are required and evaluated in the admission selection formula. Fewer poorly prepared students are accepted. (Those who are accepted must complete a rigorous summer program of instruction before matriculating in college-level courses.)

New freshmen have completed more challenging high school curricula, attained higher class rank, and achieved higher entrance test scores than did their counterparts from earlier years. The better students have stopped complaining, for the most part, that some St. Mary's courses are not as challenging as courses they took in high school. Faculty are much more satisfied with the ability and performance levels of their students. Greater satisfaction of faculty expectations has improved faculty morale and faculty attitude toward the admissions operation. Even though many people in the St. Mary's community are involved in significant ways with recruitment, most have become much more concerned about their role as agents of retention.

Since 1983, the last year before current enrollment planning strategies were implemented at St. Mary's, new undergraduate populations have grown significantly. Even if the peak recruitment year of 1987 were explained as a statistical aberration, the numbers of new students enrolled in recent years have reached a substantially higher plateau than previously reached.

It is easy, of course, to claim that the increases have occurred because of the development of an intelligent marketing plan that has been effectively implemented. It does seem, however, that some of the presuppositions of the plan have been proven correct.

First, the marketing plan emphasizes the importance of follow-up. Although publications and publicity are carefully prepared, targeted, and distributed according to a strict timetable, their function is primarily to gain attention. It is the quality of person-to-person contact that follows that usually persuades families to choose St. Mary's. The emphasis on families is intentional: parents are targeted in the recruitment process nearly as much as their children.

The Retention Task Force studied the needs of students from orientation until their departure from the university, and made appropriate recommendations to the president and to the university's several policy-making councils. As retention problems have been systematically addressed, undergraduate attrition has been reduced at an annual rate of 1.2 percent since 1980, for a total increase in retention of 10 percent. Many RTF recommendations have been implemented. More improvements that were encouraged originally by RTF activism were developed even after the committee was discontinued.

St. Mary's can point with growing satisfaction at emerging trends in retention. Today, more than 60 percent of St. Mary's entering freshmen graduate within five years. As recently as 1981, fewer than 50 percent of all entering freshmen were graduating in that time or at all.

Perhaps the most exciting aspect of the retention changes is that Hispanic and black students now graduate at the same rate as Anglo-American students. Their graduation rates at St. Mary's far exceed the graduation rates nationally, as reported in the American Council on Education's (1988) *Minorities in Higher Education,* Seventh Annual Status Report. The St. Mary's community has derived special satisfaction from both the intellectual and social dimensions of the environment it is developing — an environment that is intended to help retain all students.

It would be misleading to suggest, however, that the enrollment management efforts at St. Mary's have been continuously successful. One of the greatest strengths of the enrollment management system at St. Mary's is its collegial and informal nature. This strength is also a weakness. Some change efforts in areas that affect student retention (where the influence of enrollment management personnel is limited) have been resisted. Little support has come from some academic departments. Although several attempts have been made to involve large numbers of alumni in recruitment activities, these efforts to date have not been successful.

Despite the overall record of success at St. Mary's, all three divisions (undergraduate, graduate, and law) experienced a small enrollment decline in 1989. All indicators suggested that enrollments would increase again in 1990, but the decline serves as a reminder that no system is infallible. The factors that affect student enrollments are complex, not amenable to quick fixes, and the situation can change from year to year.

Finally, the experience of enrollment management at St. Mary's under three presidents since 1983 attests to the importance of support from the chief executive officer. When presidents have focused attention on these issues, the results have been enrollment growth. When one president chose to pursue other priorities, there was a noticeable impact on enrollment developments.

The University of Hartford

The University of Hartford is a private comprehensive university that enrolls more than 4,700 full-time and 2,700 part-time students in its eight diverse colleges: arts and sciences; basic studies; business and public administration; education, nursing, and health professions; engineering; technology; the Hartford Art School; and the Hartt School of Music. Approximately 47 percent of the enrolled students are women, and 8 percent are minorities. Located in West Hartford, Connecticut, the university serves the greater Hartford metropolitan area, widely known as a mecca of the insurance industry and world headquarters of United Technologies. Among the city's manufacturers are two divisions of United Technologies — Pratt and Whitney and Otis Elevator — as well as Stanley Tools. Over the years, these industries have offered the University of Hartford strong support; in turn, the university's Business School and Engineering Applications Center have formed partnerships with this business community as faculty and students collaborate with industry representatives on special projects. These ties reflect the University of Hartford's original community orientation — the specific niche it occupied when founded in 1957.

Since that time, the institution has shaped strong curricula in such "applied" areas as music, business, and nursing (Carlson, 1989); however, the liberal arts are receiving increased attention from President Humphrey Tonkin, and interdisciplinary courses that constitute an innovative all-university curriculum are now required of all students. The university offers over sixty majors ranging from art education to engineering to insurance. Majors with the largest enrollments include communications, accounting, and computer science.

Founded primarily to serve a commuter population, the University of Hartford has evolved — particularly during the 1980s when enrollment management activities also were initiated — into an increasingly residential, national, and even international campus. By the fall semester of 1989, newly constructed residence halls served close to 3,500 students, including 95 percent of all freshmen, and international students made up 5 percent of the student population.

Development of Enrollment Management. At the University of Hartford, unlike at St. Mary's, actual enrollment declines were not the driving force behind the emergence of an enrollment management system. Hartford, along with DePauw University, California Lutheran University, and Syracuse University, is an institution that developed an enrollment management system in order to maintain or improve both the size and quality of its enrolled student population. At the University of Hartford, a forward-thinking administration looked at the demographic projections for their market region. The rapidly dwindling population of traditional-age students convinced both faculty and administrators that the institution would have to become much more concerned about attracting and retaining students. Planning was a key to the development of an enrollment management system at the university.

Hossler (1986) and anecdotal evidence suggest that the implementation of enrollment management systems requires support from one or more senior-level administrators. The University of Hartford's experience further strengthens this assertion. In the early 1980s a dynamic vice-president for administration embarked upon a course that would alter the university's "commuter-school image." Eager to increase the recruiting power of the institution, the vice-president developed a customer-oriented approach that appealed to business people and the parents of prospective students. Among other actions, this administrator oversaw the university's move into the NCAA's highly visible Division I, and he advocated that admissions and financial aid officers be joined under one executive director and receive cross-training to answer questions in both areas. His changes coincided with the appointment of two individuals who would prove key to the successful implementation of enrollment management — a new director of admissions and financial aid and a new director of planning and institutional research. It is both interesting and significant that the director of planning and institutional research had formerly served another private institution as director of admissions and, thus, held a solid intellectual grasp of the critical issues. Ultimately the design of Hartford's comprehensive enrollment management system, including the format and content of reports, was left to these two individuals. Given the vice-president's focus on customer service, a national vendor's student information system was brought on-line in 1984 to assist with registration. At that juncture conceptualization and production of meaningful reports were secondary since it was recognized that institutional research could later provide the means to improve reporting.

To remedy an admittedly "abysmal" reporting system, the associate vice-president for academic administration (whose portfolio includes direction of the university's computer center) and the director of planning and institutional research reached a compromise: all student data would be stored and maintained on the mainframe for operational use while enrollment analyses and research would be performed by downloading those data to microcomputers in the Office of Planning and Institutional Research. Actual development of the enrollment management system occurred in that office since its microcomputers contained flexible data base software and could most readily handle large quantities of data. Moreover, institutional research personnel were skilled in statistical design and analysis. Consequently, the director of planning and institutional research worked closely with the director of admissions and financial aid to specify objectives of enrollment management, outline crucial reports, and determine what elements might be incorporated in a thorough market analysis. Through this collaboration, the director of admissions and financial aid grew to appreciate and respect his colleague's capabilities; he strongly believed in and supported the enrollment management reports produced by the Office of Planning and Institutional Research. Hence, the director of that office had a staunch ally among the senior administrators several years later when the director of admissions and financial aid became vice-president for institutional advancement. With such backing, continued investment in and refinement of enrollment management remained a high priority at Hartford.

Supportive vice-presidents who can play an advocacy role appear integral to developing and sustaining a comprehensive and effective enrollment management system. Few institutions have the kind of outside grant support that St. Mary's University had in its effort. Usually, either an ongoing planning process such as that employed at Hartford is used to focus on enrollment management issues or else a precipitous decline in enrollments results in rapid emergence of an enrollment management system.

Once the institution's academic community realized in the early 1980s that the campus could no longer rely on the lingering effects of a long period of growth, enrollment became the top priority. With this commitment by senior administrators to development of an effective enrollment management system, the associate vice-president for academic administration and the newly appointed director of institutional research focused their energies on integrating enrollment management into the strategic planning process. Muston (1984) found that integrating specific enrollment related goals into institutional goal setting was linked to success in attaining enrollment goals. The University of Hartford exemplifies the importance of such integration.

As a result of the strategic planning process, the following enrollment management goals were identified:

1. To seek ways of increasing the university's market share of prospective applicants

2. To ensure that institutional pricing and student aid policies were competitive with those of comparable institutions and to ensure the diversity of the student body

3. To seek ways of increasing admissions yield from the number of accepted applicants to provide the number and quality of entering students the university requires across its eight schools and colleges

4. To increase admissions selectivity and provide an enrollment mix that is consistent with the university's mission as a private comprehensive university serving full- and part-time students at the undergraduate and graduate level

5. To increase the accuracy of enrollment and income forecasts for budgeting purposes

6. To offer, within the limits of available resources, high-quality academic programs that are responsive to the needs and preferences of entering students

7. To offer, within the limits of available resources, high-quality campus experiences that are responsive to the needs and preferences of students

8. To find effective ways of analyzing, predicting, and improving student retention

9. To balance instructional staffing and income and expense at realistic levels considering both academic values and enrollment demand

10. To enhance the university's image and reputation for academic excellence and the quality of campus life through visible achievements of students, faculty, alumni, and staff

After identifying these goals, Hartford had to develop a research-based student information system. The goals of this system were to integrate external environmental trends and internal enrollment data across years and track student groups longitudinally from prospective applicants through application, enrollment, retention, and alumni follow-up.

The Office of Planning and Institutional Research determined that the mainframe system currently in use at the school would not provide the kind of data base and tracking system required, so admissions and institutional research created their own system, downloading data to microcomputers. Six fundamental data base structures emerged: "(1) applicants for admission; (2) prospective applicants for admission; (3) financial aid applicants; (4) characteristics of entering students; (5) summary academic history for enrolled students; and (6) course enrollment demand" (Glover, 1986, p. 19). Data from such external sources as *The College Board Handbook, The College Cost Book,* and John Minter's National Data Service were also incorporated, permitting campus managers to make interinstitutional comparisons and market analyses.

Since 1984, reports derived from these multiple but interrelated data bases have proven crucial to deliberations of the university's important Enrollment Management Committee and Budget Advisory Team. Generally convening several times a month from October through March, the Enrollment Management Committee is currently chaired by the vice-president for institutional advancement and consists of fourteen faculty and administrative representatives, including the associate vice-president for academic administration, the now-separate directors of admissions and financial aid, the director of planning and institutional research, and the director of the Counseling Center (who has been working on methods of increasing student retention). Policy recommendations of this committee regarding projected enrollments, financial aid expenditures, and marketing and retention strategies are considered by Hartford's Budget Advisory Team, which is most active throughout the same period of time. Cochaired by the senior executive vice-president for academic affairs and the vice-president for finance, the Budget Advisory Team comprises senior-level officers, deans, faculty, and other administrative staff, including the associate vice-president for academic administration and the director of planning and institutional research.

Strategy and Results. Using this student information system to drive enrollment management activities, the University of Hartford has emphasized the following areas in establishing a comprehensive, interrelated system: market research, institutional pricing and student aid, institutional competition, admissions yield, admissions selectivity, and student retention. Market research is applied social science research that enables the University of Hartford to understand which students come to the university and why they come and why other students do not come. With this information, Hartford asks how it might more effectively position itself in order to attract more of the types of students it wants. The current student information provides analyses of applied and enrolled students by home Zip code and major interest. This information can be used to identify geographical areas that promise high yield for marketing activities and to track where and how student interests have changed over time. A recent addition of geographical mapping software to this system enables the admissions office to plot potential markets from demographic data on applicants. As the new director of admissions notes, "Recruitment doesn't take care of itself. . . . Institutional research is the vital link in lots of areas."

The University of Hartford also analyzes trends in student aid and institutional pricing. The enrollment management data base permits the director of financial aid to make sure that financial aid is "getting to the right people" and to monitor tuition and fees, room and board, and total student costs over a five-year period with comparable institutions. This information enables the director to more effectively target financial aid awards and to provide sound advice to the Budget Advisory Team during the budget planning process.

The analytical focus of enrollment management activities at Hartford is also evident in the school's ability to look at its competitors. Using cluster analysis, the Office of Planning and Institutional Research has classified 221 private institutions. These classifications permit the university to compare itself to the mean scores of each group of institutions using measures such as enrollment, yield, SAT scores, tuition and fees, and faculty salaries. Analyzing the activities of competitors provides a picture of Hartford's market niche and assists campus administrators in evaluating their enrollment management efforts.

The student data base is also used to track student persistence at the university. Beginning with the transfer students and freshmen that entered the school in 1984, retention rates for each semester have been monitored. Results are presented in the form of raw numbers and percentages of students who are still in attendance, have earned two-year degrees (and are no longer enrolled), have earned four-year degrees, and have left the institution. These data confirm a need to further explore the academic, social, and emotional characteristics of students who remain at the university throughout their academic career and to better understand how profiles of such individuals differ from those of students who drop out or transfer to another institution. The director of counseling and the Office of Planning and Institutional Research have teamed up in pursuit of that vital information. The academic, social, and personal-emotional adjustment of each entering (freshman or transfer) student is assessed together with that individual's specific sense of attachment to the university using Baker and Siryk's (1989) promising new Student Adaptation to College Questionnaire (SACQ). In conjunction with information gathered unobtrusively through student activity rosters, leadership questionnaires administered through the university's Career Center, transcripts and transcript request analysis, and a reasons-for-leaving survey of withdrawing students, SACQ data can be used to construct statistical profiles of persisting and withdrawing students (Glover and Wilcox, 1989). Multivariate procedures (such as cluster, discriminant, and log-linear analyses) can identify high- or low-risk student subpopulations and enable Hartford's Counseling Center to refine and target its intervention strategies.

These activities have had an impact upon student enrollments at the university. In August 1989, the president's convocation speech noted that despite continued decline in the number of high school graduates in the university's primary market states, full-time undergraduate and total student enrollment had continued to rise. Since the initiation of enrollment management in 1984, full-time undergraduate enrollments had increased by 9.86 percent and total enrollments had increased by 15.05 percent. Between fall 1987 and fall 1988, the number of full-time undergraduates returning rose by 8.05 percent compared with declines of 4.09 percent and .92 percent between 1985 and 1986 and 1986 and 1987, respectively.

The director of admissions attributes much of this growth in applications and new-student enrollments to reports and information available from the student data base because they provide greater awareness of the characteristics of student market segments, thus permitting admissions to utilize more sophisticated marketing techniques. Similarly, the director of financial aid has been able to assess market segments and attempt to provide student aid awards tailored to the needs of various student subpopulations. It would be facile to explain the increased retention simply in terms of better student information and more sophisticated analyses. Much of the apparent rise could be due to a sizable increase in the number of new full-time undergraduates (12.58 percent increase between 1985 and 1988), although it is possible that the enrollment management system has begun to show some positive effects in the area of retention. The Office of Planning and Institutional Research is continuing to monitor and closely analyze such trends, fully expecting that analyses related to SACQ will contribute to improved retention in the not too distant future. These findings will be important to the Enrollment Management Committee as well as to President Humphrey Tonkin, who perceives himself as an activist committed to change (Carlson, 1989). Tonkin, inaugurated in October 1989, aims to fortify the university's arts and sciences programs, expand the honors programs, and, in general, "create a better sense of community on campus"—all of which should promote greater retention (Carlson, 1989, p. 35).

With its microcomputer base and constant incorporation of new elements such as SACQ and the use of mapping graphics, the University of Hartford's enrollment management system is dynamic, continuously evolving toward greater refinement. Thus, each successive year's reports offer more detailed and accurate information, and report formats themselves continue to be upgraded. Administrators and faculty, however, must be educated to expect such changes and, in fact, to request further alterations that they would find more useful. Often, reports can be standardized only after several years.

Just as at St. Mary's University, however, there are still issues to be resolved at the University of Hartford. The process of developing and using the decision support system might have proven less complex had the entire university been linked by means of a mainframe network. Data and reports were transferred on paper, via telephone, or through physical exchange of disk files (otherwise known as "sneaker net"). The network (currently being installed across Hartford's campus) would alleviate such steps, allowing the administrators to request and instantly call up the reports they need from the terminal at their own desk. At some point, also, the university must decide to base its system around a particular computer package. Ideally that package should prove compatible with IBM's operating system as well as those of other vendors.

Perhaps most important, at the university, the involvement of various administrative offices in developing an enrollment management system requires open and frequent communication. Downloading of data from the mainframe computer requires the cooperation of the Computer Center director and staff. This means, for instance, that the center must periodically inform the Office of Planning and Institutional Research of any changes in the mainframe's data base structure—changes that are crucial to the accuracy and integrity of the resulting information. In turn, the Office of Planning and Institutional Research should keep the Computer Center apprised of any apparent aberrations in the data. As previously noted, senior administrators and others who depend on such information for strategic planning also must remain in close touch with the office responsible for generating reports to ensure the timeliness of the reports as well as their long-term use and effectiveness.

Comparison of the Two Systems

St. Mary's University and the University of Hartford have developed successful enrollment management systems. At first glance, the two approaches look different. St. Mary's appears to emphasize organizational cooperation among faculty as well as academic and student affairs administrators to achieve its success. Hartford, however, emphasizes a sophisticated student information system to aid administrators in their marketing and retention efforts. Yet in both cases, these institutions have been able to focus their efforts to exert more influence over student enrollments.

At both institutions senior administrators have sanctioned enrollment management efforts and focused the attention of the entire campus on student enrollments. Institutional cooperation among key administrative areas in admissions, financial aid, institutional research, and the broader areas of academic and student affairs is also evident. Perhaps most important, enrollment management has become an integral part of the institutional planning process. At both St. Mary's University and the University of Hartford enrollment planning is a part of the strategic planning process. As such, both institutions identify enrollment goals and issues and commit time and resources to achieving these goals. Attracting and retaining students are not viewed as the sole responsibility of admissions or student affairs.

There is no single organizational template that can ensure successful enrollment management systems. Cooperation, the commitment of resources, and the integration of enrollment management into the institutional planning process make it more likely that colleges and universities will be able to attract and retain both the number and types of students they want to enroll.

Chapter 16

Tailoring Enrollment Management to Institutional Needs: Advice to Campus Leaders

John P. Bean
Don Hossler

In this book, various approaches to enrollment management have been described and the components of successful programs have been identified. The purpose of this chapter is to review the functions of enrollment management in terms of local issues, local practices, and staffing. The chapter concludes with a few comments about the future of enrollment management.

Discovering the Local Issues

A recommended course of action to increase the number of enrolled students or increase the number of minority students may or may not be useful in a particular context. A practice that greatly benefits enrollments in one context may wreak havoc in another. Enrollment management goals can only be achieved when at least three conditions are met. First, the recommended policy must be consistent with the ethos of the institution. Second, if implemented, it must ameliorate the local problem. Third, the resources needed to implement the policy must be locally available. Thus, local issues frame the contingencies of local success.

285

Just as form follows function, local practices should be designed based on a thorough understanding of enrollment issues in the local context. Eight questions need to be addressed.

What Are the Characteristics of Student Groups at This Institution? Underlying this question is the assumption that, with few exceptions, student bodies are heterogeneous. Recognizing student diversity and understanding the nature of this diversity are the core of successful enrollment management. Different recruiting, financing, orientation, retention, and placement strategies will affect different students in different ways. Programs that improve recruitment and retention for the majority student may or may not help nonmajority students. Understanding the diversity of students and providing information and services tailored to the needs of different student groups are fundamental to enrollment success.

Where Do Students at This Institution Come from? After identifying the major groups of students, enrollment managers next need to ask where these groups of students come from. The answer profoundly influences both marketing and recruitment strategies. For community colleges, the answer can be local high schools, industries, neighborhoods, churches, and so on while for liberal arts colleges, the answer can be states or regions of the country. The answer to this question tells recruiters where to look for new students with a high chance of graduating and tells marketers what markets are well served and which ones are not yet served or are poorly served.

Why Did Students Come to This Institution? Students can have a very high priority to attend a certain college or university or may end up on a campus by chance. Information on why students choose to attend the school can direct enrollment managers to effective marketing strategies — ones that emphasize institutional attributes that have image potency for target markets.

It is also useful for enrollment managers to know if students are loyal to a school upon arrival and came to the school with a goal of graduating. These students require less support and are more likely to stay and graduate than those who make a last-minute choice to attend an institution and are unclear about what exactly they are doing there. Such information is social/psychological. It can be extended with academic/pragmatic information related to the curriculum and student interests. Students who are able to take the courses they want to are more likely to stay at a college until graduation. Recruiters need to understand the curriculum in order to attract students who will be well served by the faculty upon matriculation.

How Will Students Pay for Their Education? Students who pay full tuition until graduation generate a tremendous amount of income for a college or university when compared to the part-time student who stays for only one semester. Due to multiple forms of financial aid, full-paying students may be rare. Financial aid can substantially reduce the advertised tuition rate for students, creating a low net cost. Unless accompanied by increased numbers of full-paying students or some other subsidy, financial aid will reduce tuition income. While the ethics of wealthy students subsidizing the tuition of economically disadvantaged students is subject to debate, pricing strategies are critical for attracting and retaining students. Credit hour shopping in metropolitan areas where many institutions vie for the same student dollars is a demeaning reality. Many elements must be considered in computing tuition: ability to pay, full- versus part-time registration, in-state and out-of-state rates, public and private tuition subsidies, student mix, the availability of work-study funds, student achievement, and so on. Enrollment managers must continually map the effects of tuition policy adjustments on student mix and institutional income. They must constantly seek dynamic solutions to the tuition equation.

How Can Students' Transition into School Be Eased? It is not enough for enrollment managers to simply drop a gaggle of new students at the foot of the campus statue and say, "Here is this year's class. See you next year." Easing students' transition into a college or university is another critical task for the enrollment management team; failure to do so can result in high rates of attrition. The management aspect of enrollment management will be severely tested by this task because successful transition depends on the coordinated efforts of all of the main players in enrollment management, with the possible exception of placement. Admissions officers need to know more than how many students will arrive—they need to know what these students are like academically and socially. Placing students in supportive social environments can be just as important as placing them in appropriate courses. Orientation to student life is critical for both students and their parents (or for older students, their spouses and employers). Noblitt's concept of "one at a time" is appropriate from the initial moment of contact until graduation—a school needs to provide different information, services, and experiences for different types of students, appropriate to their interests, needs, and abilities. Here again, local knowledge based on local successes is essential for modifying programs.

Why Do Students Remain Enrolled or Leave? Different types of students leave institutions for different reasons, and there is little substitute for conducting a local study into the causes of student attrition. While researchers are interested in explaining the attrition process, enrollment managers need ultimately to be concerned with the effectiveness of intervention strategies to increase retention. A data base that identifies the retention rates for different types of students is a good starting place. An analysis of the causes of attrition for each type of student is sensible in identifying problems that lead to attrition that can be remedied through proactive programming. As in the case of Marian College, described in Chapter Twelve, programs are likely to have differential impacts. Enrollment managers need to coordinate a wide variety of academic and social programs to enhance retention.

What Do Students Get out of Attending the Institution? Hypothetically, students constantly engage in a kind of quasi-rational cost effectiveness assessment of their continued enrollment. On the rational side, they look at tuition and opportunity costs (earnings forgone by going to school instead of taking a job) and balance that against future earnings based on having a degree. The quasi-rational issues — those dealing with self-image, relationships with peers, identification with the school, self-development, hedonism, relationships with faculty, sporting accomplishments, avoidance of responsibility, and so on — can create satisfaction with and an attachment to the school.

The tangible accomplishments of graduates can be documented in terms of further education and employment. Does the value added, no matter how calculated, justify for the student the commitment of time and energy and expense of attending this college? Enrollment managers, especially those who focus on numbers, must remember that much of what a student gains from a college or university cannot be meaningfully quantified. Finding out why students like a college can be very informative. Enrollment managers can also ask students what they feel they are not getting from their school. Information from such a needs assessment survey can also be useful in developing enrollment management strategies.

What Do Students Do After Graduation? Institutions find out what students do after graduation far too infrequently. Such studies can yield at least three important pieces of information. The first has to do with legitimacy; do graduates from an institution feel that they got from it what was promised? Did they learn skills useful for employment or abilities necessary for further education? Are they able to contribute to society in a manner that justifies public expenditures? The second kind of information has to do with placement. Did these students obtain the employment they wanted? Did they get into the graduate school of their choice? Third, will they recruit for (or against) the college? Again, answers to these questions can be very important in developing new or modifying old policies.

The answers to these eight questions constitute part of a scan of the internal and external environments of a college or university. Such information is essential for making informed policy choices. The mechanisms for designing and implementing these policies will next be described.

Designing Local Practices

Strategic planning, institutional research, marketing and admissions, transition, retention, and placement constitute the arena in which enrollment managers must design and enact their policies and programs. Local knowledge is essential to make sensible choices from the infinite possibilities that confront enrollment managers in any college or university.

Strategic Planning. Was it the Roman statesman Seneca who first said, "If you don't know where you're going, any road will get you there"? College and university officials must have some idea of where they are going, or they are likely to become lost in a turbulent and hostile environment. For those institutions with a sense of direction, not every road is likely to lead to institutional prosperity. Strategic planning concerns both ends and means. Colleges and universities may not need to decide anew each year their general direction, but may need to recommit to that direction at regular intervals. They will, however, constantly need to reexamine the means they use to strive toward their goals and the shifting constraints on action.

Strategic planning is appropriate for enrollment management for several reasons. First among these is that enrollment management influences the size of a student body and the type of student enrolled. The student body shapes an institution — it provides constraints and opportunities that influence the fabric of institutional life. Thus, enrollment management involves strategic decisions, and strategic planning helps keep those decisions sensible. Second, enrollment management involves a wide variety of participants, and strategic planning can integrate the activities of a large number of people at different institutional levels. Third, enrollment management needs to have a planning approach that is responsive to the external environment, and strategic planning provides such an approach.

Enrollment management activities are consistent with strategic planning approaches. Identifying the general direction of the institution (setting directions), examining institutional capabilities (internal audit) and opportunities in the external environment (environmental scanning), understanding stakeholder needs, matching opportunities with resources, and integrating symbolic acts and meaning into management activities make for good enrollment management and are consistent with strategic thinking. Institutions must know what business they are in, what their capabilities are, whom they serve, and how to match capabilities with opportunities in order to take advantage of opportunities as they arise.

Institutional Research. Without good data, good information can only be guessed at, and successful policies are a matter of luck. Few people would dispute the advantages of having good information, but at what cost? Institutional research should provide information to support decision making. Support for mechanical decisions, like how large a classroom needs to be to match course enrollments, is rather simple. Support for strategic decisions — nonrecurrent choices — can be very complex.

At a minimum, enrollment managers should be able to describe their students: who applies, who comes, who stays, who leaves, who graduates. The description can vary from a few demographic indicators, such as age, ethnicity, gender, and full- or part-time status, to detailed attitudinal information, such as parental attitude toward the institution, satisfaction, and loyalty to the school. For some groups, fairly simple information can be gathered while for others information should be very detailed. Information such as major, courses taken, and cocurricular activities engaged in can show what students do while enrolled. Alumni can be surveyed as well. Institutional researchers should help discern how existing resources can be used to meet current or potential students' needs. Institutional research and strategic planning go hand in hand with enrollment management.

Marketing and Admissions. Marketing and admissions can only be effective if an institution has an image of quality, a good faculty, a good student-life program, and attractive facilities. Although a strong marketing and admissions effort can help an institution to attract students, it cannot overcome undesirable academic programs and poor teaching. Marketing, once considered almost obscene by faculty members, is a necessity for the survival of many institutions.

When competition is weak and demand high, enrollment managers can choose an intentionally diverse and academically qualified student body. Coping with diversity becomes part of the students' education. But when competition becomes fierce and demand weak, marketing becomes an essential ingredient in developing a sensible strategic plan and an enrollment management system.

There are several difficulties with marketing in higher education. Perhaps most obvious is that the product, education, is not easily understood. Buyers cannot hold it in their hands and examine it. They must take the institution's word for the quality of the product — the product's most important aspect. This element of risk makes the selling of the product all the more difficult. In an era when advertising has greatly increased our skepticism of a seller's claims about a product's value, marketing an invisible product is not easy.

A second problem is that three of the four P's of traditional marketing theory (product, place, and price) are, if not fixed, at least extremely difficult for an institution to change in any significant amount. That gives promotion — the packaging of the product — a central role in marketing activities. Describing what a college or university can do for a student in a way that appeals to that person is essential. As student bodies become more heterogeneous, market segments increase in number and decrease in size. Finding an appropriate personal touch and meaningful appeal becomes increasingly complex.

Diversity may become the buzzword of the nineties. Students enter college with different academic capabilities, ages, genders, ethnicities, races, religions, nationalities, and life and work experiences. They come from different cultures that have different values. Marketing strategies depend on understanding how groups of students or potential students differ from each other. Successful orientation and course placement programs also depend on knowledge of student types. Factors affecting retention and attrition have a different impact on students in different groups. Understanding and coping with diversity may be higher education's most critical challenge in the nineties.

Transition. Students who feel that they do not fit in at a college or university are likely to drop out of higher education or transfer to another institution. Programs that ease the transition from high school and work to higher education or from one institution to another are essential in successful enrollment management programs. The orientation of students — academically, socially, geographically, institutionally — is key to student success.

Transition programs should take into account student differences. There is little point in making every student participate in every form of orientation. Some guidelines can be followed in designing orientation programs:

1. Students who enter school with the intention to graduate should receive more attention than those who enroll for a single course and have no intention to pursue a degree.
2. The greater the change from the old student or work roles to the new student roles, the greater the orientation effort needs to be.
3. Transition programs should be sustained for at least a semester and possibly for a year.
4. Parents of traditional-age students, especially those who did not attend college themselves, should be oriented to college life. Informed parents can be a good source of information for new students. Parental approval of the institution can greatly increase the likelihood that a student will remain enrolled. For nontraditional students, the orientation of spouses or employers can be valuable.
5. Students need support, not just financial and academic, but also social support in order to remain enrolled. Transition programs need to make sure that such support is available.

Orientation programs are often thought of as one-week bashes at the beginning of a school year during which students are given the tools to survive at the institution and have a chance to meet new friends. Enrollment managers need to be concerned with the broader issues of transition into college. The transition period is a critical one for any new member of an organization. It is also a period when the decisions about who to admit and what programs to offer are first tested. Spending resources on intelligent transition programs is often very wise.

Retention. Retention is both a moral and an economic victory for colleges and universities. It is a moral victory because a student has decided that the education a school has to offer is worth pursuing. This attachment allows an institution to provide the education it considers good for the student. The institution cannot impart such information and wisdom to a student who has left school. It is an economic victory because the student continues to pay tuition. This being the case, it is surprising that organized retention efforts pale in comparison to recruiting efforts.

Institutional responses to retention have traditionally been more diffuse than marketing, recruitment, and admissions programs. When compared to retention, these activities have been much more self-contained. Retention is an ongoing decision based on myriad factors. Anyone, inside or outside of a college or university, can influence a student to stay in or leave school. The events that can trigger departure are infinite. While there may be some critical players in retention decisions — significant others, faculty members, advisers — and critical events, like running out of money, ultimately the entire institution has to bear the responsibility for a student leaving school before achieving his or her goals. Such diffuse responsibility violates a fundamental bureaucratic principle — the ability to assign responsibility for failure. Since everyone is to blame, no one is to blame. Since it is everyone's responsibility, it is no one's responsibility.

Enrollment management offers a partial solution to this predicament. By creating and staffing a retention office as part of an overall enrollment management program, an institution is telling itself that retention is important and that retention efforts should be coordinated. Appointing a retention officer should ensure that an office on campus is tracking student retention rates and coordinating the development of retention programs.

As long as everyone is aware that a retention officer can not be held accountable for the rate of attrition or graduation, progress at reducing attrition can be made. This does not mean that a retention officer cannot be held accountable for a poorly organized retention effort or for not being up-to-date on retention programs but simply that a well-coordinated effort does not guarantee good execution. It is execution and not design that influences retention.

As higher-quality students enroll in a school, its retention rate usually goes up. When academic and social programs at a school provide for the needs of the student body, its retention rate is practically guaranteed to go up. There is, of course, no easy way to provide for the needs of a diverse group.

Enrollment managers should be constantly aware of a few guidelines for retention.

1. Develop a data base. Find out who stays and leaves.
2. Do not treat all students alike.
3. Make sure that students have the academic capabilities (skills and abilities) necessary to do the academic work required of them.
4. Provide the curriculum students want. Teach them to want what they need to achieve their academic goals.
5. Understand the importance of support — psychological, emotional, financial — for students staying in school and that when such support is lacking or is withdrawn, attrition will likely increase.
6. Admit students who are likely to fit in at a school, and help them adjust to your particular college or university.
7. Make everyone aware of the importance of attitudes toward school in influencing retention.
8. Provide rites, rituals, and other symbolic activities to enhance students' loyalty to your institution.
9. Provide in-class and out-of-class activities that help students mature, gain self-confidence, and develop skills that will serve them through life.

Retention is an area in which everybody can win: students, institution, faculty, staff, and administrators. Retention activities must completely integrate enrollment management with institutional life. To be successful, enrollment management must enhance retention.

Placement. The final responsibility of enrollment management is placement. In marketing terms, placement is a test of product viability. If an institution is promising graduates jobs but cannot place them, it is in trouble. The institution is in moral trouble because it is lying to students about the value of their education or certification for getting employment. It may also be in direct economic trouble as these disgruntled students become more sophisticated consumers and then become litigants. Indirect economic trouble arises when the institution loses credibility with its public—when it can no longer provide access to "the good life," and students choose to go elsewhere.

Responsibility for placement falls into two categories: continued education and employment. Enrollment managers need to make sure that students who graduate liked their experience while attending college and got out of it what they needed for their next role in the workplace or in graduate school. Alumni contributions build endowments and increase educational opportunities for the next generation of students. Alumni recruiters, properly trained, are extremely effective.

Staffing the Enrollment Management Office

An organization is only as good as its employees. A beautifully designed enrollment management office will fail if the office's values are not consistent with institutional values or if the employees are incompetent. In developing an enrollment management office, at least three issues need to be addressed: top-level endorsement, the use of consultants, and the use of staff in place or new staff.

Although a good argument can be made for placing the enrollment management office under the chief academic officer at a college or university, the strategic nature of the office suggests that it should be run by a vice-president. In this book, several examples of successful enrollment management efforts have been described in which the chief enrollment manager is not a vice-president. Nevertheless, most colleges and universities that place attracting and retaining students as a priority create a vice-presidential position. At those campuses where enrollment management efforts are evolving, the trend is to slowly move toward a dean or vice-president of enrollment management. Despite the desirability of establishing a vice-presidential position, budgetary constraints and campus governance issues may make it impossible.

Whether the chief enrollment manager is also the vice-president for student affairs or the vice-president for academic affairs (provost) depends on the abilities and responsibilities of these officers. If the title is given to an existing vice-president, an associate vice-president for enrollment management should be named to act as the catalyst for enrollment activities. Regardless of its administrative location, enrollment management must receive the blessings of the board and of the president. Without such an endorsement the office and its functions are not likely to be taken seriously. Hence, little change would result. When such an endorsement is made and an enrollment manager is named, jurisdiction battles are likely to ensue. The president should be prepared to deal with them as they arise. Left unresolved, such battles can undermine enrollment improvements.

A second issue is the use of consultants. Consultants can analyze local problems and help design solutions for organizing enrollment management activities. They can provide new ideas for an institution to consider when developing enrollment policies. They can provide legitimacy for changes an institution wishes to undertake. And they can help an institution that is stuck get unstuck.

A long-term reliance on consultants, however, seems unwise. They become an excuse for inactivity, people to blame when things do not go well, and their potency as catalysts diminishes each time they return. After consultants make an initial appearance or two, enrollment management functions should be assigned to resident staff and faculty.

A third issue concerns the use of existing staff or the hiring of new staff. It is worth repeating that staffing decisions are the key to the success of any program. A college or university needs to determine who should be reassigned and who needs to be hired to make enrollment management work. The functions that need to be carried out are easier to specify than the numbers of employees needed to accomplish the tasks. In small colleges, one person can be assigned several tasks, while large community colleges and complex universities may require a large staff to carry out a single function.

Once an office is in place, the chief enrollment management officer has to report to somebody. While the technical aspects of enrollment management can be carried out by mid-level managers, the policy issues involved in enrollment management are strategic and need to be dealt with at the highest levels. Three general functions need to be covered by staff: policies and strategies for enrollment management; linking of enrollment management to academic programming; and linking of enrollment management to the cocurriculum and other student affairs activities. Staffing patterns will vary depending on a number of local issues, particularly on existing staff and administrative traditions.

The roles described below should each be provided for in a comprehensive enrollment management program. Since the issues on every campus differ, there may not be a specific administrator appointed for each of these functions. The functions themselves, however, must be attended to if enrollment management efforts are to succeed. Enrollment managers may want to use this description as a checklist to determine if all aspects of enrollment management are receiving sufficient attention on their campuses.

Vice-President (or Senior Administrator) for Enrollment Management. This person is responsible for keeping institutional goals and enrollment policies consistent and mutually reinforcing and for staffing and managing the enrollment management office. This person should also be part of the strategic planning team for the institution.

Director of Policy Analysis. This person becomes the policy adviser for the vice-president. He or she should either have a staff or have access to a staff that can conduct studies in the following areas: institutional research (students, staff, faculty, facilities, resources, curriculum); admissions and marketing (student mix, yield, and so on); market research (market segmentation, institutional image studies, and so on); and financial aid and pricing strategies.

Director of Marketing, Public Relations, Recruitment, Financial Aid, and Admissions. This person should be responsible either for managing these activities or for making sure that programmatic approaches in these areas are consistent with enrollment management policies.

Student Affairs Liaison Officer. This person is responsible for seeing that many student affairs activities support the enrollment management strategy for the college or university. In particular, this person should help develop (or at some institutions have responsibility for) orientation, cocurricular programs, retention programs (like study skills centers), placement, and alumni recruitment.

Academic Affairs Liaison Officer. Faculty members commonly disdain the administration in general and areas such as admissions, financial aid, and other student affairs tasks in particular. This pejorative attitude makes the academic affairs liaison officer's task the most sensitive and difficult to carry out. The chief enrollment management officer should take on this responsibility not only because of its sensitivity but also because this link to faculty is the most critical one in enrollment management. The curriculum is the vehicle by which the main product of a college or university, education, is delivered to students. Strategic planners need to know what the curriculum is in order to assess local capabilities (for example, in deciding if new majors can be offered). They also need to consider changing the curriculum to serve new clientele. Admissions officers need to know what the curriculum is in order to attract students; marketers need to know what product they can (or cannot) sell. Institutional researchers need to track the growth and decline in enrollments in different majors, to identify which academic programs generate revenues and which generate excessive costs, and to identify which courses most often result in a student flunking out of school or changing majors.

The way in which enrollment management recommendations are presented to the faculty is critical for their acceptance. Students may shape an institution but faculty are the institution. Curricular policy recommendations that come from enrollment managers need to be delivered by academic officers in order to be implemented by the faculty. The importance of the curriculum in attracting and retaining students cannot be overemphasized.

The Future of Enrollment Management

Enrollment management is a relatively recent term, but the field is only partially a recent invention. Enrollment management addresses a continuing issue: how does a college or university attract, matriculate, and graduate students that faculty like to teach, that administrators can be proud of, and that fund raisers can rely on? It differs from other approaches to increasing enrollments by its sophistication and comprehensiveness. An effective enrollment manager should have a bright future indeed.

There are some profound issues facing higher education that will affect what enrollment managers do and what higher education institutions become. Paramount among these issues is that of demographic change. During this century, higher education changed from an eastern upper-class male activity into an endless array of postsecondary educational experiences. Access to higher education is, excluding the underclass, universal. Nontraditional students — part time or commuter or older than twenty-four years — are now in the majority. Women, ethnic minorities, and retirees generate more credit hours at many institutions than white males. To the extent that enrollment managers act as gatekeepers, they will play a key role in determining what groups of students will be served and what groups will either not be served or will have to turn to their employers for on-the-job-training programs. The total expenditure for programs outside of higher education is approximately equal to the costs of educational programs in two- and four-year colleges and universities. Enrollment managers need to be sensitive to the different needs of three groups: traditional students; nontraditional students; and potential students currently served by employee educational programs. Of course, other groups will be important to particular institutions.

Enrollment managers also need to be cognizant of the coming transformation in the composition of the faculty. The majority of current faculty members, now graying, will retire within a decade or two. During this same period, women will begin earning more doctorates than men. Institutions will have younger faculty with a much higher proportion of women faculty members than in the past. Perhaps these new faculty members will place a higher value on teaching undergraduates than did their predecessors, and teaching may have a renaissance, especially at universities now dominated by researchers. While such a presumption is highly speculative, it indicates the types of changes enrollment managers will need to understand.

At least until 1995, when traditional-age student enrollments are expected to increase for the first time in two decades, the competition for students among colleges and universities will remain intense. In locations where students have a number of options, the most sophisticated marketing techniques will likely produce the highest yields. As indicated by the case studies in this book, the results of enrollment management programs are consistent, but radical improvements will be the exception rather than the rule. It makes sense to enter the fray fully prepared rather than waiting until resources are stretched to the breaking point. There is every reason to begin an enrollment management program sooner rather than later.

This high level of competition is associated with an ethical and philosophical puzzle institutions engaged in enrollment management must consider. The puzzle revolves around the size of the student body and the purpose of the institution. It involves survival and growth of the college or university brought about by changing the school's mission. In organizational terms, it pits the goal of survival against any other organizational goal, such as providing a quality education to enrolled students. In common parlance, the tail may wag the dog.

Current budgetary trends reflect the problem. There are many instances in which the proportion of institutional funds allocated to instruction is declining while the proportion allocated for marketing, recruitment, and financial aid is on the rise. How far can such practices be taken before the basic functions of higher education are undermined?

Similarly, the extensive use of merit aid by schools to attract elite students so the institution can look like an elite institution devalues all of higher education. Colleges and universities have steadily increased their lobbying efforts to expand federal and state student aid in order to guarantee student access and choice. But where merit aid is high, campuses show little responsibility for providing access or choice, acting as if these were someone else's problem.

If enrollment policies are set to maximize tuition or status and educational considerations are ignored, both the institution and the students are losers. Institutions lose because they have abandoned their raison d'être for matters of expedience. Students lose because the education they receive is tainted by a reversal of priorities set for faculty members: to attract and retain rather than educate students. Initially, such policies may seem fiscally sound, but they are educationally and morally bankrupt.

The ultimate aim of enrollment management is to help institutions achieve educational goals. Enrollment management helps colleges and universities better understand themselves, clarify their missions, identify constituent groups, and define their positions in the marketplace. It can be a catalyst for institutional assessment and strategic planning.

Enrollment management can increase the resource base for a college or university and improve its quality, but the idea that enrollment management is primarily a resource-generating device is misbegotten. Colleges and universities should provide the best education possible for the students they serve. Enrollment management can support the institution's endeavors but it should not try to control them.

References

Ackoff, R. L. *A Concept of Corporate Planning.* New York: Wiley, 1970.

Adams, D. "The Enrollment Management Paradigm." Paper presented at the joint meeting of the American College Personnel Association/National Association of Student Personnel Administrators, Chicago, Apr. 1987.

American Council on Education. *Minorities in Higher Education, Seventh Annual Status Report.* Washington, D.C.: American Council on Education, 1988.

Andriole, S. J. *Handbook of Decision Support Systems.* Blue Ridge Summit, Pa.: Petrocelli Press, 1989.

Astin, A. W. "The Impact of Dormitory Living on Students." *Educational Record,* 1973, *54* (1), 204–210.

Astin, A. W. *Preventing Students from Dropping Out: A Longitudinal, Multi Institutional Study of College Dropouts.* San Francisco: Jossey-Bass, 1975.

Astin, A. W. *Four Critical Years: Effects of College on Beliefs, Attitudes, and Knowledge.* San Francisco: Jossey-Bass, 1977.

Astin, A. W. *Achieving Educational Excellence: A Critical Assessment of Priorities and Practices in Higher Education.* San Francisco: Jossey-Bass, 1985.

Astin, A. W., and others. *The Impact of Student Financial Aid Programs on Student College Choice.* Washington, D.C.: Office of Planning, Washington Division of Postsecondary Planning, 1980. (ED 187-368)

Baker, R., and Siryk, B. *Student Adaptation to College Questionnaire.* Los Angeles: Western Psychological Services, 1989.

Baldridge, J. V., Curtis, D. V., Ecker, G., and Riley, G. L. *Policy Making and Effective Leadership: A National Study of Academic Management.* San Francisco: Jossey-Bass, 1978.

Barnett, M. R. "State of the University Address: Six Priorities for UM-St. Louis." Unpublished manuscript in authors' possession, 1986.

Beal, P. C., and Noel, L. *What Works in Student Retention.* Iowa City, Iowa: American College Testing Program and the National Center for Higher Education Management Systems, 1980.

Bean, J. P. "Dropouts and Turnover: The Synthesis of a Causal Model of Student Attrition." *Research in Higher Education,* 1980, *12,* 155–187.

Bean, J. P. "Conceptual Models of Student Attrition: How Theory Can Help the Institutional Researcher." In E. T. Pascarella (ed.), *Studying Student Attrition.* New Directions for Institutional Research, no. 36. San Francisco: Jossey-Bass, 1982a.

Bean, J. P. "The Interaction Effects of GPA on Other Determinants of Student Attrition in a Homogeneous Population." Paper presented at the annual meeting of the American Educational Research Association, New York, Apr. 1982b.

Bean, J. P. "The Application of a Model of Turnover in Work Organizations to the Student Attrition Process." *Review of Higher Education,* 1983, *6,* 129–148.

Bean, J. P. "Interaction Effects Based on Class Level in an Explanatory Model of College Student Dropout Syndrome." *American Educational Research Journal,* 1985, *22,* 35–64.

Bean, J. P. "Assessing and Reducing Attrition." In D. Hossler (ed.), *Managing College Enrollments.* New Directions for Higher Education, no. 53. San Francisco: Jossey-Bass, 1986.

Bean, J. P., and Hull, D. "Determinants of Black and White Student Attrition at a Major Southern University." Paper presented at annual meeting of the American Educational Research Association, New Orleans, Apr. 1984.

Bean, J. P., and Metzner, B. S. "A Conceptual Model of Non-

Traditional Student Attrition." *Review of Educational Research,* 1985, *55* (4), 485–540.

Bennett, C., and Bean, J. "A Conceptual Model of Black Student Attrition at a Predominantly White University." *Journal of Educational Equity and Leadership,* 1984, *4,* 461–478.

Bensimon, E., Neumann, A., and Birnbaum, R. *Making Sense of Administrative Leadership: The "L" Word in Higher Education.* ASHE-ERIC/Higher Education Research Report, no. 1. Washington, D.C.: ERIC Clearinghouse on Higher Education and the Association for the Study of Higher Education, 1989.

Bentler, P., and Speckart, G. "Models of Attitude-Behavior Relations." *Psychological Review,* 1979, *86,* 452–464.

Bers, T. H. "Exploring Institutional Images Through Focus Group Interviews." In R. S. Lay and J. J. Endo (eds.), *Designing and Using Market Research.* New Directions for Institutional Research, no. 54. San Francisco: Jossey-Bass, 1987.

Billson, J. M., and Terry, M. B. "Search of a Silken Purse: Factors in Attrition Among First Generation Students." *College and University,* 1982, *58,* 57–75.

Boar, B. H. *Application Prototyping: A Requirements Definition Strategy for the '80s.* New York: Wiley, 1984.

Borden, N. H. "The Concept of the Marketing Mix." *Journal of Advertising Research,* 1964, *4* (2), 2–7.

Bowen, H. R. *The Costs of Higher Education: How Much Do Colleges and Universities Spend Per Student and How Much Should They Spend?* San Francisco: Jossey-Bass, 1980.

Bryson, J. M. *Strategic Planning for Public and Nonprofit Organizations: A Guide to Strengthening and Sustaining Organizational Achievement.* San Francisco: Jossey-Bass, 1988.

Buell, V. P. *Handbook of Modern Marketing.* New York: McGraw-Hill, 1986.

Buffington, S., Hossler, D., and Bean, J. "Successful Strategies in Small College Enrollment." Paper presented at the annual meeting of the Association for the Study of Higher Education, Baltimore, Md., Nov. 1987.

Carlson, B. W. "The U. of H. Meets the 90s." *Hartford Monthly,* 1989, *2* (11), 32–35, 62.

Cartter, A. "The Supply and Demand for College Teachers." *Journal of Human Resources,* 1966, *1,* 22–38.

Chaffee, E. "Strategy and Effectiveness in Systems of Higher Education." In J. C. Smart (ed.), *Higher Education: Handbook of Theory and Research.* Vol. 5. New York: Agathon Press, 1989.

Chapman, D. W. "A Model of Student College Choice." *Journal of Higher Education, 1981, 52* (5), 490–505.

Chapman, R. G., and Jackson, R. *College Choices of Academically Able Students: The Influence of No-Need Financial Aid and Other Factors.* Research Monograph, no. 10. New York: College Entrance Examination Board, 1987.

Cibik, M. A. "College Information Needs." *College and University,* 1982, *57,* 97–102.

Clark, B. *The Higher Education System.* Berkeley: University of California Press, 1983.

Clark, D. L. *New Perspectives on Planning in Educational Organizations.* San Francisco: Far West Laboratory for Educational Research and Development, 1980.

Conklin, M. E., and Dailey, A. R. "Does Consistency of Parental Encouragement Matter for Secondary Students?" *Sociology of Education,* 1981, *54,* 254–262.

Cook, R. W., and Zallocco, R. L. "Predicting University Preference and Attendance: Applied Marketing in Higher Education Administration." *Research in Higher Education,* 1983, *19,* 197–211.

Coombs, C. H. *A Theory of Data.* New York: Wiley, 1964.

Cope, R. G. *Strategic Planning, Management, and Decision Making.* AAHE-ERIC/Higher Education Research Report, no. 9. Washington, D.C.: American Association for Higher Education, 1981.

Dahl, R. W. "College Attendance and Institutional Choice: Results from the Kentucky Longitudinal Study." Paper presented at the annual forum of the Association of Institutional Research, Denver, Colo., May 1982. (ED 220 227)

Davies, A. "Organizational Aspects of Management Information Systems Change." In N. Piercy (ed.), *Management Information Systems: The Technology of Change.* New York: Nichols, 1987.

Douglas, P., and others. "Factors in the Choice of Higher Educational Institutions by Academically Gifted Seniors." *Journal of College Student Personnel,* 1982, *24,* 540–545.

Durkheim, E. *Suicide.* (J. S. Spaulding and G. Simpson, trans.) New York: Free Press, 1961.

Earl, M. J., and Hopwood, A. G. "From Management Information to Information Management." In E. K. Somogyi and R. D. Galliers (eds.), *Towards Strategic Information Systems.* Vol. 1. Cambridge, Mass.: Abacus Press, 1987.

Feldman, K. A., and Newcomb, T. M. *The Impact of College on Students.* Vol. 1. San Francisco: Jossey-Bass, 1969.

Fetters, W. B. *Withdrawal from Institutions of Higher Education: An Appraisal with Longitudinal Data Involving Diverse Institutions.* Washington, D.C.: National Center for Educational Statistics, U.S. Office of Education, 1977.

Fiedler, D., and Vance, E. B. "To Stay or Leave the University: Every Student's Dilemma." Paper presented at a meeting of the American Psychological Association, 1981.

Fishbein, M., and Ajzen, I. *Belief, Attitude, Intention, and Behavior: An Introduction to Theory and Research.* Reading, Mass.: Addison-Wesley, 1975.

Forrest, A. *Increasing Student Competence and Persistence: The Best Case for General Education.* Iowa City, Iowa: American College Testing Program National Center for the Advancement of Educational Practices, 1982.

Frank, A. C., and Kirk, B. A. "Differences in Outcomes for Users and Nonusers of University Counseling and Psychiatric Services." *Journal of Counseling Psychology,* 1975, *22,* 252–258.

Freeman, H. B. "Impact of No Need Scholarships on the Matriculating Decisions of Academically Talented Students." Paper presented at the annual meeting of the American Association of Higher Education, Chicago, Mar. 1984.

Gattiker, U. E., Gutek, B. A., and Berger, D. E. "Office Technology and Employee Attitudes." *Social Science Computer Review,* 1988, *6* (3).

Geller, W. "How Colleges Respond to Letters of Inquiry: Is Your Mail Effective?" *College and University,* 1982, *57,* 307–313.

Gilmour, J., and others. *How High School Students Select a Col-*

lege. State College: Pennsylvania State University Press, 1978. (ED 208 705)

Glover, R. H. "Designing a Decision Support System for Enrollment Management." *Research in Higher Education,* 1986, *24* (1), 15–34.

Glover, R. H., and Wilcox, J. "An Interactive Model for Studying Student Retention." Paper presented at the annual meeting of the Northeast Association of Institutional Research, Pittsburgh, Pa., Nov., 1989.

Grabowski, S. W. *Marketing in Higher Education.* AAHE-ERIC/ Higher Education Research Report, no. 5. Washington, D.C.: American Association for Higher Education, 1981.

Graff, A. S. "Organizing the Resources That Can Be Effective." In D. Hossler (ed.), *Managing College Enrollments.* New Directions for Higher Education, no. 53. San Francisco: Jossey-Bass, 1986.

Grahm, S. "Factors Related to Educational Participation Among Adults." Paper presented at the annual meeting of the Association for the Study of Higher Education, Washington, D.C., Mar. 1985.

Green, K. C., and Gilbert, S. W. (eds.). *Making Computers Work for Administrators.* New Directions for Higher Education, no. 62. San Francisco: Jossey-Bass, 1988.

Green, M. (ed.) *Minorities on Campus: A Handbook for Enhancing Diversity.* Washington, D.C.: American Council on Education, 1989.

Guiltinan, J. P., and Paul, G. W. *Marketing Management: Strategies and Programs.* New York: McGraw-Hill, 1988.

Hamming, R. W. *Coding and Information Theory.* Englewood Cliffs, N.J.: Prentice-Hall, 1980.

Hearn, J. "The Relative Roles of Academic Ascribed and Socioeconomic Characteristics in College Destinations." *Sociology of Education,* 1984, *57,* 22–30.

Hossler, D. *Enrollment Management: An Integrated Approach.* New York: College Entrance Examination Board, 1984.

Hossler, D. (ed.). *Managing College Enrollments.* New Directions for Higher Education, no. 53. San Francisco: Jossey-Bass, 1986.

Hossler, D., Braxton, J., and Coopersmith, G. "Understanding Student College Choice." In J. C. Smart (ed.), *Higher Education: Handbook of Theory and Research.* Vol. 5. New York: Agathon Press, 1989.

Hossler, D., and Gallagher, K. S. "Studying Student College Choice: A Three Phase Model and the Implications for Policy Makers." *College and University,* 1987, *23* (3), 207–221.

Hossler, D., and Schmit, J. "A Progress Report: A Longitudinal Study of the Postsecondary Plans and Activities of Indiana High School Students and Their Parents." Unpublished report of the Department of Educational Leadership and Policy Studies, Indiana University, 1990.

Huddleston, T. "Effective Organizational Structures for Enrollment Management." Paper presented at first annual Conference on Leadership for Enrollment Management. Sponsored by the Midwestern Regional Office of the College Board and Loyola University of Chicago, 1984.

Huddleston, T., and Karr, M. B. "Assessing College Image." *College and University,* 1982, *57* (4), 364–370.

Hurtubise, R. *Managing Information Systems.* Hartford, Conn.: Kumarian Press, 1984.

Ihlanfeldt, W. *Achieving Optimal Enrollments and Tuition Revenues: A Guide to Modern Methods of Market Research, Student Recruitment, and Institutional Pricing.* San Francisco: Jossey-Bass, 1980.

Ingersoll, R. *The Enrollment Problem.* New York: American Council on Education/Macmillan, 1988.

Jackson, G. A. "Financial Aid and Student Enrollment." *Journal of Higher Education,* 1978, *49,* 548–574.

Jacobi, M., Astin, A., and Ayala, F. *College Student Outcomes Assessment.* ASHE-ERIC/Higher Education Research Report, no. 7. Washington, D.C.: ERIC Clearinghouse on Higher Education and the Association for the Study of Higher Education, 1987.

Jenkins, R. "Budget Blues for the Nation's Colleges and Universities." *Academe,* 1988, *74* (5), 12–16.

Johnson, M., and Richard, H. "A Framework for Evaluating Institutional Planning." In R. Fenske (ed.), *Conflicting Pressures in Post-Secondary Education.* Tallahassee, Fla.: AIR Press, 1976.

Jones, D. P. *Data and Information for Executive Decisions in Higher Education.* Boulder, Colo.: National Center for Higher Education Management Systems, 1982.

Jones, L. Y., Lindzey, G., and Coggeshall, P. E. (eds.). *An Assessment of Research Doctorate Programs in the United States.* 5 vols. Washington, D.C.: National Academy Press, 1982.

Kealy, M. J., and Rockel, M. L. "Student Perceptions of College Quality: The Influence of College Recruitment Policies." *Journal of Higher Education,* 1980, *57* (6), 683–703.

Keller, M. J., and McKewon, M. P. "Factors Contributing to Postsecondary Enrollment Decisions of Maryland National Merit Scholarship Semifinalists." Paper presented at annual meeting of the Association for the Study of Higher Education, Chicago, Mar. 1984.

Kemerer, F., Baldridge, J. V., and Green, K. *Strategies for Effective Enrollment Management.* Washington, D.C.: American Association of State Colleges and Universities, 1982.

Kesler, G. *Academic Strategy: The Management Revolution in American Higher Education.* Baltimore, Md.: Johns Hopkins University Press, 1983.

Konnert, W., and Giese, R. "College Choice Factors of Male Athletes at Private NCAA Division III Institutions." *College and University,* 1987, *63* (1), 23–48.

Kotler, P. *Marketing for Nonprofit Organizations.* Englewood Cliffs, N.J.: Prentice-Hall, 1982.

Kotler, P. *Principles of Marketing.* Englewood Cliffs, N.J.: Prentice-Hall, 1986.

Kotler, P., and Fox, K. *Strategic Marketing for Educational Institutions.* Englewood Cliffs, N.J.: Prentice-Hall, 1985.

Kuh, G. D., and Wallman, G. H. "Outcomes-Oriented Marketing." In D. Hossler (ed.), *Managing College Enrollments.* New Directions for Higher Education, no. 53. San Francisco: Jossey-Bass, 1986.

Kuh, G. D., Whitt, E. J., and Shedd, J. D. *Student Affairs, 2001: A Paradigmatic Odyssey.* Alexandria, Va.: American College Personnel Association, 1987.

Kulage, K. "A Follow Up Study of Non-Returning Students to the University of Missouri, St. Louis." Unpublished manuscript, Office of Institutional Research, University of Missouri, St. Louis, 1985.

Kuntz, S. S. "A Study of Student's Cognitive Structure for Colleges." Paper presented at the annual meeting of the American Educational Research Association, Washington, D.C., Apr. 1987.

Kuznik, A. "Resident Hall Influence on Student Attrition." *Contact,* Winter 1975, pp. 9–12.

Lamden, L. "Changing Through Cooperation." *Change,* 1982, *14* (2), 27–29.

Land, F. F. "Adapting to Changing User Environments." In E. K. Somogyi and R. D. Galliers (eds.), *Towards Strategic Information Systems.* Vol. 1. Cambridge, Mass.: Abacus Press, 1987a.

Land, F. F. "Social Aspects of Information Systems." In N. Piercy (ed.), *Management Information Systems: The Technology of Change.* New York: Nichols, 1987b.

Land, F. F., Le Quesne, P., and Wijegunaratne, I. "Effective Systems: Overcoming the Obstacles." *Journal of Information Technology,* 1989, *4* (2), 37–45.

Lasch, C. *The Culture of Narcissism: American Life in an Age of Diminishing Expectations.* New York: Norton, 1978.

Lay, R., and Maguire, J. "Identifying the Competition in Higher Education." *College and University,* 1980, *56* (1), 53–65.

Lay, R., and Maguire, J. "Coordinating Market and Evaluation Research on the Admissions Rating Process." *Research in Higher Education,* 1981, *14,* 71–85.

Leister, D. V. "Identifying Institutional Clientele: Applied Metamarketing in Higher Education Administration." *Journal of Higher Education,* 1975, *46,* 381–398.

Lenning, O. T. "Variable Selection and Measurement Concerns." In E. T. Pascarella (ed.), *Studying Student Attrition.* New Directions for Institutional Research, no. 36. San Francisco: Jossey-Bass, 1982.

Lenning, O., and Cooper, E. M. *Guidebook for Colleges and Universities: Presenting Information to Prospective Students.* Boulder, Colo.: National Center for Higher Education Management Systems, 1978. (ED 156098)

Levitt, T. "Marketing Product Intangibles and Intangible Products. *Harvard Business Review,* 1981, *59,* 94–102.

Levitt, T. *Marketing the Imagination.* New York: Free Press, 1983.

Lewis, B. J. *A Consultants Guide to Effective Recruiting.* Union, N.J.: Lewis, 1987.

Lewis, G. H., and Morrison, J. *A Longitudinal Study of College Selection.* Technical Report, no. 2. Pittsburgh, Pa.: School of Urban Public Affairs, Carnegie-Mellon University, 1975.

Lin, C. "User-Friendly Applications Development in a Relational Data Base Environment." *Journal of Information Systems Management,* 1988, *5* (2), 45–52.

Lincoln, Y. S., and Guba, E. G. *Naturalistic Inquiry.* Newbury Park, Calif.: Sage, 1985.

Litten, L. H. "Market Structure and Institutional Position in Geographic Market Segments." *Research in Higher Education,* 1979, *11* (1), 59–83.

Litten, L. H. "Different Strokes in the Applicant Pool: Some Refinements in a Model of Student College Choice." *Journal of Higher Education,* 1982, *53* (4), 383–402.

Litten, L. H. "Perspectives on Pricing." In D. Hossler (ed.), *Managing College Enrollments.* New Directions for Higher Education, no. 53. San Francisco: Jossey-Bass, 1986.

Litten, L. H. "You Can't Get Much from Watching the Radio." *Journal of College Admissions,* 1989, *119,* 7–17.

Litten, L., and Brodigan, D. "On Being Heard in a Noisy World." *College and University,* 1982, *57* (3), 242–264.

Litten, L. H., and Hall, A. E. "In the Eyes of Our Beholders: Some Evidence on How High-School Students and Their Parents View Quality in Colleges." *Journal of Higher Education,* 1989, *60,* 302–324.

Litten, L. H., and others. *Applying Market Research in College Admissions.* New York: College Entrance Examination Board, 1983.

Lolli, A., and Scannell, J. "Admissions Market Research: An Alternative to Decline in the Eighties." *College and University,* 1983, *58,* 135–151.

Louis, K. S., Colten, M. E., and Demeke, G. *Freshmen Experiences at the University of Massachusetts at Boston.* Boston: University of Massachusetts Press, 1984. (ED 242 251)

Lovelock, C. H. *Services Marketing.* Englewood Cliffs, N.J.: Prentice-Hall, 1984.

Lovelock, C. H., and Weinberg, C. B. *Marketing for Public and Non-Profit Managers.* New York: Wiley, 1984.

McCarthy, J. E., and Perreault, W. D. *Basic Marketing: A Managerial Approach.* Homewood, Ill.: Irwin, 1984.

McCredie, J. W. (ed.). *Campus Computing Strategies.* Bedford, Mass.: Digital Press, 1983.

McDade, S. A. *Higher Education Leadership.* ASHE-ERIC/Higher Education Research Report, no. 5. Washington, D.C.: ERIC Clearinghouse on Higher Education and the Association for the Study of Higher Education, 1987.

MacLean, L. S. "The University of Missouri-St. Louis: Student Recruitment and Retention Program." Unpublished manuscript, Office of the Vice-Chancellor for Student Affairs, University of Missouri, St. Louis, 1986.

Maguire, J., and Lay, R. "Modeling the College Choice Process." *College and University,* 1981, *56* (2), 123–139.

Martorana, S. V., and Wattenbarger, J. L. "Principles, Practices, and Alternatives in State Methods of Financing Community Colleges and an Approach to Their Evaluation, with Pennsylvania a Case State." In L. Leslie and R. Anderson (eds.), *ASHE Reader on Finance in Higher Education.* Lexington, Mass.: Ginn Press, 1986.

Masland, A. T. "Administrative Computing in Higher Education." In J. C. Smart (ed.), *Higher Education: Handbook of Theory and Practice.* Vol. 1. New York: Agathon Press, 1985.

Metzner, B., and Bean, J. P. "The Estimation of a Conceptual Model of Student Attrition." *Research in Higher Education,* 1987, *27,* 15–38.

Meyers, E. M. "A Comparative Analysis of Persisters, Permanent Dropouts, Dropouts Who Transfer, and Stopouts at St. Cloud State University." *Dissertation Abstracts International,* 1981, *42,* 105A.

Mills, H. D., Linger, R. C., and Hevner, A. R. *Principles of Information System Analysis and Design.* New York: Academic Press, 1986.

Morehead, G. G., and Johnson, J. C. "Some Effects of a Faculty

Advising Program." *Personnel and Guidance Journal*, 1964, *43* (2), 139–144.

Muffo, J. A., and Whipple, T. W. "The Use of an Expectancy Value Model in Studying a University's Image." Paper presented at the annual forum of the Association of Institutional Research, Denver, Co., May 1982.

Murphy, P. E., and McGarrity, R. A. "Marketing Universities: A Survey of Student Recruitment Activities." *College and University*, 1978, *53*, 249–261.

Muston, R. "Enrollment Management Strategies Among Selected State Universities." Paper presented at the annual meeting of the Association for the Study of Higher Education, Chicago, Mar. 1984.

Noel, L., and Levitz, R. (eds.). *How to Succeed with Academically Underprepared Students*. Iowa City, Iowa: American College Testing Program National Center for the Advancement of Educational Practices, 1982.

Noel, L., Levitz, R., Saluri, D., and Associates. *Increasing Student Retention: Effective Programs and Practices for Reducing the Dropout Rate*. San Francisco: Jossey-Bass, 1985.

Nora, A. "Campus-Based Aid Programs as Determinator of Retention Among Hispanic Community College Students." *Journal of Higher Education*, May/June 1990, *61* (3).

Novak, T., and Weiss, D. "Trends in Enrollment Management." Unpublished manuscript, College Entrance Examination Board, 1985.

O'Malley, C. "Connectivity Made Simple." *Personal Computing*, Mar. 20, 1990.

Pantages, T. J., and Creedon, C. F. "Studies of College Student Attrition: 1950–1975." *Review of Educational Research*, 1978, *48*, 49–101.

Pascarella, E. T. "Student-Faculty Informal Contact and College Outcomes." *Review of Educational Research*, 1980, *50* (4), 545–595.

Pascarella, E. T. (ed.). *Studying Student Attrition*. New Directions for Institutional Research, no. 36. San Francisco: Jossey-Bass, 1982.

Pascarella, E. T., and Terenzini, P. T. "Student-Faculty Infor-

mal Relationships and Freshman Year Educational Outcomes." *Journal of Educational Research,* 1978, *71,* 183–189.

Pascarella, E. T., and Terenzini, P. T. "Student Faculty Informal Contact and College Persistence: A Further Investigation." *Journal of Educational Research,* 1979, *72,* 214–218.

Pascarella, E. T., and Terenzini, P. T. "Predicting Voluntary
Freshman Year Persistence/Withdrawal Behavior: A Path
Analytic Validation of Tinto's Model." *Journal of Educational
Psychology,* 1983, *75,* 215–226.

Peat Marwick. *Enrollment Management in Higher Education.* New
York: Peat Marwick, 1987.

Peters, T., and Waterman, R., Jr. *In Search of Excellence: Lessons from America's Best-Run Companies.* New York: Warner
Books, 1982.

Pliskin, N. "Human Resource Management: Guidelines for Effective Introduction of Microcomputer Technology." Journal of Information Systems Management, Spring 1989.

Ponce, F. "Minority Student Retention: A Moral and Legal Im-
perative." In M. Terrell and D. Wright (eds.), *From Survival
to Success: Promoting Minority Student Retention.* Washington,
D.C.: National Association of Student Personnel Administrators, 1988.

Price, J. *The Study of Turnover.* Ames: Iowa State University
Press, 1977.

Price, J. L., and Mueller, C. W. *Handbook of Organizational Measurement.* Marshfield, Mass.: Longwood Press, 1986.

Rainsford, G. N. "One Plus One Equals Three: The Senior Ad-
ministrator in Enrollment Management." Paper presented at
"Enrollment Planning: A Total Institutional Approach," New
Orleans, June 1986.

Ramist, L. *College Student Attrition and Retention.* New York: College Entrance Examination Board, 1981.

"Review of Data Management." *PC World,* Mar. 1990, pp.
164–171.

Ricker, R. P. "Data and Information, Are They Synonyms?"
Journal of Systems Management, Sept. 1979, *7,* 78–90.

Ries, A., and Trout, J. *Positioning: The Battle for Your Mind.* New
York: McGraw-Hill, 1980.

Rokeach, M. *Beliefs, Attitudes, and Values: A Theory of Organization and Change.* San Francisco: Jossey-Bass, 1968.

Rose, H. A. "Prediction and Prevention of Freshman Attrition." *Journal of Counseling Psychology,* 1965, *12* (4), 399–403.

Rothwell, W. J., and Kazanas, H. C. "Training: Key to Strategic Management." *Performance Improvement Quarterly,* 1989, *3* (1), 42–56.

Ryland, J. N. "Distributed Computing." In K. C. Green and S. W. Gilbert (eds.), *Making Computers Work for Administrators.* New Directions in Higher Education, no. 62. San Francisco: Jossey-Bass, 1988.

Saluri, D. "Case Studies and Successful Programs." In L. Noel, R. Levitz, D. Saluri, and Associates, *Increasing Student Retention: Effective Programs and Practices for Reducing the Dropout Rate.* San Francisco: Jossey-Bass, 1985.

Schein, E. H. *Organizational Culture and Leadership: A Dynamic View.* San Francisco: Jossey-Bass, 1985.

Scherer, C., and Wright, N. "Sound Beginnings Support Freshman Transition into University Life." *Journal of College Student Personnel,* 1982, *23* (5), 378–383.

Schoell, W. F., and Ivy, T. T. *Marketing: Contemporary Concepts and Practices.* Newton, Mass.: Allyn & Bacon, 1982.

Sexton, V. S. "Factors Contributing to Attrition in College Populations: Twenty-Five Years of Research." *Journal of General Psychology,* 1965, *72,* 301–326.

Seymour, J., and Dvorak, J. C. "A Debate on LANs." *PC/Computing,* Mar. 1990, pp. 21–22.

Simpson, C., Baker, K., and Mellinger, G. "Conventional Failures and Unconventional Dropouts: Comparing Different Types of University Withdrawals." *Sociology of Education,* 1980, *53,* 203–214.

Smith, L. N., Lippitt, R., Noel, L., and Sprandel, D. *Mobilizing the Campus for Retention: An Innovative Quality of Life Model.* American College Testing Program, 1980.

Somogyi, E. K., and Galliers, R. D. (eds.). *Towards Strategic Information Systems.* Vol. 1. Cambridge, Mass.: Abacus Press, 1987.

Spady, W. "Dropouts from Higher Education: An Interdisciplinary Review and Synthesis." *Interchange,* 1970, *1* (1), 64–85.

Spady, W. "Dropouts from Higher Education: Toward an Empirical Model." *Interchange,* 1971, *2* (3), 38–62.

Spies, R. *The Effects of Rising Costs on College Choice. A Study of the Application Decision of High Ability Students.* New York: College Entrance Examination Board, 1978.

Starr, A., Betz, E. L., and Menne, J. "Differences in College Student Satisfaction: Academic Dropouts, Non-Academic Dropouts, and Non-Dropouts." *Journal of Counseling Psychology,* 1972, *19,* 318–322.

Stewart, N. R., and others. "Counselor Impact on College Choice." Paper presented at the annual meeting of the American Educational Research Association, Washington, D.C., Apr. 1987.

Straumanis, E. "Positioning and Trade-Off Analysis." In R. S. Lay and J. J. Endo (eds.), *Designing and Using Market Research.* New Directions for Institutional Research, no. 54. San Francisco: Jossey-Bass, 1987.

Terenzini, P. T., and Pascarella, E. T. "The Relation of Freshman Students' Social and Academic Integration to Attrition." Paper presented at the annual forum of the Association for Institutional Research, Los Angeles, May 1976.

Terenzini, P. T., and Pascarella, E. T. "The Relation of Students' Pre-College Characteristics and Freshman Year Experience to Voluntary Attrition." *Research in Higher Education,* 1978, *9,* 347–366.

Terenzini, P. T., Pascarella, E. T., and Lorang, W. C. "An Assessment of the Academic and Social Influences on Freshman Year Educational Outcomes." *Review of Higher Education,* 1982, *5,* 86–110.

Thomas, R. O. "Student Retention at Liberal Arts Colleges: The Development and Test of a Model." Unpublished doctoral dissertation, Department of Educational Leadership and Policy Studies, Indiana University, 1988.

Tierney, M. "The Impact of Financial Aid on Student Demand for Public/Private Higher Education." *Journal of Higher Education,* 1980, *51,* 527–545.

Tierney, M. "Student College Choice Sets: Toward an Empirical Characterization." *Research in Higher Education,* 1983, *18,* 271–284.

Tinto, V. "Dropout from Higher Education: A Theoretical Synthesis of Recent Research." *Review of Educational Research,* 1975, *45* (1), 89–125.

Tinto, V. *Leaving College: Rethinking the Causes and Cures of Student Attrition.* Chicago: University of Chicago Press, 1987.

van Gennep, A. *The Rites of Passage.* (M. Vizedon and G. Caffee, trans.) Chicago: University of Chicago Press, 1960.

Wakstein, J. "Identifying Market Segments." In R. S. Lay and J. J. Endo (eds.), *Designing and Using Market Research.* New Directions for Institutional Research, no. 54. San Francisco: Jossey-Bass, 1987.

Webster, D. *Academic Quality Rankings of American Colleges and Universities.* Springfield, Ill.: Thomas, 1986.

Weick, K. *The Social Psychology of Organizing.* Reading, Mass.: Addison-Wesley, 1979.

Zeithaml, V. A. "Consumer Perceptions of Price, Quality, and Value: A Means-End Model and Synthesis of Evidence." *Journal of Marketing,* 1988, *52,* 2–22.

Zemsky, R., and Oedel, P. *The Structure of College Choice.* New York: College Entrance Examination Board, 1983.

Index

Adm.	FA	Reg.	
ILA	BILL	LINDY	
CAROLYN	KENT	MARY	9
RHONDA			
AH SA			
STUDENT 1			

HOWARD	DEBBIE	ELIZABETH	
RODNEY		CLERK	9
MERRILY	NICOLE		
LAURA			
GALEN			

STUDENT 2	KRIS	CLERK ?	4
	RHONDA ?	COUNTER	